THE
NAVY CROSS

THE
NAVY CROSS

EXTRAORDINARY HEROISM IN
IRAQ, AFGHANISTAN, AND OTHER CONFLICTS

★ ★ ★

James E. Wise Jr. and Scott Baron

NAVAL INSTITUTE PRESS
Annapolis, Maryland

Naval Institute Press
291 Wood Road
Annapolis, MD 21402

Library of Congress Cataloging-in-Publication Data

Wise, James E., 1930-
  The Navy Cross : extraordinary heroism in Iraq/Afghanistan and other conflicts / James E. Wise, Jr. and Scott Baron.
      p. cm.
  Includes bibliographical references and index.
  ISBN 978-1-59114-945-3 (alk. paper)
  1. Navy Cross (Medal) 2. United States. Navy–Biography. 3. United
States. Marine Corps–Biography. 4. Heroes–United States–Biography.
5. Sailors–United States–Biography. 6. Marines–United
States–Biography. 7. Courage–Anecdotes. 8. United States–History,
Naval–20th century–Anecdotes. 9. United States–History, Naval–21st
century–Anecdotes. I. Baron, Scott, 1954- II. Title.
VB333.W57 2007
359.1′342–dc22
                                                                                2007017334

Printed in the United States of America on acid-free paper ∞

14 13 12 11 10 09 08 07   9 8 7 6 5 4 3 2

First printing

*Dedicated to our courageous military men and women
who have served and continue to serve in the
Iraq/Afghanistan war zone. And especially
to those who have displayed extraordinary heroism
in combating enemy terrorism.*

CONTENTS

PREFACE

The word "hero" has been abused to the point where today anyone—a celebrity, an athlete, a politician, or just someone doing the right thing—might be crowned with the title. In truth, however, a hero is someone who puts his or her life on the line for others. Military men and women, law enforcement officers, firefighters, emergency medical teams—in other words our "first responders" in crisis situations—are America's true heroes. Their dedication to keeping our country and our citizens safe and to protecting the freedom we enjoy is too often taken for granted.

Today the United States is a bastion for freedom as a way of life. In the past century we fought in world wars, limited conflicts, and the forty-year Cold War to preserve that freedom. But in the days to come we as a nation will be challenged more and more by forces that want to destroy America and what it stands for, by terrorism, subterfuge, or outright confrontation. We have met such threats before and have prevailed. In today's world of possible nuclear weapons proliferation, our task will be more difficult. Only time will tell where America will stand in the years to come.

There is no question that our military men and women, all volunteers, who are serving their country in Iraq and Afghanistan are heroes. In fighting an insurgency war there is no safe haven. There are no rear lines or front lines. Soldiers can be killed where they sleep, where they work, on patrol in dangerous environments, or just attempting to help people who live, suffer, and die in those countries.

Unfortunately, these military men and women receive little coverage in the American media, except when they are wounded or killed. The public is constantly exposed to images of military burial ceremonies or coffins being taken off military planes, and, yes, even photos of flag-draped caskets being removed from the cargo compartments of commercial airliners while passengers stare blankly at the proceedings from inside the plane. Where are the stories of our young people who have been decorated with some of our nation's highest awards honoring bravery and courage? It has been over five years since we went to war (Afghanistan in 2001, Iraq in 2003), and all we see are statistics of our people who have been killed to date, complete with bar charts and the names of personnel lost. Periodically, newspapers will run photos of those lost. On Veterans Day 2006, only one national newspaper, *USA Today*, ran a feature article on the bravery of our bemedaled military. A British magazine, *The Economist*, published an article on the bravery of our military in its Veterans Day 2006 issue (Washington, D.C., section) titled, "The Underdecorated: Serving at High Risk, and No Medals to Show for It," referring to the lack of medals being awarded to our fighting men and women in the Middle East and Afghanistan. Fewer than 30 Navy Crosses have been awarded for actions in Iraq and Afghanistan. Compare that number to the 345 Navy Crosses bestowed in the three-year Korean War (1950–1953) and the 483 Navy Cross medals awarded during the seven-year Vietnam conflict (1965–1972). *The Economist* article noted that "the Pentagon announced that it would take a look at its award process. The review will take several more months to complete. In the meantime, valor will have to remain its own reward."

At this writing, our young military men and women, all volunteers, have been put in a precarious situation. Their mission is to help to stabilize Iraq by training Iraqi policemen and soldiers to assume the task themselves, while at the same time they are fighting a growing insurgency. Unfortunately, American politicians have learned nothing from the Vietnam insurgency war, and the obsession to win has clouded our nation's leaders to the point where winning a war now has become elusive. This country has won only three wars since 1945—World War II, the Persian Gulf War, and the Cold War (if the latter fits appropriately in this category)—while being stalemated in Korea and losing in Vietnam, Somalia, and now perhaps Iraq and Afghanistan.

There is no lack of bravery among the members of our military who fight in foreign lands. Time and again they have shown great courage and determination in completing their assigned missions. In talking to wounded soldiers back from the ongoing war, one is deeply inspired by their love for their country and for those they have fought with and left behind. Although many are maimed, they are optimistic about their future. More than one has voiced the desire to return to their comrades.

Too few of our military men and women have received medals for their valor and sacrifices. As mentioned, less than thirty Navy and Marine Corps combatants have been cited for their extraordinary heroism during this ongoing war, and these few have been decorated with the Navy Cross, America's second highest military award. These individuals and their stories, together with other Navy Cross recipients from earlier wars, are the focus of this book.

For Iraq and Afghanistan, we have included all recipients of the medal up to the date of delivering our manuscript to our publisher, the Naval Institute Press. For the earlier conflicts, space permitted the inclusion of only a small number of recipients of the Navy Cross. Whether covered in this book or not, the valor of all Navy Cross recipients should be recognized by all generations of Americans, now and into the future.

Just as the book was going into production, Sgt. Aubrey McDade, USMC, became the latest recipient of the Navy Cross for his actions on 11 November 2004 in Fallujah, Iraq. At a Parris Island ceremony on 19 January 2007, Sergeant McDade said, "This award, I'm accepting it for me, but at the same time I'm accepting it for all the Marines who go before me and after me."[1]

The story of the bravery of the U.S. armed forces must be told so that future generations of Americans are continually reminded of the high cost of freedom.

ENDNOTE

1. *Leatherneck,* http://www.leatherneck.com.

ACKNOWLEDGMENTS

There are many to thank for assisting us in our work. Natalie Hall, our indispensable team member, has continued to mold our drafts into readable prose, correcting our grammatical and punctuation errors while improving our work with her editorial skills. We've worked together on several of our books, and she will always remain our "rock" as we prepare our finished manuscripts. We owe special gratitude to Dianne Dellatorre-Stevens, Ted Altenberg, Kevin Reem, Douglas Sterner and his magnificent Web site Homeofheroes.com, and Col. Matthew Dodd, USMC (Ret.).

Additionally, we would like to thank Glenn Helm, Jack Green, Roger Cirillo, Paul Wilderson, and the editors and production staff of the Naval Institute Press.

Authors' Note: The table of contents and lead page for each individual include the most recent rank of the active duty awardees, as well as the rank of personnel upon their retirement. Many were of lower rank when they performed the heroic acts for which they were awarded the Navy Cross.

INTRODUCTION

History of the Medal, Criteria for Award, and Early Awards

As of 1 November 2006, the Navy Cross has been awarded 6,921 times, including 20 times for actions in Iraq and Afghanistan during the current war on terror. A handful of men have won the medal twice, three times, four times—and, in two cases, five times. Four women have been awarded the medal, but none since 1918. It has been awarded for saving lives as well as taking them. After it was created in 1919, the Navy Cross was awarded retroactively for acts of valor arising out of the campaigns in Haiti and Nicaragua (1915–1918) and the First World War (1917–1918). It has been awarded to Sailors, Soldiers, Coast Guardsmen, Marines, and, in one case, a civilian. It has been awarded for fighting fires, fighting the flu, trans-Atlantic flights, and salvage and rescue operations. Originally the Navy's third-ranking decoration, following the Medal of Honor and the Navy Distinguished Service Medal, it was bumped up in precedence in 1942 to rank behind only the Medal of Honor.

The Navy Cross was established by an Act of Congress (Public Law 253, 65th Congress) and approved on 4 February 1919, and is equivalent to the Distinguished Service Cross (Army) and Air Force Cross (Air Force). The criteria for the award of the Navy Cross are as follows:

> The Navy Cross may be awarded to any person who, while serving with the Navy or Marine Corps or (in time of war) Coast Guard, distinguishes himself in action by extraordinary heroism not justifying an award of the Medal of Honor. The action must take place under one of three circumstances: while engaged in action against an enemy of the United States; while engaged in military operations involving conflict with an opposing foreign force; or, while serving with friendly foreign forces engaged in an armed conflict in which the United States is not a belligerent party. To earn a Navy Cross the act to be commended must be performed in the presence of great danger or at great personal risk and must be performed in such a manner as to render the individual highly conspicuous among others of equal grade, rate, experience, or position of responsibility. An accumulation of minor acts of heroism does not justify an award of the Navy Cross.[1]

The original legislation authorized the award of the Navy Cross for distinguished noncombat acts, but on 7 August 1942, legislation changed the criteria of
the award to acts of combat heroism.[2]

The medal itself was designed by James Earle Fraser (1876–1953), an apprentice to Augustus Saint Gaudens and a member of the nation's Fine Arts Committee.
Fraser also designed the obverse of the World War I Victory Medal and an early
version of the Navy Distinguished Service Medal. His other creations of note include
the iconic sculpture, *End of the Trail,* a statue of Alexander Hamilton at the Treasury
Building in Washington, D.C., and the Indian Head (Buffalo) nickel.

The Navy Cross medal is a modified cross patee with rounded ends one-and-
a-half inches wide on the obverse. In the center of the cross is a sailing vessel on the
waves, crossing to the left. The ship, a caravel circa 1480–1500, represents both naval
service and the tradition of the sea. On the reverse are crossed anchors and the letters
USN. The medal is suspended from a navy blue ribbon with a white center stripe.
The blue represents naval service; the white represents purity of service. Additional
awards are denoted by a gold star five-sixteenths of an inch in diameter.

ENDNOTES

1. Ronald E. Fischer, "The Navy Cross," *Journal of the Orders and Medals Society of America,* 45, no. 2
   (March 1994).
2. Evans Kerrigan, *American Medals and Decorations* (New York: Mallard Press, 1990).

AFGHANISTAN AND IRAQ

The course of events that led to the war on terrorism began to take shape in the latter decades of the twentieth century. Early terrorist-initiated incidents included the takeover of the U.S. Embassy in Iran in 1979; the suicide truck-bombing of the U.S. Marine barracks in Beirut in 1983, which resulted in the deaths of 241 American servicemen; the bombings in 1983 and 1984 of the U.S. Embassy in Beirut; the hijacking of TWA Flight 847 in 1985; and the bombing of the World Trade Center in New York in 1993. After the U.S. embassies in Kenya and Tanzania were bombed in 1998, President Bill Clinton ordered the air attacks on targets thought to be associated with the al Qaeda terrorist network in Sudan and Afghanistan, code-named Operation INFINITE REACH.

On 12 October 2000, an attack by two al Qaeda suicide bombers on the guided-missile destroyer USS *Cole* (DDG-67) while she was harbored at Aden, Yemen, killed seventeen American sailors. This was followed by the terrorist attacks in New York and Washington on 11 September 2001. Terrorism had arrived in the United States, and the American people demanded a decisive response.

Following the 11 September 2001 attacks, the United States, supported by the United Kingdom and a coalition of other countries and the NATO alliance, began the military invasion of Afghanistan in October 2001, which included the bombing of Taliban and al Qaeda–related camps.

On 20 March 2003 the United States, supported by a coalition, invaded Iraq in Operation IRAQI FREEDOM, ultimately removing Saddam Hussein from power. Although major combat ended in Iraq on 1 May 2003, intense operations against insurgents in Iraq and Afghanistan are continuing at this writing. Twenty-one Navy Crosses have been awarded to date in the war on terrorism.

It is uncertain when the war on terrorism will end. What is certain is that it is likely that more Navy Crosses will be awarded as the United States continues to fight to bring stability to areas that have been unstable for centuries.

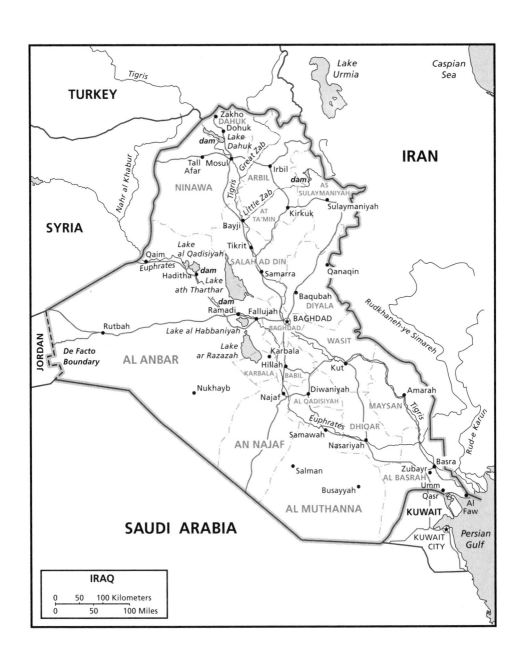

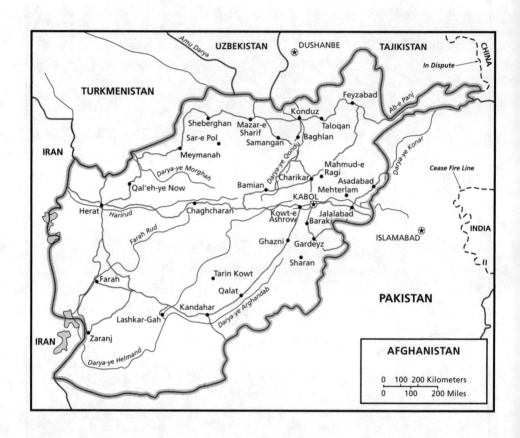

GM2 Danny P. Dietz, USN (SEAL)

ST2 Matthew G. Axelson, USN (SEAL)

Hindu Kush Mountains, Afghanistan
27–28 June 2005

The Navy Cross is awarded to Gunner's Mate Second Class Danny Phillip Dietz, United States Navy, for extraordinary heroism in actions against the enemy while serving in a four-man Special Reconnaissance element with SEAL Delivery Vehicle Team ONE, Naval Special Warfare Task Unit, Afghanistan from 27 to 28 June 2005. Petty Officer Dietz demonstrated extraordinary heroism in the face of grave danger in the vicinity of Asadabad, Konar Province, Afghanistan. Operating in the middle of an enemy-controlled area, in extremely rugged terrain, his Special Reconnaissance element was tasked with locating a high-level Anti-Coalition Militia leader, in support of a follow-on direct action mission to disrupt enemy activity. On 28 June 2005, the element was spotted by Anti-Coalition Militia sympathizers, who immediately revealed their position to the militia fighters. As a result, the element directly encountered the enemy. Demonstrating exceptional resolve and fully understanding the gravity of the situation and his responsibility to his teammates, Petty Officer Dietz fought valiantly against the numerically superior and positionally advantaged enemy force. Remaining behind in a hailstorm of enemy fire, Petty Officer Dietz was wounded by enemy fire. Despite his injuries, he bravely fought on, valiantly defending his teammates and himself in a harrowing gunfight, until he was mortally wounded. By his undaunted courage in the face of heavy enemy fire, and absolute devotion to his teammates, Petty Officer Dietz will long be remembered for the role he played in the Global War on Terrorism. Petty Officer Dietz' courageous and selfless heroism, exceptional professional skill, and utmost devotion to duty reflected great credit upon him and were in keeping with the highest traditions of the United States Naval Service. He gallantly gave his life for the cause of freedom.[1]

Navy Cross citation for GM2 Danny P. Dietz, USN (SEAL)

The Navy Cross is awarded to Sonar Technician Second Class Matthew Gene Axelson, United States Navy, for extraordinary heroism in actions against the enemy while serving in a four-man Special Reconnaissance element with SEAL Delivery

Vehicle Team ONE, Naval Special Warfare Task Unit, Afghanistan from 27 to 28 June 2005. Petty Officer Axelson demonstrated extraordinary heroism in the face of grave danger in the vicinity of Asadabad, Konar Province, Afghanistan. Operating in the middle of an enemy-controlled area, in extremely rugged terrain, his Special Reconnaissance element was tasked with locating a high-level Anti-Coalition Militia leader, in support of a follow-on direct action mission to disrupt enemy activity. On 28 June 2005, the element was spotted by Anti-Coalition Militia sympathizers, who immediately revealed their position to the militia fighters. As a result, the element directly encountered the enemy.

Demonstrating exceptional resolve and fully understanding the gravity of the situation, Petty Officer Axelson's element bravely engaged the militia, who held both a numerical and positional advantage. The ensuing firefight resulted in numerous enemy personnel killed, with several of the Navy members suffering casualties. Ignoring his injuries and demonstrating exceptional composure, Petty Officer Axelson advised the teammate closest to him to escape while he provided cover fire. With total disregard for his own life and thinking only of his teammate's survival, he continued to attack the enemy, eliminating additional militia fighters, until he was mortally wounded by enemy fire. A champion of freedom, Petty Officer Axelson will be remembered for his self-sacrificing actions in the continuing Global War on Terrorism. By his undaunted courage, fortitude under fire, and unwavering dedication to duty, Petty Officer Axelson reflected great credit upon himself and upheld the highest traditions of the United States Naval Service. He gallantly gave his life for the cause of freedom.[2]

Navy Cross citation for ST2 Matthew Gene Axelson, USN (SEAL)

ON 13 SEPTEMBER 2006, family members, fellow SEALs (Sea, Air, Land commandos), and friends gathered at the broad outdoor plaza that forms the amphitheater of the Navy Memorial, directly across Pennsylvania Avenue from the National Archives and Records building in downtown Washington, D.C.

Some three hundred American military personnel and civilians had come to honor two Navy SEALs who had been killed in Afghanistan in the summer of 2005. The attendees included Navy Secretary Donald C. Winter; Chief of Naval Operations Adm. Mike Mullen; Rear Adm. Joseph Maquire, USN, commander of the Naval Special Warfare Command; and military and civilian dignitaries, including members of Congress. With flags on ships' masts flying under a gray evening sky, Admiral Maquire opened the ceremony with the words "These were our men." Following his remarks the families of the two SEALs were brought forward, and Secretary Winter presented Navy Cross medals to the widows of GM2 Danny P. Dietz and ST2 Matthew G. Axelson.[3]

Navy SEAL ST2 Matthew G. Axelson, killed by enemy forces in Afghanistan on 28 June 2005. (U.S. Navy)

On 27 June 2005 the American military in Afghanistan initiated Operation RED WING, in which a four-man SEAL team consisting of Lt. Michael P. Murphy, Dietz, Axelson, and one other SEAL were inserted behind enemy lines east of Asadabad to find, capture, or kill Taliban militia leader Ahman Shah. As the team moved through the mountainous terrain, it was detected by anti-coalition sympathizers who immediately informed Taliban fighters. The Taliban quickly engaged the SEALs with an overwhelming force of thirty to forty militiamen, attacking the team from a high-ground position. The firefight started at an elevation of ten thousand feet amid rugged terrain along the Afghanistan-Pakistan border. With three of the four SEALs wounded, the team was forced into a deep ravine, where Lieutenant Murphy radioed for help.

An MH-47 Chinook helicopter with eight SEALs and eight army "Night Stalkers" on board rushed into the area to rescue the men and immediately faced a life-or-death dilemma. The pilots could either try to land and make a rescue during a fierce firefight or wait while their comrades on the ground were overrun. They chose the former, but while attempting to land, the Chinook was struck by a rocket-propelled grenade and crashed, killing all sixteen on board.[4]

Dietz and Axelson, though wounded, provided cover fire for one of their partners to escape. That SEAL, whose name is being withheld to protect his identity (and who received the Navy Cross at an earlier ceremony), evaded the enemy for several days before being rescued.

Murphy, Dietz, and Axelson died from enemy fire. Their bodies were recovered by a combat search-and-rescue operations team on 4 July 2005 in Kunar province.[5] The loss of the three SEALs and the Chinook rescuers was the worst death toll in a single day since the U.S. invasion of Afghanistan in October 2001 and the largest single loss of life for the Naval Special Warfare forces since the invasion of Normandy in World War II.

Danny Dietz was brought up in Littleton, Colorado, where he played football in high school. His teachers were aware of his goal to join the Navy and become a SEAL, and they remember his later visit to the school in full uniform as a SEAL. To prepare himself for SEAL training, Dietz spent hours lifting weights and swimming while still in school. He joined the Navy three months after graduating from Heritage High School in 1999.

In November 2001 Dietz reported for duty at the Little Creek Naval Amphibious Base at Virginia Beach, Virginia, where he completed Navy SEAL training. He was twenty-one and single. He eventually married Maria Paz Leveque, who had served as an aviation maintenance administrator with Navy Fighter Squardon 11 at Oceana Naval Station in Virginia, and was assigned to SEAL Delivery Team One. At the age of twenty-five, Dietz, now a father of two children, was deployed to Afghanistan in April 2005. His wife remembers his words the day he left to join the war: "All the training I have [undergone] for years is going to pay off with this trip, and I'm going to do something special for this country and for my team." When Dietz was killed, he was on his final mission in Afghanistan and scheduled to return home in two weeks.

In a statement released at his SEAL base in Virginia Beach, Mrs. Dietz said that he "was not just my husband, but he was my other half, my friend, my role model and my hero." She went on to say that her husband "probably wouldn't have wanted to die any other way, but only trying to protect his fellow teammates and his country. . . . I want the world to know that it has lost an incredible man, an outstanding Navy SEAL, and a hero. . . . People around the world don't hear much about the U.S. Naval Special Forces men and what they do for this country, but as a proud SEAL team wife, I can tell that the world as a whole owes those men more than it can imagine."[6]

At the ceremony honoring Dietz and Axelson, a Navy spokesman stated that Lieutenant Murphy, who was based in Pearl Harbor, Hawaii, would be awarded the Silver Star medal and the Purple Heart. All three members of the team who were killed had received the Silver Star initially, but since Murphy's award had not been upgraded to a Navy Cross there is talk that he might be under consideration for the Medal of Honor at some point. His father commented, "We're just proud of everything he's accomplished in such a short period of time."[7]

Dr. Donald C. Winter, Secretary of the Navy, presents the Navy Cross (posthumous) to the wife of GM2 (SEAL) Danny P. Dietz at the Navy Memorial in Washington, D.C., on 13 September 2006. (U.S. Navy / MC1 Chad J. McNeeley)

Many at the ceremony in Washington talked about these young men and their dedication and gallantry. One SEAL spoke of his close friend, Matt Axelson, with great affection. "He was laid back, a golfer, a quiet leader, a generous man who loved his dogs and would hand out $20 bills to strangers." The SEAL became emotional when he repeated an inscription Matt had written on the back of a photo of the two men that Axelson's wife had given him: "But within the willingness to die for family and home, something inside us longs for someone to die beside. Someone to lock step with, another man with a heart like our own." The SEAL commented, "I can't tell you how much I wish I could have been there for him."[6]

ENDNOTES

1. Navy Cross citation for GM2 Danny P. Dietz, USN. www.homeofheroes.com/valor/1_citation/nc_21wot.html.
2. Navy Cross citation for ST2 Matthew G. Axelson, USN, www.homeofheroes.com/valor/1_citation/nc_21wot.html.
3. Ann Scott Tyson, "Two SEALs Receive Navy Cross," *Washington Post*, 14 September 2006.
4. Navy Newstand: The Source of Navy News, www.navy.mil/search/displayasp?story_id=25573. "Navy SEAL from Colorado dies in Afghanistan," www.militarycity.com/valor/958396.html. Tyson, Two SEALs Receive Navy Cross."
5. Ibid.
6. Ibid. "Fallen Heroes: Navy Petty Officer 2nd Class Danny P. Dietz," http://livinglegendteam.blogspot.com/2006/01/navy-petty-officer2nd-class-danny-p.html. "Navy SEAL Heroes," www.floppingaces.net/2005/07/10/navy-seal-heroes.
7. Ibid.
8. Tyson, "Two SEALs Receive Navy Cross."

Unidentified (Navy SEAL)

SEAL Delivery Team One

Naval Special Warfare Task Unit, Afghanistan
27–28 June 2005

The Navy Cross is awarded to a member of SEAL Delivery Team One, Naval Special Warfare Task Unit, Afghanistan, whose identity remains classified, for extraordinary heroism in actions against the enemy while serving in a four-man Special Reconnaissance element with SEAL Delivery Vehicle Team ONE, Naval Special Warfare Task Unit, Afghanistan, from 27 to 28 June 2005. This Navy SEAL, who remains on active duty and whose identity has not been revealed, demonstrated extraordinary heroism in the face of grave danger in the vicinity of Asadabad, Konar Province, Afghanistan. Operating in the middle of an enemy-controlled area, in extremely rugged terrain, his Special Reconnaissance element was tasked with locating a high-level Anti-Coalition Militia leader, in support of a follow-on direct action mission to disrupt enemy activity. On 28 June 2005, the element was spotted by Anti-Coalition Militia sympathizers, who immediately revealed their position to the militia fighters. As a result, the element directly encountered the enemy. Demonstrating exceptional resolve and fully understanding the gravity of the situation and his responsibility to his teammates, the unidentified SEAL fought valiantly against the numerically superior and positionally advantaged enemy force.[1]

Navy Cross citation for an Unidentified Navy Seal

NAVY CROSSES WERE ALSO AWARDED to two other members of this unit, Navy SEALs Danny Dietz and Matthew Axelson. Their heroic actions are described in the preceding chapter.

ENDNOTE

1. Navy Cross citation for an Unidentified Navy SEAL, www.homeofheroes.com/valor/1_citation/nc_21wot.html.

BMC Stephen Bass, USN (SEAL-1)

British Special Boat Service (Attached)

Quala-I-Jangi Fortress, Mazar-i-Sharif, Northern Afghanistan
25–26 November 2001

For extraordinary heroism while serving with the British Special Boat Service during combat operations in Northern Afghanistan on 25 and 26 November 2001. Chief Petty Officer Bass deployed to the area as a member of a Joint American and British Special Forces Rescue Team to locate and recover two missing American citizens, one presumed to be seriously injured or dead, after hard-line al Qaeda and Taliban prisoners at the Quala-I-Jangi fortress in Mazar-i-Sharif overpowered them and gained access to large quantities of arms and ammunition stored at the fortress. Once inside, Chief Petty Officer Bass was engaged continuously by direct small arms fire, indirect mortar fire and rocket propelled grenade fire. He was forced to walk through an anti-personnel minefield in order to gain entry to the fortress. After establishing the possible location of both American citizens, under heavy fire and without concern for his own personal safety, he made two attempts to rescue the uninjured citizen by crawling toward the fortress interior to reach him. Forced to withdraw due to large volumes of fire falling on his position, he was undeterred. After reporting his efforts to the remaining members of the rescue team, they left and attempted to locate the missing citizen on the outside of the fortress.

As darkness began to fall, no attempt was going to be made to locate the other injured American citizen. Chief Petty Officer Bass then took matters into his own hands. Without regard for his own personal safety, he moved forward another 300–400 meters into the heart of the fortress by himself under constant enemy fire in an attempt to locate the injured citizen. Running low on ammunition, he utilized weapons from deceased Afghans to continue his rescue attempt. Upon verifying the condition and location of the American citizen, he withdrew from the fortress. By his outstanding display of decisive leadership, unlimited courage in the face of enemy fire, and utmost devotion to duty, Chief Petty Officer Bass reflected great credit upon himself and upheld the highest traditions of the United States Naval Service.[1]

Navy Cross citation for BMC Stephen Bass, USN (SEAL)

FOLLOWING THE ATTACKS ON the World Trade Center and the Pentagon on 11 September 2001, the United States attributed the actions to Osama bin Laden and his al Qaeda followers. Bin Laden was then in Afghanistan, where he had forged an alliance with the governing Taliban regime. The United States issued an ultimatum to the Taliban, demanding the capture of al Qaeda leaders; release of all imprisoned foreign nationals; destruction of terrorist training camps and infrastructure within Afghanistan; and delivery of terrorists and their supporters to appropriate authorities.[2]

The Taliban's response was not acceptable, and the United States made preparations for a military invasion of Afghanistan. The U.S. Central Command (CENTCOM), located at MacDill Air Force Base in Tampa, Florida, and commanded by General Tommy Franks, had charge of U.S. military operations in Afghanistan, Central Asia, and the Middle East (excluding Israel). Operations against the Taliban would involve the full weight of U.S. military power, along with significant contributions from the international community. By 2002 the allied coalition included sixty-eight countries, with twenty-seven nations having representatives at CENTCOM. Supported by the coalition and numerous agencies of the U.S. government, CENTCOM executed a multiple line-of-operation tactics that attacked the enemy on several fronts simultaneously.

The main attacks were concentrated on the leadership of al Qaeda and the Taliban, while at the same time providing humanitarian aid to civilians who had suffered for four years under the rule of the Taliban. The coalition also sought to destroy the Taliban military by using unconventional forces together with Afghan opposition groups.

By 20 October 2001, all Taliban air defenses had been destroyed, allowing devastating air attacks on the Taliban capital of Qandahar. At the same time, detachments of Special Forces (elite commandos from coalition countries) joined anti-Taliban forces and coordinated highly successful reconnaissance and firefighting support on numerous fronts. On 30 November the northern provincial capital of Mazar-i-Sharif was captured, and in quick succession the cities of Herat, Kabul, and Jalalabad fell to coalition forces. By the following month the U.S. Marines were in control of the Qandahar airport, and the city was under the control of anti-Taliban forces. In a few short weeks the Taliban resistance had been reduced to a few small pockets of soldiers determined to fight to the end. Seventy-eight days after the beginning of the campaign, General Franks traveled to Kabul to attend a ceremony marking the inauguration of the Afghan interim government headed by Hamid Karzai.[3]

Although the campaign against the Taliban had been swift and successful, there were fierce battles yet to be fought. One occurred in late November 2001 at Qala-I-Jangi, a ruined nineteenth-century fortress located ten miles west of the city of Mazar-i-Sharif, where hundreds of lives would be lost in a prisoner revolt.

On 24 November 2001 three hundred al Qaeda fighters laid down their arms and surrendered after fleeing the U.S. bombardment of Kunduz, the last Taliban stronghold in northern Afghanistan. Flat-bed trucks carrying the al Qaeda prisoners arrived at the Qala-I-Jangi fortress late in the afternoon of 24 November. They were interned in the prison block and guarded by one hundred soldiers of the Northern Alliance. The fortress was imposing, and it dominated the landscape. Built of adobe-style bricks, the structure contained moats, ramparts, scarps (ditches) and counter-scarps, and parapets. Its walls were ten feet high and fifteen feet thick, with hundreds of firing ports.[4] During the twentieth century it had been used by various forces–the Royal Afghan Army, the Soviet Red Army, the Northern Alliance, and the Taliban.

The surrender of the Taliban fighters at Kunduz was good news for the anti-Taliban Northern Alliance forces and the two dozen U.S. Special Forces (SF) soldiers from the 3rd Battalion 5th SF Group positioned at a forward operating base (FOB 53) in the newly liberated city of Mazar-i-Sharif. But neither the Northern Alliance nor their American advisers were prepared for what was to follow.

When the Taliban prisoners arrived at Qala-I-Jangi, the Northern Alliance warlord overseeing the fortress, General Abdul Rashid Dostum, didn't order the prisoners to be searched, fearing that a fight would ensue. His intention was eventually to free Afghan members of the Taliban as a gesture of reconciliation to help unite the country's warring tribes, while foreign fighters would be detained and handed over to the U.N. Once inside the fortress, the Taliban prisoners were asked to empty their pockets. Two prisoners pulled grenades from their pockets and pulled the pins, killing two Northern Alliance commanders and several guards. The three hundred prisoners were quickly pushed into underground cell blocks that already housed scores of captured Taliban fighters.[5] The following morning (25 November), two American CIA agents, Johnny Michael Spann (a former U.S. Marine) and Dave Dawson, went to the fortress to identify al Qaeda members among the prisoners. Instead of interrogating them one by one, Spann and Dawson met with a group of prisoners in an open area outside the cell compound. The prisoners immediately became belligerent and attacked the two interrogators. According to eyewitness accounts later told to a German TV camera crew that had rushed to the scene, Spann killed three of the prisoners and Dawson killed two, using their sidearms, before being overwhelmed by the mob. Dawson grabbed an AK-47 from an Alliance guard and killed three more Taliban before escaping and eventually hiding with the German TV crew.

Early that afternoon the Joint Special Operations Task Force North, located in Uzbekistan, informed the America advisers in Mazar-i-Sharif that the prisoners at the fortress had killed two Americans. A follow-on radio contact corrected the first message with clarification that one American had been wounded and another was trapped in the fortress. Both reports turned out to be somewhat inaccurate.

Almost immediately the FOB 53 operations officer formed a rescue assault team consisting of a squad of British Special Boat Service (SBS) commandos (British Royal Navy Special Forces unit) with a U.S. Navy attachment that had been operating in the Mazar-i-Sharif area, and sent them to Qala-I-Jangi.[6] The Navy attachment included Navy SEAL CPO Stephen Bass.

Meanwhile, at the fortress the prisoners had overpowered Alliance guards and killed them with their own weapons. The Taliban fighters then rushed to the underground prison block and freed their comrades, but they soon found themselves trapped in the southwest corner of the fort. They were well armed, however, having stormed an armory and carried off AK-47s, grenades, mines, rocket launchers, mortars, and ammunition. A fierce exchange of fire between the Taliban and Northern Alliance troops ensued. Two Northern Alliance tanks began to fire into the Taliban-held compound.

At 2:00 PM two minivans and a pair of open-sided white Land Rovers with mounted machine guns pulled up outside the fortress gates, carrying the team from FOB 53. The eight British SBS commandos and nine Special Forces Americans were to assist Northern Alliance soldiers in keeping the Taliban from breaking out of the fortress and perhaps retaking Mazar-i-Sharif. The Americans each carried a snub-nosed M-4 automatic rifle; the British were armed with M-16s. After quickly discussing the situation with the on-scene Northern Alliance commanders, the British and American contingent took positions along the fort's ramparts and poured massive gunfire into the Taliban-held south compound. The Americans directed aerial strikes, often positioning themselves as close as 150 feet from Taliban targets.[7]

Chief Petty Officer Bass was sent to locate and recover the two missing Americans, Spann and Dawson, not knowing what had occurred since FOB 53 had first been informed of their status. As he moved toward the fort, he was constantly engaged by small-arms fire, indirect mortar fire, and rocket propelled grenades. He was forced to traverse an antipersonnel minefield to gain entry, then crawl through withering fire to establish the possible location of the Americans while still dodging a barrage of enemy fire. One of the Americans, Johnny Michael Spann, had been severely wounded, while Dave Dawson was uninjured. Bass made two attempts to rescue Spann and Dawson by crawling toward the fortress interior to reach them. He was forced to withdraw because enemy fighters had zeroed in on his position and had increased their firing. Bass returned to the rescue team and reported his actions. The team subsequently learned that the uninjured American, Dawson, had escaped and made his way out of the fortress and hitched a ride to Mazar City.[8]

As darkness fell the rescue force withdrew to its base within the city to plan for the next day's operations, but no attempt was going to be made to rescue the injured American that night. At this point Chief Bass took the matter into his own hands. Under cover of darkness, he again tried to make the rescue, moving into the heart of the fortress while under constant enemy fire. His own ammunition gone, he used the weapon of a fallen enemy to return fire. After finally locating the wounded Spann and verifying his condition, he withdrew from the fortress.[9]

The following morning (26 November), four more special-operations soldiers and eight men from the American 10th Mountain Division arrived at a position about three hundred yards outside the fort to the northeast, and the air assault continued. The rescue force was almost wiped out, however, when an errant 2,000-pound bomb pulverized a section of the massive fortress wall. Five American and four British troops were wounded and evacuated. Some eighty Afghans were also killed or wounded. That night, two AC-130 Spectre gunships orbited the fort and poured 40-mm and 105-mm cannon fire into the compound.[10]

By Tuesday the Taliban counterfire began to wane. It was estimated that only fifty Taliban survivors remained alive out of the original six hundred. Northen Alliance troops fought their way into the southern compound with the support of tank fire. Room-to-room engagements rooted out the last small pockets of resistance. By the next day Taliban resistance at Qala-I-Jangi had ended as the last enemy fighters surrendered. Among the recaptured prisoners was American John Walker Lindh, who did not identify himself until a few days later. Lindh, a twenty-year-old Californian, had undergone a journey of spiritual zeal, linguistic and cultural education, and battlefield training by al Qaeda, which led to his fighting on the Taliban front lines in Afghanistan. Called the "American Taliban," he was later tried, convicted, and sentenced in a Virginia court to twenty years of imprisonment.

Alliance soldiers found the body of CIA agent Johnny Michael Spann and delivered him to the Anglo-American rescue team. Spann was the first American to be killed in combat in Afghanistan.[11]

ENDNOTES

1. Navy Cross citation for BMC Stephen Bass, USN, www.homeofheroes.com/valor/1_Citations/nc_21wot.html.
2. "Operation Enduring Freedom–Afghanistan," http://www.globalsecurity.org/military/ops/enduring freedom.htm.
3. Ibid.
4. "Uprising at Qala-I-Jangi: The Staff of the 3/5th SF Group," *Special Warfare Quarterly*, Sept. 2002, U.S. Army John F. Kennedy Special Warfare Center and School, Fort Bragg, North Carolina.
5. Alex Parry, "Inside the Battle at Qala-I-Jangi," 1 December, 2001, http://time.com/time/nation/article/0,8599,186592,00.html.
6. "Uprising at Qala-I-Jangi."
7. Parry, "Inside the Battle at Qala-I-Jangi."
8. "Sergeant 'Scuff' McGough, Royal Navy Special Boat Service (SBS)," obituary, Telegraph Co. UK, www.telegraph.co.uk/news/main.jhtml?xml=/ news/2006/06/24/db2403.xml.
9. Ibid.
10. "Uprising at Qala-I-Jangi."
11. Ibid.

SCPO Britt Slabinski, USN (SEAL)

Sniper Element, Joint Special Operations Unit

Shahikot Valley, Afghanistan
3–4 March 2002

For extraordinary heroism as Sniper Element Leader for a joint special unit conducting combat operations against enemy forces during Operation ANACONDA, Shahikot Valley, Afghanistan, on 3 and 4 March 2002, in support of Operation ENDURING FREEDOM. On the evening of 3 March Senior Chief Petty Officer Slabinski led his seven-man reconnaissance team onto the snow covered, 10,000 foot mountaintop known as Takur Ghar, to establish a combat overwatch position in support of U.S. Army forces advancing against the enemy on the valley floor. As their helicopter hovered over the mountain it was met by unrelenting rocket propelled grenade (RPG) and small arms fire by entrenched enemy forces. As a result of several RPG hits, a member of Senior Chief Petty Officer's team was ejected from the helicopter into the midst of the fortified enemy positions. The badly damaged helicopter conducted a controlled crash, at which time Senior Chief Petty Officer Slabinski immediately took charge and established security on the crash location until the crew and his team were recovered to a support base. At this point, Senior Chief Slabinski, fully aware of the overwhelming, fixed, enemy forces over the mountain, but also knowing the desperate situation of his missing teammate, now reportedly fighting for his life, without hesitation made the selfless decision to lead his team on an immediate, bold rescue mission. He heroically lead the remainder of his SEAL element back onto the snow-covered, remote, mountaintop into the midst of the numerically superior enemy forces in a daring and valiant attempt to rescue one of their own. After a treacherous helicopter insertion onto the mountaintop, Senior Petty Officer Slabinski led his close quarter firefight. He skillfully maneuvered his team and bravely engaged multiple enemy positions, personally clearing one bunker and killing several enemy within. His unit became caught in a withering crossfire from other bunkers and the closing enemy forces. Despite mounting casualties, Senior Chief Petty Officer Slabinski maintained his composure and continued to engage the enemy until his position became untenable. Faced with no choice but a tactical withdrawal, he cooly directed fire from airborne assets to cover his team. He then led an arduous movement through the mountainous terrain, constantly under fire, covering over one kilometer in waist-deep snow, while carrying a seri-ously wounded teammate. Arriving at a defensible position, he organized his team's security posture and stabilized his casualties. For over fourteen hours, Senior Chief Petty Officer Slabinski directed the defense of his position through countless engagements, personally engaging the enemy and directing close air support onto the enemy positions until the enemy was ultimately defeated. During this entire sustained engagement, Senior Chief Petty Officer Slabinski exhibited classic grace under fire in steadfastly leading the intrepid rescue operation, saving the lives of his wounded men and setting the conditions for the ultimate vanquishing of the enemy and the seizing of Takur Ghar. By his heroic display of decisive and tenacious leadership, unyielding courage in the face of constant enemy fire, and utmost devotion to duty, Senior Chief Petty Officer Slabinski reflected great credit upon himself and upheld the highest traditions of the United States Naval Service.

Navy Cross citation for SCPO Britt Slabinski, USN (SEAL)

IN THE EARLY MORNING hours of 4 March 2002, on a mountaintop called Takur Ghar in southeastern Afghanistan, al Qaeda soldiers fired on an MH-47E Chinook helicopter carrying a Special Operations Forces (SOF) reconnaissance element (code-named Mako 30) led by SCPO Britt Slabinski, USN (SEAL). This fire caused SEAL PO1 Neal Roberts to fall out of the helicopter and began a chain of events culminating in one of the most intense small-unit firefights of the war against terrorism. All of the al Qaeda terrorists defending the mountaintop were killed, and seven U.S. servicemen died. Despite these losses, the U.S. forces distinguished themselves by conspicuous bravery. Their countless acts of heroism demonstrated the best of America's Special Operational Forces as Army, Navy, and Air Force special operators fought side by side to save each other, and in the process secured the mountaintop and inflicted serious loss on the al Qaeda fighters.

For well over a month the U.S. SOF unit had been monitoring a large pocket of enemy forces in the Shahikot Valley, southeast of Gardez, Afghanistan. In February the headquarters for U.S. ground forces in Afghanistan, Task Force (TF) Mountain, commanded by Maj. Gen. Franklin Hagenbeck, USA, conceived a classic military "hammer and anvil" maneuver, Operation ANACONDA, to clear out this threat. U.S. and Afghan forces in Gardez would push from the west in an effort to clear an area of reported high concentrations of al Qaeda in the western part of the Shahikot Valley. ANACONDA planners believed this maneuver would cause the enemy to flee into the blocking positions of awaiting American soldiers from the 10th Mountain Division and 101st Airborne Division located in the eastern sector of the valley. Small reconnaissance teams would augment the conventional forces. These teams were drawn from U.S. and coalition SOF; they included U.S. Navy SEALs, U.S. Army Special Forces, and U.S. Air Force special-tactics operators. The plan was to position these reconnaissance (recce) teams at strategic locations where they would establish observation posts (Ops) to provide information on enemy movements and direct air strikes against observed enemy forces. The Ops were placed in several locations, resulting in effective air strikes on al Qaeda positions and the death of hundreds of al Qaeda in the Shahikot area.

In war, however, things rarely go exactly as planned, and Operation ANACONDA proved to be no exception. Rather than flee, these disciplined and well-trained al Qaeda soldiers stood and fought, and at times were reinforced, all along a series of draws and trails at the southern end of the valley near Marzak, dubbed the "ratline." The enemy halted the Afghan forces pushing east toward "the whale," a humpback ridgeline almost nine thousand feet high, over four miles long, and almost a mile wide southeast of Gardez, and the Afghan forces withdrew back to Gardez. Because of a brief period of bad weather and the unexpectedly heavy enemy resistance, only a portion of the TF Mountain troops had been inserted into their positions by D-day. Some of those that did insert fought under intense mortar and small-arms fire. The SOF units, well-hidden in their observation posts, used direct-fire weapons and coordinated close air-support bombing onto enemy fighting positions. This provided some relief for the TF Mountain forces, especially in the south at Helicopter Landing Zone (HLZ) Ginger, east of Marzak. General Hagenbeck repositioned his soldiers to the northern end of the Shahikot valley and attacked the al Qaeda from that direction. As the battle became more fluid, Hagenbeck recognized the need to put U.S. "eyes" on the southern tip of the valley and the ratline. Additional observation posts near HLZ Ginger were needed in order to provide surveillance and to call in U.S. air power on the numerous concentrations of enemy forces. Takur Ghar, a snow-capped mountain of ten thousand feet, appeared to be a perfect location for an observation post because it dominated the southern approaches to the valley and offered excellent visibility into Marzak, two kilometers to the west. The mountaintop also provided an unobstructed view of the whale on the other side of the valley. Unfortunately, the enemy also thought that Takur Ghar was a perfect site for an observation post and had installed a concealed, fortified force that included a heavy machine gun perfectly positioned to shoot down coalition aircraft flying in the valley below.

On 2 March 2002, U.S. forces began planning to insert forces into two observation posts the following night. Two MH-47E helicopters from 2nd Battalion, 160th Special Operations Aviation Regiment (Airborne), would insert two teams; one MH-47E (call sign Razor 04) would emplace a team to the north, while the other MH-47E (Razor 03) would deploy a team of Navy SEALs and an Air Force combat controller (CCT) led by Senior CPO Slabinski on Takur Ghar. Late the next evening, the two helicopters took off from their base north of the "box," as the ANACONDA operational area became known to U.S. soldiers.

At approximately 3:00 AM local time, Razor 03, carrying Slabinski's team, including PO1 Roberts, approached its landing zone on a small saddle atop Takur Ghar. As Razor 03 approached, the pilots and the men in the back all saw the same thing—fresh tracks in the snow, goatskins, and other signs of human activity. Immediately, the pilots and team discussed a mission abort, but it was too late. A rocket-propelled grenade (RPG) struck the side of the aircraft, wounding one crewman, while machine-gun bullets ripped through the fuselage, cutting hydraulic and oil lines and causing fluid to spew about the ramp area of the helicopter. The pilot struggled to get the Chinook off the landing zone and away from the enemy fire. Roberts stood closest to the ramp, poised to exit onto the landing zone. He and an aircrew member were knocked off balance by the explosions and the sudden burst of power applied by the pilot. Roberts and the crewman reached to steady each other, but both slipped on the oil-soaked ramp and fell out of the helicopter. As the pilots fought to regain control of the helicopter, other crewmen pulled the crewman, who was tethered, back into the aircraft. The untethered Roberts fell a few feet onto the snowy mountaintop. The pilots managed to keep the aircraft aloft until it became apparent it could fly no more, then executed a controlled crash landing some seven kilometers north of where Roberts had fallen. He was now alone in the midst of an enemy force.

Nobody knows exactly what happened over the next few minutes on that mountaintop. There were no surveillance aircraft over the area at the time Roberts fell from the helicopter. Based on forensic evidence subsequently gathered from the scene, it is believed that Roberts survived the short fall, activated his signaling device, and engaged the enemy with his squad automatic weapon (SAW). He was mortally injured by enemy gunfire as they closed in on him.

Following Razor 03's controlled crash landing, Slabinski did a quick head count that confirmed what he already knew—Petty Officer Roberts was missing. TSgt. John A. Chapman, the team's combat controller, immediately contacted a nearby AC-130 gunship for protection. At the same time, Slabinski took charge and established security at the crash location. A short time later, Razor 04, after inserting its recce team, arrived on the scene and picked up the downed crewmen and SEALs, taking them to Gardez. Slabinski and his SEAL team and the pilots of Razor 04 quickly formulated a plan to go back in and rescue Roberts, despite the fact that they knew a force of heavily armed al Qaeda manned positions on Takur Ghar. An AC-130 gunship flew over Takur Ghar and reported seeing what they believed to be Roberts, surrounded by a half-dozen enemy fighters. Knowing how the al Qaeda brutally treated prisoners, Roberts' teammates and commanders knew that time was running out on the SEAL. Razor 04, with its cargo (team) of five SEALs and TSgt. Chapman, departed Gardez and returned to Roberts' last known location on the mountaintop. There were no suitable landing zones other than where Roberts had fallen. But inserting the rescue team at the base of the mountain was not an option—it would take two to three hours to climb up the mountain. Their only real chance of success was to reinsert in the same proximity of where Razor 03 had already taken intense enemy fire.

At about 5:00 AM, Razor 04 approached the landing zone atop Takur Ghar. Despite enemy fire cutting through the helicopter, all six members of what had been a recce element were safely inserted, and the Chinook, although damaged, returned to base. Once on the ground near Roberts' last known location, and using the waning darkness for cover, Slabinski assessed the situation and moved his team quickly to high ground. The most prominent features on the hilltop were a large rock and tree. As they approached the tree, Sergeant Chapman saw two enemy personnel in a fortified position under the tree. Chapman and Slabinski opened fire, killing both. The Americans immediately began taking fire from another bunker position some twenty meters away. A burst of gunfire hit Chapman, mortally wounding him. Another SEAL climbed up on the rock beside the bunker and fired his M-60 machine gun into it at almost point-blank range, and the fire from the bunker stopped. By now at least two SEALs were exposed up on the rock. Then more fire burst from another bunker. A SEAL threw two grenades into it; each detonated, and the fire stopped. As the SEALs attempted to flank the bunker, however, a grenade flew out and exploded, wounding one of the SEALs in his left leg. More fire burst from the bunker, hitting the wounded SEAL again, this time in his other leg.

Having already lost one teammate and with another wounded, and with increasing enemy fire coming from numerous sites, Slabinski decided to break contact and move his men out of range of the enemy. As they moved off the mountaintop to the northeast they shot several more al Qaeda fighters; however, in the continuing exchange two more SEALs were wounded. As they left the mountaintop, Slabinski pulled out his hand-held radio and asked a circling AC-130 ("Grim 32") gun ship to cover their retreat. He also contacted another observation post, which relayed a message to Bagram from Slab: "Mako 30 was requesting the quick reaction force (QRF)." Slabinski arduously moved his men through mountainous terrain, constantly under fire, covering more than a kilometer in waist-deep snow while carrying seriously wounded teammates. Arriving at a defensible position, he organized his team's security posture and stabilized his casualties.

Back at the U.S. staging base, the Ranger quick reaction force, a designated unit on standby for just these situations, was put on alert and directed to move forward to a safe landing zone at Gardez, where it would be able to respond within fifteen minutes. The twenty-three-man QRF loaded on two Chinook helicopters and took off from the base, having little knowledge about what was actually happening on Takur Ghar. As the aircraft flew toward the Takur Ghar landing zone, the QRF was unaware that a squad of al Qaeda fighters, who by this time had already killed two Americans, was poised and expecting their arrival. The sun was just beginning to crest the mountains to the east when the first helicopter approached from the south. On final approach, an RPG round exploded on the helicopter's right side, while small arms peppered it from three directions. The pilots attempted to abort the landing, but the aircraft had taken too much damage. The helicopter dropped ten feet and landed hard on the snow-covered slope of the landing zone, seriously wounding both pilots in the crash. The impact of the crash knocked everyone to the helicopter floor. The Rangers, CCT, and the eight-man Chinook crew struggled under intense fire to get up and out of the helicopter fuselage. A helicopter side gunner and three Rangers were killed during the crash and chaotic exit from the downed aircraft. The surviving Rangers quickly assembled at the helicopter ramp to assess the situation and fix the enemy locations. With their M-4s the Rangers killed two more al Qaeda, including an RPG gunner. Using rock outcroppings as cover, they began maneuvering toward better positions. The Ranger platoon leader formulated a plan to assault the bunkers on top of the mountain, but after an initial attempt to do so he quickly realized he would need a larger force. Instead, the Air Force combat controller worked to get close air support on station. Within minutes, U.S. aircraft began to bomb and strafe the enemy positions, dropping 500-pound bombs within fifty meters of the SOF positions. By 7:00 AM the Rangers were no longer in danger of being overrun. They consolidated their position and established a casualty point to the rear of the helicopter.

After the shootdown of the first Ranger QRF helicopter, the second aircraft was directed to a safe area to await further instructions. Later, the helicopter inserted the other half of the QRF with its force of ten Rangers and an additional SEAL at an "offset" landing zone, approximately eight hundred meters down the mountain to the east and more than two thousand feet below the mountaintop. The Navy SEAL linked up with Slabinki's recce element, which was now about a thousand meters from the mountaintop. The Rangers' movement up the hill was a physically demanding, two-hour effort under heavy mortar fire and in thin mountain air. They climbed the extremely steep slope, most of it covered in three feet of snow, weighed down by their weapons, body armor, and equipment.

By 10:30 the men were completely exhausted, but still had to defeat the enemy controlling the top of the mountain, now a mere fifty meters from their position. With the arrival of the second QRF force (ten Rangers), the Rangers prepared to assault the enemy bunkers. As the Air Force CCT called in a last airstrike on the enemy bunkers and with two machine guns providing suppression fire, seven Rangers stormed the hill as quickly as they could in the knee-deep snow, shooting and throwing grenades. Within minutes the Rangers took the hill, killing several al Qaeda. The Rangers began to consolidate their position on the top of the mountain, which the platoon leader deemed more defendable and safer for their wounded. The Rangers, Army crew members, and Air Force personnel began moving the wounded up the steep slope.

At about 8:15 PM, four helicopters from the 160th Special Operations Aviation Regiment (SOAR) extracted the Rangers on Takur Ghar and Slab and his four surviving SEALs (two wounded), who were down the mountainside. Two hours later the survivors and their fallen comrades were back at their base. A team of medical staff of the 247th Forward Surgical Team, operating out of the Bagram airport tower, awaited the eleven wounded personnel. By morning, all the wounded were headed to hospitals in Germany and elsewhere.

Operation ANACONDA would continue for another nineteen days. These same units continued to play a decisive role in defeating the al Qaeda in the largest coalition ground combat operation up to that time in the war against terrorism.

ENDNOTES

The following reference sources were used to write this chapter: Navy Cross citation for SPCO Britt Slabinski, USN (SEAL), www.homeofheroes.com/valor/1_Citations/nc_21wot.html; Department of Defense, "Executive Summary of the Battle of Takur Ghar," released 24 May 2002; Navy Cross citation for Senior Chief Petty Officer Britt Slabinski, USN (SEAL), www.freerepublic.com/focus/f-news/14373/ posts; Operation ANACONDA, www.time.com/time/covers/110102318/popup; Naylor, Sean. *Not A Good Day To Die.* (New York: Penguin Group Inc., 2005), pp. 300–3, 305–7, 309–14, 316–18, 323–27, 332–37, 358–60, 366–68.

1st Lt. Brian R. Chontosh, USMC

Platoon Commander, Weapons Company, 3rd Battalion, 5th Marines

Highway 1 Leading to Ad Diwaniyah, Iraq
25 March 2003

For extraordinary heroism as Combined Anti-Armor Platoon Commander, Weapons Company, 3rd Battalion, 5th Marines, 1st Marine Division, I Marine Expeditionary Force in support of Operation IRAQI FREEDOM on 25 March 2003. While leading his platoon north on Highway 1 toward Ad Diwaniyah, First Lieutenant Chontosh's platoon moved into a coordinated ambush of mortars, rocket propelled grenades, and automatic weapons fire. With coalition tanks blocking the road ahead, he realized his platoon was caught in a kill zone. He had his driver move the vehicle through a breach along his flank, where he was immediately taken under fire from an entrenched machine gun. Without hesitation, First Lieutenant Chontosh ordered the driver to advance directly at the enemy position enabling his .50 caliber machine gunner to silence the enemy. He then directed his driver into the enemy trench where he exited his vehicle and began to clear the trench with an M16A2 service rifle and 9 millimeter pistol. His ammunition depleted, First Lieutenant Chontosh, with complete disregard for his safety, twice picked up and discarded enemy rifles and continued his ferocious attack. When a Marine following him found an enemy rocket grenade launcher, First Lieutenant Chontosh used it to destroy yet another group of enemy soldiers. When his audacious attack ended, he had cleared over 600 feet of enemy trench, killing more than 20 enemy soldiers and wounding several others. By his outstanding display of decisive leadership, unlimited courage in the face of heavy enemy fire, and utmost devotion to duty, First Lieutenant Chontosh reflected great credit upon himself and upheld the highest traditions of the Marine Corps and the United States Naval Service.[1]

Navy Cross citation for 1st Lt. Brian R. Chontosh, USMC

Capt. Brian R. Chontosh, USMC. (Chontosh collection)

CAPT. BRIAN CHONTOSH, USMC, is one of those rare men who, despite the odds against him, is a "go forward" warrior. He exemplified this trait on 25 March 2003 when, as commander of a combined anti-armor platoon of the 3rd Battalion, 5th Marines (the 3/5), he was in the lead vehicle of seven thin-skinned Humvees following four M1-A1 Abrams tanks on Highway 1, rolling toward Ad Diwaniyah, Iraq. His platoon had traveled hundreds of miles and seen little action, but that would soon change.

Riding in the Humvee with Chontosh were four Marine corporals, Armand McCormick, Robert Kerman, Thomas "Tank" Franklin, and Korte. McCormick was driving, while Franklin and Kerman were at the turret and Korte manned the radio. McCormick and Chontosh were of the same breed and mentality. McCormick considered the six foot, chisel-faced Chontosh to be a leader "above and beyond," and the two would act like one when it came time to face combat. Corporal Kerman had been a freshman at the University of Nevada, Reno, when the attacks of 9/11 occurred, and he left school to do something meaningful—to serve his country in the same unit, the 3/5, that his father had served in during the Vietnam War. Corp. Thomas "Tank" Franklin was one of the best .50-caliber machine gunners in the Corps. Although he was on terminal leave at the time Chontosh was putting his team together, Franklin, at Chontosh's urging, stayed in the Corps and showed his mettle when all hell broke loose on Highway 1 in Iraq.[2]

As it made its way up the highway, the convoy was slowed by a white pickup truck ahead of it. Chontosh noticed a tall man-made berm (a narrow path at the bottom of the shoulder of a road) to the side of the highway that looked suspicious and had Korte notify the rest of the Humvees to keep their eye on it. As the tanks stopped, the column was attacked by rocket-propelled grenades (RPGs). The tankers dropped inside and closed their hatches as mortars, machine guns, and RPGs zeroed in on the column. With the unprotected Humvees stuck in the middle of a kill zone, the Marines began to take heavy casualties. Chontosh made the instant decision to find the source of the enemy fire and ordered his driver to off-road his vehicle. As it moved to the side of the column, Chontosh looked for a way to lead his men to safety. Finding a way through the berm, he was fired on by a machine gun coming from a bunker directly ahead. He ordered McCormick to floor the Humvee right into the enemy emplacement while Franklin fired a .50-caliber machine-gun barrage into the five Iraqis manning the gun. Franklin's accurate shooting from the moving vehicle killed all five of the enemy.[3]

A trench full of enemy fighters lay adjacent to the bunker, and Chontosh ordered his driver to take the Humvee directly into it. Once the vehicle was over the embattlement, Chontosh, Kerman, and McCormick leapt to the ground and raced into the trench, leaving Franklin behind to man the .50-caliber machine gun and Korte to man his radio. It has been officially estimated that the three Marines ran into an enemy force of fifty to two hundred Iraqi fighters, many of whom scattered as Franklin raked the area. The fighters that remained fought back in groups of five or six, and the adversaries were often only an arm's length away from each other. Chontosh killed more than twenty of the enemy with his M-16 rifle and 9-mm pistol. The Iraqi fighters were armed with AK-47 automatic machine guns, 9-mm pistols, and RPGs. The rest of the platoon, up on the highway, had no idea what was happening in the trench and were ordered by radio to stay away to prevent an incident of friendly fire.

When Chontosh ran out of ammunition, he grabbed one of the AK-47s that littered the ground and emptied it on the remaining enemy fighters. He found a second AK-47 and once again fired until all ammunition was gone. As the fighting in the trench quieted, the three Marines still had to make their way back to the Humvee under enemy fire. As they raced back through the trench, McCormick picked up an RPG and tossed it to Chontosh. When Chontosh turned to fire the RPG, but before he could squeeze the trigger, the grenade fired and clusters of Iraqi fighters ran for cover. The Marines made it to the Humvee, McCormick floored the vehicle, and they made it back onto Highway 1.

After the engagement it was estimated that Chontosh had cleared two hundred yards of entrenched Iraqis, killed over twenty enemy fighters, and wounded many more. The date was not only significant because of his heroic action but also because it happened on his twenty-first birthday. Although Chontosh and his men did not engage the enemy again in a similar close-quarter firefight, they did take fire every day during the rest of their tour.[4]

On 6 May 2004, at a ceremony at the Marine Corps Air Ground Combat Center (MCAGCC), Twentynine Palms, California, Gen. Michael W. Hagee, Commandant of the Marine Corps, and Sergeant Major of the Marine Corps John L. Estrada were on hand for the presentation of awards. General Hagee presented the Navy Cross to Capt. Brian Chontosh and the Silver Star to Cpl. Armand McCormick and Cpl. Robert Kerman for their "conspicuous gallantry and intrepidity." In his remarks General Hagee stated, "They are the reflection of the Marine Corps type where service to the Marine Corps and country is held above their own safety and lives."[5]

Corporal McCormick was scheduled for discharge after the 6 May ceremonies, but upon hearing that his buddies back in Iraq weren't getting out until September or October, he extended his time in the Corps to join them for the remainder of their tour. Today he is a full-time criminology major at the University of Northern Iowa. McCormick states that during his time in Iraq 80 percent of the Iraqi people favored the American military presence and hoped that we would remain. But his best memories are of the Iraqi children, who he believes give hope for the future of the country. American soldiers are continually surrounded by these young smiling faces—one could always see them sitting outside American camps, hoping to "hang out" with the soldiers. Like many of our servicemen and -women, he finds that some university faculty and students are hostile to him when the subject of Iraq comes up. Most of the veterans either don't talk about their service or they ignore group discussions on the subject. Chontosh also believes that the American main-stream media distort the situation in Iraq and Afghanistan to such a degree that the American public has grown more and more pessimistic about the war, even though he witnessed many positive developments.

Most military men and women who have received medals for valor say the same thing, that they were just doing their job. Chontosh comments that he's the same person as he was before. That he's just an average Joe. That there's no heroism about it. That he was just lucky to have the day to show what he was capable of doing.[6]

Chontosh returned to Iraq during the second half of 2004 as the commanding officer of India Company, 3rd Battalion, 5th Marines. During this time his company took part in Operation PHANTOM FURY, the second assault on Fallujah in November 2004. Of the 158 Marines he commanded, only 3 were killed in action and 25 wounded. During this time his company was also the focus of a Fox News documentary titled "Breaking Point: Company of Heroes." Captain Chontosh is married with two children. As of this writing he was assigned as an instructor at The Basic School at Marine Corps Base Quantico.[7]

ENDNOTES

1. Navy Cross citation for Capt. Brian R. Chontosh, USMC, www.homeofheroes.com/valor/1_Citations/nc_21wot.html.

2. Caspar W. Weinberger and Wynton C. Hall, *Home of the Brave: Honoring the Unsung Heroes in the War on Terror* (New York: Tom Doherty Associates, LLC, 2006), 21–26.

3. "Brian Chontosh," www.snopes.com/politics/military/chontosh.asp.

4. Ibid. See also Weinberger and Hall, *Home of the Brave*, 25–31.

5. Cpl. Jeremy M. Vought, "3/5 Marines Awarded for Heroism," *Marine Corps News*, 13 May 2004.

6. Weinberger and Hall, *Home of the Brave*, 32–36.

7. "Brian Chontosh."

HA Luis E. Fonseca Jr., USN

Company C, 1st Battalion, 2nd Marines, RCT 2

Highway 1 Leading to An Nasiriyah, Iraq
23 March 2003

The Navy Cross is presented to Luis E. Fonseca Jr., Hospitalman Apprentice, U.S. Navy, for conspicuous gallantry and intrepidity in action against the enemy while serving as Corpsman, Amphibious Assault Vehicle Platoon, Company C, First Battalion, Second Marines, Regimental Combat Team 2 on 23 March 2003. During Company C's assault and seizure of the Saddam Canal Bridge, an amphibious assault vehicle was struck by a rocket-propelled grenade inflicting five casualties. Without concern for his own safety, Hospitalman Apprentice Fonseca braved small arms, machine gun, and intense rocket propelled grenade fire to evacuate the wounded Marines from the burning amphibious assault vehicle and tend to their wounds. He established a casualty collection point inside the unit's medical evacuation amphibious assault vehicle, calmly and methodically stabilizing two casualties with lower limb amputations by applying tourniquets and administering morphine. He continued to treat and care for the wounded awaiting evacuation until his vehicle was rendered immobile by enemy direct and indirect fire. Under a wall of enemy machine gun fire, he directed the movement of four casualties from the damaged vehicle by organizing litter teams from available Marines. He personally carried one critically wounded Marine over open ground to another vehicle. Following a deadly artillery barrage, Hospitalman Apprentice Fonseca again exposed himself to enemy fire to treat Marines wounded along the perimeter. Returning to the casualty evacuation amphibious assault vehicle, he accompanied his casualties South through the city to a Battalion Aid Station. After briefing medical personnel on the status of his patients, Hospitalman Apprentice Fonseca returned North through the city to Company C's lines and to his fellow Marines that had been wounded in his absence. His timely and effective care undoubtedly saved the lives of numerous casualties. Hospitalman Apprentice Fonseca's actions reflected great credit upon himself and upheld the highest traditions to the Marine Corps and the United States Naval Service.[1]

Excerpt from Navy Cross citation for HA Luis E. Fonseca Jr., USN

THE 23RD OF MARCH 2003 was a day that offered both success and setbacks for U.S. forces in the early days of Operation IRAQI FREEDOM:

- In the first three days, American troops advanced over two hundred miles into enemy-held territory, a feat unprecedented for speed and depth of penetration. By the 23rd, coalition forces were 130 miles north of the city of An Nasiriyah, and the Air Force successfully completed an airlift of approximately 280 Army and Air Force special operations troops into Kurdish-held territory.[2]
- At Camp Pennsylvania in Kuwait, Sgt. Hasan Akbar, a combat engineer with the 101st Airborne, tossed two live grenades into tents where officers were sleeping. He then opened fire with small arms, and two officers, Army Capt. Christopher Seifert and Air Force Maj. Gregory Stone, were killed, and fourteen others were wounded.
- On the Kuwaiti border, a U.S. Patriot missile team accidentally fired on a British RAF Tornado GR4 jet as it was returning from a mission over Baghdad, killing both RAF crew members. Two U.S. Apache helicopter pilots, CWOs David Williams and Ronald Young, were luckier. Shot down while on a combat mission over Baghdad, they were taken prisoner and displayed on Iraqi television, then held as POWs until being rescued by advancing Marines on 13 April near Tikrit.
- Pfc. Jessica Lynch and six other members of the U.S. Army's ill-fated 507th Maintenance Company were taken prisoner after their convoy was ambushed when it took a wrong turn into the city of An Nasiriyah. Eleven others were killed, and the remainder were rescued by advancing Marines.

NAVY HA LUIS FONSECA performed heroic actions on 23 March during the American forces' advance northward from Kuwait into the city of An Nasiriyah. In what would be one of the bloodiest battles of the war, Fonseca, while serving as a corpsman with the Marines, repeatedly ignored enemy fire to rescue and care for wounded Marines, actions for which he would receive one of the two Navy Crosses awarded that day, the first of the war.[3]

Luis E. Fonseca Jr. was born in 1980, the son of retired Army SFC Luis Fonseca Sr., and grew up near Fort Bragg, North Carolina. He enlisted in the Navy at eighteen and met his wife, HM3 Maria Crisostomo Fonseca, when the two attended the hospital school together. After completing his training, Fonseca was assigned to the 2nd Marines at Camp Lejeune, North Carolina. "I was in a Marine unit for four years, two months of my first five years in the Navy."[4]

The Marines were part of Task Force Tarawa, a Marine Expeditionary Brigade (MEB) made up of elements of the 2nd Marine Division and the 1st Marine Expeditionary Force. Arriving in Kuwait in early 2003, Task Force Tarawa crossed into Iraq on 20 March, the first day of the ground war, and secured the airfield at Jalibah, forty miles south of the city of An Nasiriyah. On 22 March it was tasked with securing two key bridges adjacent to the city.

Secretary of the Navy Gordon R. England presents the Navy Cross to HA Luis E. Fonseca Jr. at Camp Lejeune, N.C., in March 2003. (U.S. Navy / HM2 Wayne Neims)

In the predawn hours of 23 March, Fonseca was with the Amphibious Assault Vehicle Platoon, supporting Charlie Company, 1st Battalion, under the command of Capt. Dan Wittnam. Marine commanders wanted to advance on Baghdad using Highways 1 and 7. The plan was for Lt. Col. Paul Dunahoe's 3rd Battalion, 2nd Marines (3/2) to take the far western bridges and for Lt. Col. Ricky Grabowski's 1st Battalion, 2nd Marines (1/2) to move up Highway 7 to secure the eastern bridges over the Euphrates River and Saddam Canal. As they prepared for the assault on the bridges, Grabowski's Marines watched dumbfounded as eighteen supply and maintenance vehicles of the Army's 507th Maintenance Company sped past their position.

Capt. Troy King of the 507th had led his convoy of thirty-three clerks, cooks, and mechanics across the Euphrates bridge, through An Nasiriyah, and across the Saddam Canal without incident before realizing that he had missed a turnoff and had become lost. He ordered his convoy back through the city to retrace its path back to Highway 1. Iraqi forces consisting of some twenty thousand Saddam fedayeen, Al-Qud, Republican Guard, and Iraqi Army fighters, now alerted, directed intense and accurate fire on the American convoy as it passed back through the city. The convoy was forced to split into three sections. The lead element of three vehicles sped up to escape the kill zone. The middle section of five vehicles was immediately engaged, its ten soldiers taking up defensive positions. And the slower, heavier vehicles at the rear of the convoy were disabled and destroyed, resulting in eleven killed and six captured, including Pfc. Jessica Lynch. Five of the missing would be paraded on Iraqi television, and the search for Lynch would engage the nation for the next several weeks.

The Abrams M-1 tanks of Maj. Bill Peeples' Alpha Company, 8th Tank Battalion, met Captain King's lead Humvee. Apprised of the situation, Major Peebles sent the tanks forward to engage the advancing Iraqis and relieve the beleaguered middle element. But they arrived too late to help the vehicles at the rear, where they found only smoking vehicles and the dead, and realized that six soldiers were missing.

Grabowski's Marines (1/2) continued north and returned to their primary mission of securing the bridges. Bravo Company was first across the Euphrates bridge and turned to the east, skirting the eastern edge of the city. Alpha Company followed, setting up a defensive perimeter to secure the bridge. Charlie Company, riding in eleven assault amphibian vehicles (AAVs), proceeded through An Nasiriyah to secure the northern bridge across the Saddam Canal.[5]

Because the four-kilometer strip between the Euphrates River bridge and the Saddam Canal bridge ran through the eastern side of downtown An Nasiriyah and was so easy for the Iraqis to defend, it was dubbed "Ambush Alley." As soon as Charlie Company, lacking the M1-A1 Abrams tanks that normally spearhead a column (the tanks had left the column for refueling), crossed the Euphrates River bridge and proceeded north into Ambush Alley, it was met by intense fire from small arms, mortars, and rocket-propelled grenades (RPGs). It seemed like lethal fire was coming from all directions. Thousands of Iraqis fired from rooftops, windows, alleyways, and surrounding grassy fields. As the AAVs pushed forward and returned fire with 40-mm and .50-cal machine guns, several Iraqis ran to the middle of the road in front of them and fired RPGs point-blank. Many were duds, while others just bounced off the vehicles. It seemed that one out of every four fighters was armed with an RPG. Others stood before the advancing AAVs firing a continuous stream of AK-47 bullets until they were run over. There were so many enemy fighters on the road that many tried to climb onto the AAVs.

The column had nearly cleared the four kilometers of Ambush Alley and gotten to the Saddam Canal bridge when an RPG hit the right rear of AAV C211, the next to last in the column, exploding within the crowded troop compartment and wounding five Marines. Disabled, the smoking vehicle was able to make it across the bridge to the northern side of the canal.[6]

"Our track got hit—blew up—and I was knocked unconscious," recalled Capt. Noel Trevino. "I was pulled to safety, but I blanked in and out. First I was in a house, then on a tank and then put into a helo."[7]

Fonseca was in the last AAV, C212 (his medevac vehicle), behind the burning C211, and he and other Marines dismounted to assist any injured Marines. As a hail of mortar and small-arms fire and RPGs filled the air around him, Fonseca raced three hundred meters to the damaged vehicle and found five injured Marines lying on the ground. The RPG had ripped open the protective aluminum walls inside, and the explosion had nearly amputated the lower limbs of two of the Marines. Fonseca applied tourniquets and bandages to stop the profuse bleeding from the injuries and injected morphine to stem their pain. (At the time, he doubted if the legs could be saved. Miraculously, they were saved, and both Marines are still recovering).[8] While other Marines assisted in moving the injured, Fonseca ran back to his medevac AAV through the gauntlet of enemy fire. This time, the 5 foot, 5 inch, 140-pound corpsman had a 6 foot, 210-pound Marine draped over his back.[9]

Fonseca set up a casualty collection point inside his medevac AAV. He tended the wounded awaiting evacuation until enemy mortar shells damaged his vehicle, necessitating the transfer of the wounded while under fire. He got his injured Marines out of the vehicle just before an enemy shell from a recoilless rifle exploded inside the AAV. Fonseca dragged his two most seriously wounded Marines, Cpl. Randy Glass and Cpl. Mike Mead, both of whom had severe leg wounds, and placed them in a ditch. He sent the others away with other corpsmen but refused to leave Glass and Mead alone. Finally, he heard the rumble of an AAV. He managed to stop the vehicle, put his injured on board, and jump in. Eventually they ran across Marines of the 2nd Battalion, 8th Marines, and found an ambulance. Fonseca located another corpsman, relayed information regarding the condition of the two men, and after saying good-bye, got into another vehicle and headed off to rejoin his company.[10]

After assisting Alpha Company in securing the Euphrates bridge, Major Peeples left two tanks with Alpha Company and ordered his tank north, along with Capt. Scott Dyer in a second Abrams, to support Charlie Company, whose Marines were dispersed and fighting a fierce enemy force. Peebles and Dyer raced their vehicles through a hail of gunfire and RPGs along Ambush Alley while directing fire on targets identified by Capt. Dan Wittnam as he stood exposed, outside the turret. Aboard Dyer's tank was Maj. Scott Hawkins, a forward air controller (FAC) responsible for assisting in coordinating air/ground operations. Hawkins called in an air strike to suppress enemy fire, but because of poor communications in the confusion of battle the two Air Force A-10 Thunderbolts ("Warthogs") and the Cobra attack helicopters that responded were unaware that Charlie Company was north of the Saddam Canal in the target area. Iraqi emplacements and vehicles were targeted and engaged by eight 500-pound bombs, three Maverick missiles, and 30-mm Gatling guns, but collateral damage included some Marine AAVs hit by stray rounds, and several Marines were wounded, one fatally.[11]

Once again, Fonseca exposed himself to enemy fire as he moved along the perimeter, treating wounded Marines. "The job of a corpsman is to go through hell and back for your Marines," he later told a group of corpsmen in Rota, Spain. "My brothers needed me, so I was going to be there for them."[12]

Fonseca gathered the wounded onto an evacuation AAV and accompanied them south through the city to a battalion aid station, then returned north through the city to Charlie Company's position—twice traversing Ambush Alley. Arriving back to the north, he resumed treating Marines wounded in his absence.

By the end of the day, both bridges were secure. The 1st Battalion accomplished its mission, opening the way for the 1st Marine Division's advance on Baghdad, but at a cost of eighteen Marines dead and another fifteen wounded. Credited with saving numerous lives, Fonseca emerged with only a minor scratch from shrapnel.

Fonseca returned home in June 2003, but four months after that he was back in combat, this time assigned to the 2nd Battalion, 8th Marines, for a six-month deployment to Afghanistan. He came home again in May 2004, and at this writing is assigned to the Naval Hospital, Camp Lejeune, North Carolina, but he continues to volunteer for combat assignments. "It's hard just sitting here when all your brothers are over there. . . . If the Navy would let me do twenty years [in] a Marine unit, I would happily do it."[13]

On 11 August 2004, while U.S. and Iraqi forces were preparing to battle insurgents loyal to radical Shiite Muslim cleric Muqtadar al-Sadr in the holy city of Najaf, HA Luis Fonseca Jr. stood at attention as he was presented the Navy Cross by Secretary of the Navy Gordon R. England in a ceremony at Camp Lejeune. Called "the finest of the finest" by Secretary England, Fonseca doesn't believe that he did more than any other corpsman would have done in his situation. "Some of us might have done more than what I did, some of us might have done less, and then you've got those that don't do anything at all because of fear. There's no training that I can think of to train someone to think that way. You just have to put it into your mindset to act."[14]

His advice is simple for those going to war: "One day you will die. It might be today, it might not be for a hundred years, but one day you will die, and the only thing I ask of you, the only thing the Marines will ask of you, is to just do your job until that day comes."[15]

ENDNOTES

1. Navy Cross Citation for HA Luis E. Fonseca, USN, www.homeofheroes.com/valor/1_Citations_21wot.html.
2. C. Mark Brinkley, "March 23rd Is a Day Remembered All Too Well," *Army Times*, 17 March 2004.
3. Some sources give the spelling as "Louis." The U.S. Navy Web site lists it as "Luis." A second Navy Cross was awarded to a Marine, GySgt. Justin D. Lehew.
4. C. Mark Brinkley, "Finest of the Finest: Corpsman Awarded Navy Cross for An Nasiriyah Valor," *Marine Corps Times*, 23 August 2004.
5. Richard S. Lowry, *Marines in the Garden of Eden* (New York: Berkeley, 2006).
6. Ibid.
7. Eric Steinkopf, "Marines Saved during Battle at An Nasiriyah," *Jacksonville (North Carolina) Daily News*, 12 August, 2004.
8. Official U.S. Navy Cross award citation.
9. Brinkley, "Finest of the Finest."
10. Casper Weinberger and Wynton C. Hall, *Home of the Brave: Honoring the Unsung Heroes in the War on Terror* (New York: Tom Doherty Associates, 2006), 117–22.
11. Lowry, *Marines in the Garden of Eden*.
12. Cara Maib, "Navy Cross Recipient Talks about Experiences with Rota Sailors," *Navy Newsstand*, 22 November 2004.
13. Brinkley, "Finest of the Finest."
14. Maib, "Navy Cross Recipient Talks about Experiences."
15. Ibid.

GySgt. Justin D. Lehew, USMC

An Nasiriyah, Iraq
23–24 March 2003

The Navy Cross is awarded to Gunnery Sergeant Justin D. Lehew, United States Marine Corps, for extraordinary heroism as Amphibious Assault Platoon Sergeant, Company A, 1st Battalion, 2d Marines, Task Force Tarawa, I Marine Expeditionary Force in support of Operation IRAQI FREEDOM on 23 and 24 March 2003. As Regimental Combat Team 2 attacked north towards An Nasiriyah, Iraq, lead elements of the Battalion came under heavy enemy fire. When the beleaguered United States Army 507th Maintenance Company convoy was spotted in the distance, Gunnery Sergeant Lehew and his crew were dispatched to rescue the soldiers. Under constant enemy fire, he led the rescue team to the soldiers. With total disregard for his own welfare, he assisted the evacuation effort of four soldiers, two of whom were critically wounded. While still receiving enemy fire, he climbed back into his vehicle and immediately began suppressing enemy infantry. During the subsequent company attack on the eastern bridge over the Euphrates River, Gunnery Sergeant Lehew continuously exposed himself to withering enemy fire during the three-hour urban firefight. His courageous battlefield presence inspired his Marines to fight a determined foe and allowed him to position his platoon's heavy machine guns to repel numerous waves of attackers. In the midst of the battle, an Amphibious Assault Vehicle was destroyed, killing or wounding all its occupants. Gunnery Sergeant Lehew immediately moved to recover the nine Marines. He again exposed himself to a barrage of fire as he worked for nearly an hour recovering casualties from the wreckage. By his outstanding display of decisive leadership, unlimited courage in the face of heavy enemy fire, and utmost devotion to duty, Gunnery Sergeant Lehew reflected great credit upon himself and upheld the highest traditions of the Marine Corps and the United States Naval Service.[1]

Navy Cross citation for GySgt. Justin D. Lehew, USMC

GySgt. Justin Lehew was never alone on the battlefield of An Nasiriyah, Iraq. He carried with him the memory of his father, Arthur, a veteran Army infantryman who survived the landing at Omaha Beach on 6 June 1944 to come home and instill the values of sacrifice and dedication to duty in his children. Perhaps that's why Justin Lehew chose a career in the Marine Corps.

GySgt. Justin D. Lehew, USMC. (U.S. Marine Corps / Cpl. Daniel J. Fosco)

As Lehew advanced north across the Kuwaiti border into Iraq as a gunnery sergeant with Company A, 1st Battalion, 2nd Marines, Task Force Tarawa (RCT-2), 1st Marine Expeditionary Force, he recalled his earlier experiences in the Gulf War. Unlike then, when the Iraqis surrendered in overwhelming numbers, Lehew expected the resistance to be greater this time out. In DESERT STORM, they were throwing the Iraqis out of Kuwait. This time, they'd be invading Iraq.[2]

At 3:00 AM on 23 March, Task Force Tarawa waited outside An Nasiriyah, a city of 535,000 in southern Iraq, preparing to move in and secure the bridges across the Euphrates River and Saddam Canal. The 3rd Battalion, 2nd Marines (3/2), would secure the western bridges, and the 1st Battalion (1/2) would secure the eastern bridges. Lehew waited with Alpha, Bravo, and Charlie Companies, each equipped with twelve assault amphibian vehicles (AAVs) to carry the infantrymen, and accompanied by the M-1 Abrams tanks of Alpha Company, 8th Tank Battalion.

The 160-plus Marines of Alpha Company had dismounted outside An Nasiriyah and were clearing the small farms on the city's outskirts when Lehew heard radio reports that U.S. Army units were forward of the Marines' position. This confused the commanders of Task Force Tarawa because they were supposed to spearhead the drive into An Nasiriyah. Even more confusing, the forward soldiers were reported to be on foot. Lehew was ordered to take two vehicles to investigate the grid where they were observed.[3]

The vehicles advanced about two-and-a-half kilometers and found nothing in the area, so they proceeded forward to make contact with their tanks, which had advanced forward. "All of a sudden, we pass these American vehicles that are on fire in the center of the road. They were still flaming. It was a tanker, a wrecker truck, various support vehicles, and a couple of Humvees," Lehew recalled. First Sgt. James Thompson, riding with Lehew, spotted several Army soldiers about two hundred meters off the road waving and signaling frantically, and he and Lehew approached them. An Army warrant officer with the stranded group reported that thirteen of his soldiers were unaccounted for.[4]

Those soldiers, members of the 507th Maintenance Company, had lost their way and mistakenly driven through An Nasiriyah. Upon realizing their mistake, they retraced their path back through the city, where they took heavy fire and casualties from Iraqi rocket-propelled grenades (RPGs) and small-arms fire. The ambush separated the convoy into three groups. The first group, comprised of small, light vehicles, had accelerated and escaped the kill zone. Lehew made contact with the second group, which had taken defensive positions to resist the Iraqi assault. The group had taken casualties, and Marine corpsmen had gone to work with the medics to treat the wounded. The third group had all been killed or captured, including three female soldiers. All that remained were the burning hulks of their vehicles.

Under sporadic enemy fire, Lehew used the .50-caliber machine gun mounted on his AAV to lay down suppressing fire as his vehicles withdrew back to medical stations with ten rescued soldiers. After turning the soldiers over to the medics, Lehew rejoined his unit. A short time later, the order was given to prepare to advance on the bridges. It was approximately 7:00 AM.

Unknown to coalition commanders at the time, about twenty thousand Iraqi troops, members of the Iraqi 11th Infantry Division and Saddam Hussein's fedayeen, waited in An Nasiriyah to resist the American advance. The coalition forces had expected little resistance because there had been reports, erroneous it later turned out, that eight thousand Iraqi troops had surrendered. That expectation was a colossal error. To make matters worse, no airstrike or artillery barrage preceded the advance into the city. "We heard over the radio that we were going to put infantry into the city," said Lehew. "I thought, and all the rest of us thought, we were going to hit this city with artillery, and were going to hit it with air [strikes] because you always prep the target before you send in ground troops."[5]

The order was given, and 1st Battalion moved forward. Bravo Company crossed first, skirting the eastern edge of the city, followed by Alpha Company, which took up defensive positions to secure the southern bridge across the Euphrates River. Charlie Company was last across, and its eleven AAVs (one AAV had been disabled crossing the railroad bridge south of the Euphrates River bridge) raced north through what was known as "Ambush Alley" on its mission to secure the northern bridge across the Saddam Canal.[6]

Alpha and Charlie Companies were also without tank support because the large M-1 Abrams needed refueling, but they were ordered to advance anyway. Almost immediately the two companies were engaged by hostiles firing RPGs from a civilian van. The column zigzagged back and forth as it advanced to the southern bridge along building-lined streets. They took occasional small-arms fire, but there was little resistance as they crossed the southern bridge and took up positions in three sections of four AAVs each. The first section was farthest down the road, the third section closest to the bridge, and Lehew's AAV was positioned at a four-way intersection. The Marines dismounted and took up positions against the buildings. Lehew recalled, "No one was shooting. It was quiet. And it seemed really weird. That lasted about seven minutes. And then all at once, at the eighth minute, it was like the entire world exploded."[7] Taking the bridge had been easy. Holding it proved to be significantly more difficult.

RPGs and small-arms fire began raining down on Alpha Company from windows, alleys, and rooftops. "The Iraqis were getting into vigilante-type swarms. We have also got some artillery coming in, and we don't know where from. We assumed these were Iraqi mortar and artillery rounds. All at the same time." Thus began an urban battle of four-and-a-half hours in which the Marines were besieged from all sides. The enemy combatants, some in uniform but most in civilian clothes, attacked from taxicabs, ambulances, and private cars. Women and children were used as spotters. Hostiles attacked from south of the bridge, and Lehew found his command surrounded. "I remember thinking this is how Custer must have felt at the Battle of the Little Big Horn."[8]

The Marines of Alpha Company withstood assault after assault for ninety minutes. Finally, four tanks arrived under the command of Maj. Bill Peeples, and Capt. Michael Brooks, Alpha Company commander, began directing fire on points of resistance as Peeples deployed his tanks, two to the front and two in the rear. One by one, the tanks' main guns reduced the points of resistance to rubble.

Later, as the tide of the battle turned, Lehew returned to his vehicle to check on battle positions by radio when his driver, Pfc. Edward Sasser, noticed an AAV driving rapidly toward the southern bridge with its rear ramp down and dragging on the road. It was C206, one of Charlie Company's AAVs, returning from the north. The AAV had nearly reached the southern bridge when it was struck in the side by an RPG. Almost simultaneously, a second RPG flew into the open back, exploding inside. A burning Marine fell out.

Lehew recalled, "The vehicle came to a rolling stop right in front of us, not more than thirty meters away, and I saw the crewmen who were on fire but still moving. They were hanging out of the hatches or maybe trying to climb out, and the men that were in the back were falling out, and they were on fire. There were seven to nine [wounded] Marines in there."[9]

Without donning helmets and flak vests or grabbing weapons, Lehew and a nineteen-year-old hospitalman, Alex Velasquez, ran across open terrain under massive enemy fire to reach the smoldering vehicle's open ramp. Body parts and dead Marines were everywhere, and Lehew thought everyone killed, as they triaged the tangle of bodies. But as he moved forward to destroy the radio and check if the .50-caliber was salvageable, he heard a groan. He and Velasquez moved bodies to find Cpl. Matthew Juska trapped beneath a collapsed hatch. As they worked to extract him, they realized they were working in a time bomb. One of the RPGs had punctured the AAV's fuel tank, and the dead Marines, ammunition, and vehicle interior were soaked in gasoline. If one more enemy RPG hit the AAV, it would become a flaming coffin.

Assisted by other Marines who'd responded to calls for help, it still took almost forty-five minutes to extract Corporal Juska and carry him to Lehew's AAV. As Velasquez tended to Juska's wounds, Lehew radioed for a medevac helicopter.

In the interim, the company executive officer, Lt. Mathew Martin, had set up a casualty collection point on the bottom floor of a nearby house, but it had only been a "hasty clear." Weaponless, Lehew sprinted through gunfire to check out the house before risking transporting Juska through gunfire. Several wounded Marines were inside, with others coming and going. In the confusion, Lehew realized that nobody had been tasked with defending the wounded Marines. Worse, he heard Iraqi voices coming from the back of the house.

Dodging enemy fire, Lehew ran back into the street to gather weapons, then placed a wounded AAV crewman in charge of guarding the wounded Marines, positioning him at the door to the hallway and telling him, "If anyone comes from my direction, don't shoot. If anyone comes from the opposite direction [back of the house], shoot them."

Lehew ran back into the street and, advised by his platoon commander, Lieutenant Brenize, that the medevac was en route, Lehew and the battalion executive officer, Major Tuggle, began clearing a landing zone at a safe distance from the intersection. They marked it with purple smoke to guide Maj. Eric Garcia of Medium Marine Helicopter Squadron 162, MAG-29, as he flew his CH-46 into heavy fire for the pick-up. (Garcia was later awarded the Distinguished Flying Cross for repeatedly flying into contested landing zones.)

An accidental discharge of green smoke near the intersection, which Garcia took to indicate a safe landing zone, led him to set the helicopter directly adjacent to the intersection, the most dangerous spot in the battle. Through RPG explosions and small-arms fire, Lehew, Velasquez, 1st Sergeant Martin, Major Tuggle, and several other Marines toted the 240-pound Juska to the chopper, while Lieutenant Martin and a second group guided and carried the casualties from the collection point to the waiting medevac helicopter. As soon as Juska was loaded, Garcia took off.

With the bridge secure and the wounded safely evacuated, Captain Brooks ordered his Marines to load up, and they moved north through Ambush Alley to go to the aid of Charlie Company at the Saddam Canal bridge. Six of their AAVs had returned south through An Nasiriyah, only one reaching the southern bridge. As Alpha Company raced up Ambush Alley, guns firing at hostiles on the rooftops, it passed the burning hulks of Charlie Company's AAVs. Alpha Company's vehicles were needed to transport Charlie Company's casualties, some of which had been caused by friendly fire. Lehew's Marines helped evacuate the wounded and secure the area north of the northern bridge. Not one Alpha Company Marine died that day, but Task Force Tarawa lost eighteen Marines, with forty more wounded. But their mission was accomplished, and the way was open for the 1st Marine Division's historic race for Baghdad.[10]

After leaving An Nasiriyah, the task force secured the highways to the rear of the 1st Marines, and on 3 April it secured the town of Ad Diwaniyah. The task force then pushed into Al Amarah on 7 April. It finally ended the invasion outside of Baghdad, following security and stabilization operations in Al Kut on 11 April. Task Force Tarawa retrograded to Kuwait on 14 May.

First Sergeant Lehew was back in Iraq on 24 July 2004, when Lt. Gen. James T. Conway, commanding general of the 1st Marine Expeditionary Force, presented him with the Navy Cross, awarded for his actions in An Nasiriyah. Velasquez was awarded a Bronze Star with a V for Valor. Lehew finished his second tour in Iraq in February 2005.

Lehew is humbled by the award of the Navy Cross and will tell you that he saw countless acts in Iraq worthy of the Medal of Honor. There is no way he accepts the title "hero." "We're just Marines. This is what we do. A six-year-old kid trying to beat cancer—that's the fight of your life. That's a hero."[11]

ENDNOTES

1. Navy Cross Citation for GySgt. Justin D. Lehew, USMC, www.homeofheroes.com/valor/1_Citations/nc_21wot.html.
2. Trish Wood, *What Was Asked of Us: An Oral History of the Iraq War by the Soldiers Who Fought It* (New York: Little Brown, 2006).
3. Caspar Weinberger and Wynton Hall, *Home of the Brave: Honoring the Heroes on the War on Terror* (New York: Tom Doherty Associates, 2006).
4. Ibid.
5. Ibid.
6. Richard S. Lowry, "The Battle of An Nasiriyah," www.militaryhistoryonline.com/iraqifreedom/articles/GardenofEden.aspx.
7. Weinberger and Hall, *Home of the Brave.*
8. Lisa Burgess, "This Is How Custer Must Have Felt," *Stars and Stripes*, 14 June 2005.
9. Wood, *What Was Asked of Us.*
10. Weinberger and Hall, *Home of the Brave.*
11. Ibid.

Cpl. Marco A. Martinez, USMC

1st Fire Team Leader, 2nd Squad, 1st Platoon, Company G, 2nd Battalion, 5th Marines

Tarmiya, Iraq
12 April 2003

The Navy Cross is awarded to Corporal Marco A. Martinez, United States Marine Corps, for extraordinary heroism while serving as 1st Fire Team Leader, 2nd Squad, 1st Platoon, Company G, 2nd Battalion, 5th Marines, 1st Marine Division, I Marine Expeditionary Force in support of Operation IRAQI FREEDOM on 12 April 2003. Responding to a call to reinforce his Platoon that was ambushed, Corporal Martinez effectively deployed his team under fire in supporting positions for a squad assault. After his squad leader was wounded, he took control and led the assault through a tree line where the ambush originated. As his squad advanced to secure successive enemy positions, it received sustained small arms fire from a nearby building. Enduring intense enemy fire and without regard for his own personal safety, Corporal Martinez launched a captured enemy rocket propelled grenade into the building temporarily silencing the enemy and allowing a wounded Marine to be evacuated and receive medical treatment. After receiving additional fire, he single-handedly assaulted the building and killed four enemy soldiers with a grenade and his rifle. By his outstanding display of decisive leadership, unlimited courage in the face of heavy enemy fire, and utmost devotion to duty, Corporal Martinez reflected great credit upon himself and upheld the highest traditions of the Marine Corps and the United States Naval Service.[1]

Navy Cross citation for Cpl. Marco A. Martinez, USMC

MARCO MARTINEZ DREAMED OF seeing combat as a Marine as far back as sixth grade. He realized that dream in Iraq. Through decisive leadership, courageous action in battle, and determined dedication to his men and country, he displayed a true warrior's mettle.

Raised in Las Cruces, New Mexico, Martinez marveled at the stories his father told about his Ranger experiences while engaged in counter-drug operations in South America. At the age of seventeen, Marco signed up with the Marine Corps and during his senior year in high school worked out continuously so he would be ready for the arduous thirteen weeks of boot training. In fact, he missed his senior prom, preferring to continue his training routine by jogging through the darkened streets of Las Cruces. He never lost focus of what was most important to him—becoming a Marine and seeing combat. For Martinez, being a Marine was the most honorable way of serving his country. He envisioned being among Marines who were first in and last out in wartime engagements, men who would readily die for their country and comrades.

In April 2003 Corporal Martinez was in Baghdad, Iraq, as a member of the 1st Platoon, Company G, 2nd Battalion, 5th Regiment. His unit was using the University of Baghdad as its base of operations. Gold 2/5 (the code name for his unit) was on alert to engage enemy fighters moving within their zone. When intelligence wanted to know if the bridge at At Tarmiyah would support the weight of tanks, Gold 2/5 was ordered there to assess the situation.

Four assault amphibious vehicles (AAVs) loaded with Marines (twenty-two men in each vehicle) departed their base for the rural town. As they came within three miles of Tarmiya, Marine drivers noted that local inhabitants were quickly evacuating their homes.

The lead AAV, carrying the 1st and 3rd Squads, crossed a small bridge and waited. The other two AAVs remained behind while officers back at the base formulated a tactical plan, after which the vehicles of the 1st Squad and 2nd Squad moved slowly into the town. Lone individuals ran into buildings or down side alleys. The Marines sensed that enemies lurked in the shadows and that an attack could come at any moment. The 3rd Squad was now in the town, but nothing stirred for the first ten minutes. Then the air erupted with enemy AK-47 gunfire and rocket-propelled grenades (RPGs). The 3rd Squad's AAV was hit and immobilized. Luckily, the Marines had already left the vehicle and had begun patrolling the road. The driver, mechanic, and gunner of the vehicle were all wounded. The enemy was everywhere. Fire was coming from building windows, and many fedayeen fighters were hidden in the bushes and tall grass that lined the main road into the town. The Marines had been ambushed by an overwhelming enemy force.

The AAVs of the 2nd Squad and the command track came under attack by charging enemy fighters. A number of them were cut down by the Marines. As the AAVs moved forward, Martinez could hear AK-47 rounds hitting his vehicle and RPGs screaming overhead. Martinez, 1st fire team leader, 2nd Squad, and Cpl. Timothy C. Tardif, who was in charge of the 2nd Squad, exited their vehicles and moved toward several buildings. Miraculously neither was hit, though they were totally exposed. The fire was so intense and the rounds so close and loud that Martinez suffers from hearing loss today.

By this time the remainder of the platoon's Marines were engaging clusters of enemy fighters firing from neighborhood houses and rooftops. The eight-foot walls surrounding each house (or compound of houses) had to be holed by gunners with shoulder-launched multipurpose assault weapons (SMAWs). After a hole was blown out, the Marines would charge through to fight the enemy. Once inside, they were trapped and could only escape by killing the fedayeen soldiers.

As they fought their way forward, Tardif was severely wounded by a grenade that almost took his leg off. The Marine refused to leave his men; he told them not to move him from the battle scene until the fight was over, then they could take him to a medevac point. The Marines subsequently killed the enemy fighter who threw the grenade that wounded Tardif. Martinez was now in charge of the fifteen-man squad. Remembering his father's words about leadership, he immediately issued quick, decisive orders.

The second fire team was to stay outside of the first house they were going to clear. Once Martinez and his team entered the house, the second fire team was to kill anyone who tried to follow them in. A SMAW blew a hole in the wall enclosing the house, and Martinez and three of his men went in and killed the entire group of fifteen fedayeen fighters.

Sprinting across the street to a second compound, Martinez and his men faced intense fire as they moved through a SMAW-blown hole in the surrounding wall. Once inside, they encountered numerous insurgents firing from spider holes dug in the courtyard and a group of fighters occupying a distant small house. The barrage of firing seemed almost overwhelming. Martinez and his men immediately dropped to the ground and used a rolling maneuver to kill many of the Iraqis. Except for a line of palm trees, however, the yard lacked few obstacles to hide behind. Martinez raced to a position behind one of the trees. As bullets flew around him, one of his men, LCpl. Dave Gardner, motioned to the wall behind them. Looking behind him, Martinez saw a heavily bullet-ridden wall that was marked by one discernable feature, the outline of the palm tree that he was hiding behind as the bullets created a silhouette on the wall. The enemy was just seventy-five feet away, and Martinez could clearly see the armed Iraqi fighters in the house.

Because the Marines were running short of ammunition, Martinez knew that something dramatic had to happen quickly or they'd all be dead. The fighters in the house had to be silenced. Suddenly a break in the action came when one of the guns in the house jammed and the Iraqis had to spend critical moments to check it out while also reloading their weapons. Taking advantage of this slight pause in the battle, Martinez left his position and began a full-frontal charge as three lance corporals—Garcia, Gardner, and Jaramillo—laid down suppression fire. While Martinez was in full sprint towards the house, however, the enemy fighters resumed firing. Martinez suddenly found himself stranded and exposed to being hit by a fatal round at any second. He turned and raced for a palm tree forty feet away. Crouching low as he ran, he instinctively grabbed an enemy RPG launcher that lay among the weapons littering the yard. The rocket wasn't locked in, and it fell out. However, Martinez was able to retrieve it.

He made it to the palm tree with the RPG-7 launcher and rocket, but now came the hard part. He didn't know how to load the rocket nor use the launcher, which had an intricate dual-trigger system. But under the circumstances he became a quick learner. He loaded the rocket and stepped from behind the tree and pulled the trigger. Nothing happened. He reloaded the rocket, checked the sights, and gave it another try. The launcher still didn't fire. Thinking it was a dud, he checked the launcher once again and noticed a feature on the trigger he had missed. As Martinez was about to attempt a third firing, Gardner was hit and went to the ground writhing in pain. The Iraqis were quick to notice the downed Marine and began to zero in on him, hoping to kill him.

Martinez quickly fired the RPG, this time successfully. The rocket tore through the building, killing two of the enemy. A pause of ten or fifteen seconds followed, during which the squad was able to remove Gardner from the line of fire. Then the enemy fighters resumed their fire, aiming specifically at the Marines who were carrying their wounded comrade to safety.

Martinez, enraged by this audacious action, once again charged the remaining terrorists in the house. As he moved forward spraying the enemy with his M-16, he ran out of ammunition. With bullets pinging off the gear he was carrying, he dropped his M-16 and prepped a hand grenade as he neared the house. When he reached the wall of the building, he threw the grenade through the open window from which the terrorists were firing. The blast found its mark, and Martinez saw arms and legs flying through the air. Because he was only two feet from them, their blood splattered on him. The noise of the grenade going off was deafening, and his ears rang.

The yard was now silent. As Martinez went around to the back of the building, a fedayeen fighter who had lain hidden confronted him. Martinez took him out with a quick shot. When his men praised him for his act of bravery, Martinez replied that he couldn't let the guys who shot one of his men get away.

Martinez spent eight months in Iraq and was engaged in several battles. Not one Marine under his leadership died as a result of the Tarmiya ambush. Both Tardif and Gardner survived their wounds, although Gardner today remains paralyzed from the waist down. Tardif was awarded the Silver Star, and for his extraordinary heroism Sergeant Martinez was awarded the Navy Cross. He is a member of the Legion of Valor and one of the few Hispanic Americans to receive the Navy Cross since the Vietnam War.

Upon his return home from Iraq, Martinez decided to leave the Marine Corps and seek a college degree, something none of the male members in his family had ever attained. He is presently a full-time psychology major at Saddleback College, a junior college in Mission Viejo, California. He plans to continue his education at

UCLA or Cal State Fullerton. He keeps his military service experiences to himself while on campus. In one instance, when a woman on campus learned that he had been a Marine, she called him a disgusting human being and hoped that he would rot in hell.

Martinez openly admits how much he misses the Corps and his Marine comrades. He has given some thought to joining the Corps as a commissioned officer once he completes his education. He hopes that someday his children will read about his experiences in Iraq and enjoy the stories he will tell them, much like those told by his father that so enthralled him and set him on a course in life in which his dreams and goals came true.[2]

ENDNOTES

1. Navy Cross citation for Cpl. Marco A. Martinez, USMC, www.homeofheroes.com/valor/1_Citations/nc_21wot.html.

2. Caspar Weinberger and Wynton C. Hall, *Home of the Brave: Honoring the Unsung Heroes in the War on Terror* (New York: Tom Doherty Associates, LLC, 2006), 49–64; "Navy Honors Four Marines' Valor in Combat," www.signonsandiego.com/news/military/20040504-9999-Im4awards.html; "Sergeant Marco Martinez to Be Recognized by City Council," www.las-cruces.org/news/news_item.asp?News ID=94; "Campus Rads vs Our Vets," by Wynton C. Hall and Peter Schweizer, www.nationalreview.com/script/printpage.p?ref=/comment/hall_schweizer2005082; "The Soldiers You Never Hear About," www.nationalreview.com/script/printpage.p?ref=/kob/kob200405280824.asp; "Trio Face Enemy Fire in Battle for Baghdad," www.usatoday.com/news/nation/2006-11-09-medal-battle-baghdad_x.htm.

Sgt. Scott C. Montoya, USMC

Baghdad, Iraq
8 April 2003

The Navy Cross is awarded to Sergeant Scott C. Montoya, United States Marine Corps, for extraordinary heroism while serving as a Scout Sniper, Scout Sniper Platoon, 2d Battalion, 23d Marines, 1st Marine Division, I Marine Expeditionary Force in Support of Operation IRAQI FREEDOM on 8 April 2003. During the battle for Baghdad, Sergeant Montoya's sniper team arrived within Company F's position as they came under heavy small arms fire from a determined enemy force. He immediately encouraged Marines to deploy and return fire. Noticing a disabled civilian vehicle on the road in the line of fire and with complete disregard for his own life, he rushed forward amidst a hail of gunfire and dragged a wounded Iraqi civilian to safety. Returning to the front, he spotted a wounded Marine struggling to get off the same fire swept street, he risked his life to lead the Marine to safety. Returning to the front, he spotted a wounded Marine lying in the street. Ignoring the hailstorm of bullets, Sergeant Montoya rushed into the street for a third time to carry the injured Marine to safety. Sergeant Montoya returned a fourth time to evacuate an unconscious Marine. Returning to the front again, he dashed into the contested street and assisted a Marine to safety who had been dazed by an explosion. Sergeant Montoya ensured medical attention was administered and verified that evacuations were ongoing. By his outstanding display of decisive leadership, unlimited courage in the face of heavy enemy fire, and utmost devotion to duty, Sergeant Montoya reflected great credit upon himself and upheld the highest traditions of the Marine Corps and the United States Naval Service.[1]

Navy Cross citation for Sgt. Scott C. Montoya, USMC

SCOTT MONTOYA IS A WARRIOR. He believes in values like duty and honor. He takes pride in his colors and his regiment. He is compassionate, faithful in his obedience to orders, and loyal to his comrades. These traits all show in his bearing, his words, and his actions. Ask him what he is passionate about, and he'll tell you about his horses or his dogs, or his devotion to martial arts. Unspoken is his love of God, country, and the Marines.

Sgt. Scott C. Montoya, USMC. (U.S. Marine Corps / LCpl. Daniel J. Redding)

It was that love that caused him to enlist in the Marine Reserve on 15 May 1995. After boot camp at San Diego and infantry training with a line company, Montoya returned to reserve status and to his job as a deputy sheriff for Orange County, California.

His unit, the 2nd Battalion, 23rd Marine Regiment (2/23), was a reserve infantry battalion with a history that included action at Saipan and Iwo Jima, and in Desert Storm. The 2/23 was activated in February 2002, partly in response to the attacks on 9/11, to serve as a quick reaction force (QRF). The 2/23 trained at Camp Pendleton, California, in squads, companies, and as a battalion, learning skills they might be called upon to use in combat. Toward the end of their one-year mobilization, they were extended on active duty, with demobilized members recalled. The commanding general of the 1st Marine Division had specifically requested that 2/23 be part of Regimental Combat Team One (RCT-1). As the battalion's new commander, Lt. Col. Jeffrey Cooper stated, "I was concerned the Marines might be disheartened by the extension and was caught off-guard because they went from being really motivated to being extremely motivated. Now they had a mission."[2]

Montoya, already on active duty, had to sign a waiver to extend in order to accompany his unit to Iraq, and he arrived with them at Camp Commando in Kuwait. Twelve hours after the start of the Iraq War, Montoya's unit crossed the Kuwait border into Iraq and was on the road to Baghdad. "We were with the forward element. We're moving north at such a pace that we were running out of gas. We had to wait for our supply lines to keep up with us for food, water, and gas. We just kept pushing, pushing forward."[3]

Elements of the 2/23 were with Task Force Tarawa at An Nasiriyah and Task Force Tripoli as part of the vanguard into Tikrit, Saddam Hussein's hometown. Then, on the afternoon of 8 April, Montoya, a sniper with the Scout Sniper Platoon, found himself on the outskirts of Baghdad. "We were moving forward, but on that day [8 April] we had a lull. As sniper scouts, we were spread out among the companies. We got some mail in, the first time in a couple of weeks, and we went up to Fox Company to give some other snipers their mail, magazines, and some smokes. While we were there, a warrant officer came up and asked if we'd patrol with him through the city. We had a Humvee, and we dismounted and began walking with two platoons of line company Marines."

Highway 8 was lined with small shops, markets, apartment buildings, and a military compound. Most of the roads were paved. Resistance had melted in the face of superior air and armor resources. The Marines' mission was to locate the enemy and destroy him by fire and maneuver.

"We were on patrol when the other platoon, 1st Platoon, got in a firefight," Montoya recalled. "We heard it over the radio, and we heard firing in the interim. Their radioman had got shot, and that's how the firefight got started. . . . In a firefight, there's a lot of confusion and a lot of noise. There's a lot going on. These civilians were cruising along Highway 8, or whatever road they were on, going back and forth, and they got caught in the crossfire. A lot of Saddam's militia were using them as bait. They'd lay prone on the ground, and as a car went by they would shoot at us."[4]

In one car the driver had been shot, and his car stalled in the middle of the road, right in the line of fire. Another man, two women, and a child were also inside. Ignoring the intense small-arms fire, the heavily laden Montoya charged across three hundred yards of open terrain to reach the vehicle. The driver was dead, and the male passenger had a leg wound that had shattered his tibia. As Fox Company Marines provided suppressing fire, Montoya dragged the wounded man bit by bit, fifteen to twenty feet at a time. Taking time to rest, it took him ten minutes. "I got him around the corner. I called for a corpsman, and we set up a casualty collection point. There were other wounded, so we set up to consolidate medical resources and have a location to pick up Marines that were injured and get them out of there." The women and child also made it safely to cover.

Montoya then saw a Marine down in the street, wounded and trying to crawl for cover. Again, he rushed into enemy fire to assist him to safety. He returned to help another wounded Marine, and yet again to carry a Marine, knocked unconscious by the impact of an RPG hitting a wall, out of harm's way. And one more time, Montoya ran into the open to lead a Marine dazed from an explosion to cover.

"I didn't do anything heroic," he said. "We don't leave Marines behind. It's what Marines do. If what I did was exceptional, then all Marines are exceptional. I saw amazing things done every day."

The battle lasted throughout the night and was only brought to a close when airpower bombed the neighborhood. "It was like God grabbed the Earth like a big carpet and shook it out. Here was this flapping sound as the buildings swayed from the energy that was transferred into the Earth. That pretty much ended the resistance. The next morning, the tanks came and popped holes in the wall and we entered the compound."

For his actions that day, Sergeant Montoya was awarded the Navy Cross. He returned to the States with his battalion in June 2003 but remained on active duty until December, teaching martial arts to Marines in San Diego.

"People are generally the same, no matter what country I've been in," he said. "They want to worship their God the way they want to. They want to raise their family the way they want to, and be left alone. Regardless of whether they are Muslim, Christian, or Jew. They want to live their lives the way the want to. They're not that different from Americans. It's just those people who choose to engage the U.S. for malicious means or just plain power. Those are the evil men. Those are the men of tyranny. Those are the men we were sent to fight!"[5]

ENDNOTES

1. Navy Cross Citation for Sgt. Scott C. Montoya, USMC, www.homeofheroes.com/valor/1_Citations/ nc_21wot.html.
2. SSgt. Jeffrey Langille, "Trailbrazing Reserve Unit Demobilizes," U.S. Department of Defense News, About the War on Terrorism, 19 June 2003, www.defendamerica.mil/articles/june2003/ a062003a.html.
3. Scott Montoya, interview by Scott Baron, 28 January 2007.
4. Ibid.
5. Ibid.

LCpl. Todd Corbin, USMC

Hadithah, Iraq
7 May 2005

The Navy Cross is awarded to Lance Corporal Todd Corbin, United States Marine Corps, for extraordinary heroism as Medium Tactical Vehicle Replacement Driver, Weapons Company, 3d Battalion, 25th Marines, Regimental Combat Team 2, 2d Marine Division, II Marine Expeditionary Force (Forward) in support of Operation IRAQI FREEDOM in Hadithah, Iraq. On 7 May 2005, enemy forces ambushed Lance Corporal Corbin's platoon using a suicide vehicle borne improvised explosive device, rocket-propelled grenades, and machine guns. Instantly, three of the four vehicles were severely damaged and 11 of 16 Marines suffered casualties. Lance Corporal Corbin immediately repositioned his truck directly between the enemy and many of the wounded. He radioed the situation to the battalion and leapt into the enemy fire, directing Marines to engage and marking targets. He ran to his fallen patrol leader, threw him onto his shoulder and carried him to safety while firing at the enemy with his off-hand. He re-crossed the kill zone, made his way to his fallen corpsman, bound his wounds and began carrying him. As he began to move, the enemy engaged at close range and Lance Corporal Corbin threw himself on a wounded Marine and shielded him as friendly machine gun fire suppressed the enemy. Organizing Marines to suppress and repel the ambush, he then, on five occasions, ran through enemy fire, recovered dead or wounded personnel, and returned them to his truck. When the casualties were loaded onto his heavily damaged vehicle, he activated its emergency systems and drove it out of the kill zone and through the city to a battalion aid station five miles away. Due to his heroism, no Marine lost his life after the initial attack. By his outstanding display of decisive leadership, courage in the face of heavy enemy fire, and utmost devotion to duty, Lance Corporal Corbin reflected great credit upon himself and upheld the highest traditions of the Marine Corps and the United States Naval Service.[1]

Navy Cross citation for LCpl. Todd Corbin, USMC

THE CITY OF AL HADITHAH is on the Euphrates River at the midpoint between Baghdad and Al Qa'im on the Syrian border. It is also at the crossroads of a major highway that leads to Mosul in the north. Marines of the 3rd Battalion, 25th

Marines, nicknamed "three deuce five," were tasked with training the Iraqi Security Forces (ISF) and conducting stability and security operations in the area.[2]

The three deuce five is a reserve infantry battalion headquartered out of Brookpark, Ohio, with a proud history that includes action at Saipan and Iwo Jima, and in Operation DESERT STORM. The battalion was activated on 4 January 2005 and deployed to Iraq in March, following predeployment training at Marine Corps Air Ground Combat Center, Twentynine Palms, in the California desert.

The weapons company of 3/25 consisted of nine mobile assault platoons (MAPs), each platoon with three armored Humvees and one six-wheeled, seven-ton armored truck. The lead Humvee in each platoon was armed with an M240 machine gun and usually carried the platoon leader. The second Humvee carried an M-2 .50-caliber machine gun, and it was followed by the seven-ton truck. The third Humvee was armed with another M240 MG. The nine MAPs of 3/25 were collectively designated Kabar 1 through 9.

On 7 May 2005, as Operation MATADOR began in western Iraq, the Marines of Weapons Company, 3rd Battalion, 25th Marines, were returning to their base at Hadithah Dam. LCpl. Todd Corbin was looking forward to some down time following a twenty-four-hour patrol on the eastern side of the Euphrates. Corbin, a deputy sheriff from Sandusky, Ohio, was serving as a tactical vehicle driver. That evening, he would repeatedly expose himself to intense enemy fire to rescue wounded Marines.

As Corbin's platoon leader, SSgt. Randall Watkins, would later recall, "We had just come off a twenty-four-hour patrol on the east side of the Euphrates the day prior, and that was supposed to be our down day, but a civil affairs mission into Hadithah that morning kept us on alert. Then Kabar 1 hit a land mine and we had to go recover their downed vehicle. We only had hours before going back out on another twenty-four-hour security mission to the east. . . . Sergeant Cepeda and I heard the mortars hit the dam. He rushed to get the platoon on the trucks and I went to get order from the COC. . . . By the time I got on the trucks I heard that Kabar 1 was taking fire, [and] that is the main reason we wanted to get out the gate so fast."[3]

Unlike other occasions, when mortar fire had come from the eastern side of the Euphrates River, these rounds were coming from Hadithah. Kabar 1 was on the eastern side of the river and feared firing into the city and hitting innocent civilians. Marines were rapidly organized into a quick reaction force (QRF), and MAP-7 (sixteen Marines in three Humvees, a seven-ton truck, and two tanks) moved into the city to locate and envelop the insurgents.[4]

The Marines were in the vicinity of Hadithah Hospital at about 8:30 PM when they passed a map mark they were assigned to investigate. Sergeant Watkins ordered the patrol to turn around—not an easy task on the narrow rubble-strewn streets of Hadithah. Doing so put the tanks at the rear of the convoy and the Humvee

"Victor-1," containing LCpl. Lance Graham, LCpl. Stan Mayer, and LCpl. Emanuel Fellousis, at the front.

The turnaround required the Marines to dismount to guide and direct the large vehicles. Sgt. Michael Marzano, Sgt. Aaron Cepeda, and a corpsman, HM3 Jeffery Wiener, were on the ground when a white van, identified as a suicide vehicle-borne improvised explosive device (SVBIED), emerged from an alley and exploded directly to the rear of Victor-1. As Corbin remembered, "All hell broke loose." Cpl. Jeff Schuller agreed, "It was a total nightmare."[5]

The explosion's blast blew the turret of Graham's Humvee thirty feet, instantly killing him as well as Marzano, Cepeda, and Wiener. Two Marine staff sergeants, Randall Watkins and Daniel Priestly, were critically wounded, and five other Marines were seriously wounded. Miraculously, Mayer and Fellousis survived the blast but were injured in the explosion. Only five Marines remained combat operational.

The survivors were immediately peppered with rocket-propelled grenades (RPGs) and small-arms fire from within Hadithah Hospital. Patients and medical staff were used as shields while insurgents fired on the Marines from fortified positions.[6]

Corbin maneuvered his truck to shield the wounded Marines, placing it between the insurgents and the convoy. He radioed a situation report back to battalion headquarters, then exited the vehicle and began directing return fire. He ran under direct fire to where Watkins lay critically wounded, hoisted him over his shoulder, and carried him to the truck, returning fire with his off hand.

During this time, Schuller was engaging insurgents with his Humvee's M240G machine gun, firing at targets on the roof, in the windows of the hospital, and on nearby buildings. Schuller had taken over for LCpl. Mark Kalinowski, who had been wounded in the wrist by shrapnel. When Schuller exhausted his ammo, Kalinowski handed up Schuller's M-16 with a full magazine, and he fired on targets while Kalinowski loaded a new box of 7.62 ammo. Schuller and Kalinowski provided covering fire, moving back and forth between targets for nearly forty minutes. After the MK 19 (belt-fed grenade launcher) on the seven-ton truck jammed, Schuller was the only gunner left firing.[7]

Corbin can't recall how many times he ran into the open to retrieve dead or wounded comrades and carry them back to the truck, but his citation credits him with at least seven. On one of the forays he entered the kill zone with another wounded Marine and carried the corpsman, Wiener, to the truck as small-arms fire erupted from close range. Corbin shielded Wiener until Schuller's suppressing fire eliminated the threat. At least five more times, Corbin retrieved dead or wounded personnel.

Out of ammunition, Schuller helped Corbin recover a dead Marine, assisted Kalinowski to the truck, then provided covering fire with an M-16 as the remaining Marines loaded aboard the seven-ton truck. Every Marine who could fire a weapon fired at insurgents. Exploding ammunition had kept the Marines from recovering Graham's body, but the remaining Marines of MAP-7, living and dead, were aboard the truck as Corbin got the vehicle moving despite three flat tires and a shot-up radiator.

"The whole platoon rolled out in that seven-ton," Schuller said. "It's a testament to Corporal Corbin's knowledge of that vehicle that he kept it running. . . . Corbin was flipping switches the whole time he drove the five miles back to the battalion aid station."[8]

The two tanks stood watch over Graham until MAP-9, a makeshift rifle platoon, arrived and secured the scene thirty minutes later. They flushed insurgents from the hospital, killing one and capturing one, provided cover as the medical staff evacuated patients to safety, and conducted a sweep of the immediate area.

The 3/25 returned from Iraq in October 2005. In its seven-month deployment in Al Anbar Province, the battalion lost forty-six Marines and two Navy corpsmen killed in action, one of the largest casualty rates for any unit in Iraq.[9]

On 4 July 2005, at a ceremony at the headquarters of 3/25 in Brookpark, Ohio, Corbin was presented the Navy Cross, and Schuller received the Silver Star. Modest about the award, Corbin said, "In hindsight, would I do it again? Hell, I don't know. It's a situation you want to say yeah, every time, but you don't know. It's just what you're trained for . . . and you do it for your buddies."

ENDNOTES

1. Navy Cross Citation for LCpl. Todd Corbin, USMC, www.homeofheroes.com/valor/1_Citations/nc_21wot.html.
2. Third Battalion/25th Marines Unit History, http://www.mfr.usmc.mil/4thmardiv/25thMar/3dBn/History.htm.
3. "Memorial to LCpl. Lance T. Graham," http://www.corpsstories.com/graham-whatwhenwhere1.htm.
4. Ibid.
5. Beth Zimmerman, "Navy Cross, Silver Star Awarded for Actions in Deadly Firefight," *Marine Corps Times*, September 2006.
6. "Three Marines, One Sailor Killed in Hadithah," www.centcom.mil, 9 May 2005.
7. Zimmerman, "Navy Cross, Silver Star."
8. Ibid.
9. Third Battalion/25th Marines Unit History.

LCpl. Joseph B. Perez, USMC

Baghdad, Iraq
4 April 2003

The Navy Cross is awarded to Lance Corporal Joseph B. Perez, United States Marine Corps, for extraordinary heroism as Rifleman, Company I, 3d Battalion, 5th Marines, 1st Marine Division, I Marine Expeditionary Force in support of Operation IRAQI FREEDOM on 4 April 2003. While clearing near Route 6 during the advance into Baghdad, 1st Platoon came under intense enemy fire. As the point man for the lead squad and the most exposed member of the platoon, Lance Corporal Perez came under the majority of these fires. Without hesitation, he continuously employed his M16A4 rifle to destroy the enemy while calmly directing accurate fires for his squad. He led the charge down a trench destroying the enemy and while closing and under tremendous enemy fire, threw a grenade into the trench that the enemy was occupying. While under a heavy volume of fire, Lance Corporal Perez fired an AT-4 rocket into the machine gun bunker, completely destroying it and killing four enemy personnel. His actions enabled the squad to maneuver safely to the enemy position and seize it. In an effort to link up with 3d Platoon on his platoon's left flank, Lance Corporal Perez continued to destroy enemy combatants with precision rifle fire. As he worked his way to the left, he was hit by enemy fire, sustaining gunshot wounds to his torso and shoulder. Despite being seriously injured, Lance Corporal Perez directed the squad to take cover and gave the squad accurate fire direction to the enemy that enabled the squad to reorganize and destroy the enemy. By his outstanding display of decisive leadership, unlimited courage in the face of heavy enemy fire, and utmost devotion to duty, Lance Corporal Perez reflected great credit upon himself and upheld the highest traditions of the Marine Corps and the United States Naval Service.[1]

Navy Cross citation for LCpl. Joseph B. Perez, USMC

"WHEN YOU'RE OUT THERE, you don't think about any of this stuff. I was thinking about keeping the boys alive and keeping out of trouble. . . . Mom, this is what Marines do, we take care of our boys."

Those humble and responsible words were spoken by a twenty-three-year-old Marine, LCpl. Joseph B. Perez, when asked about the Iraqi battlefield exploits detailed in his Navy Cross citation. His "stuff" is shared with you below, and "taking care of our boys" is what every American should be thanking him for today.

The Navy Cross is the nation's second-highest award for valor, surpassed only by the Medal of Honor. As of this writing, fifteen Marines have received the Navy Cross for their battlefield heroics in Operation IRAQI FREEDOM.

The analysis by Marine Lt. Col. Matthew Dodd of Lance Corporal Perez's heroic actions on 4 April 2003 in Iraq (in italics below) breaks down each phrase of his citation.[2] It amplifies for the reader what this brave Marine faced as he met the enemy. Excerpts from Perez's citation follow, interspersed by the comments of Colonel Dodd, in italics.

"For extraordinary heroism as Rifleman, Company I, 3d Battalion, 5th Marines, 1st Marine Division, I Marine Expeditionary Force in support of Operation IRAQI FREEDOM on 4 April 2003. While clearing near Route 6 during the advance into Baghdad, 1st Platoon came under intense enemy fire. As the point man for the lead squad and most exposed member of the platoon, Lance Corporal Perez came under the majority of these fires."

Just being the point man for the lead squad and the most exposed member of his intensely under fire platoon advancing into Baghdad warrants some sort of recognition for "extraordinary heroism" in my book. Add to that mix the fact that he came under the majority of those fires, and you have the kind of stuff of which heroes are made.

"Without hesitation, he continuously employed his M16A4 rifle to destroy the enemy while calmly directing accurate fires for his squad."

Obviously, being the most exposed and most vulnerable made him also the most alert and most ready to handle the situation. Others may have been easily overwhelmed by the weight of the danger and the uncertainty of the situation, but Lance Corporal Perez was trained, equipped, and empowered to deal with it. Here was a young man who truly exemplified "grace under fire." Every Marine is a rifleman, but it takes a special breed of warrior to direct (lead) fellow Marines under fire in destroying the enemy.

"He led the charge down a trench destroying the enemy and while closing and under tremendous enemy fire, threw a grenade into a trench that the enemy was occupying. While under a heavy volume of fire, Lance Corporal Perez fired an AT-4 rocket into the machine gun bunker, completely destroying it and killing four enemy personnel. His actions enabled the squad to maneuver safely to the enemy position and seize it."

Having risen to the occasion, he continued to lead. The presence of mind—Marine Corps defined as "thinking and acting effectively in an unexpected emergency or under periods of prolonged stress"—of Lance Corporal Perez was truly remarkable. He was able to employ three different tools of his trade at different times against different targets under incredible stress and got the same results every time—destroyed enemy positions and many dead enemies.

Perez, as point man, set a great example for any leader or follower to emulate. Boldness, competence, initiative, and relentless determination is a tough combination to beat. A good leader will recognize those qualities in subordinates and set them up for success by putting them in situations where those qualities can be used effectively. Navigating through confusion and formidable obstacles takes courage and confidence, and sometimes all it takes is one brave person to enable many others. These kinds of point men are invaluable force-multipliers when effective organizations have the leadership and resources to readily exploit any opportunities uncovered by their point man's efforts. Perez's squad was no doubt a truly effective combat organization. Perez made his squad better, and his squad made him better.

"In an effort to link up with 3rd Platoon on his platoon's left flank, Lance Corporal Perez continued to destroy enemy combatants with precision rifle fire. As he worked his way to the left, he was hit by enemy fire, sustaining gunshot wounds to his torso and shoulder. Despite being seriously injured, Lance Corporal Perez directed the squad to take cover and gave the squad accurate fire direction to the enemy that enabled the squad to reorganize and destroy the enemy."

By this point, whatever was left of the enemy must have been wondering, What does it take to stop this Marine? The answer clearly was "More than you have."

What an inspirational sight Lance Corporal Perez must have been for his fellow Marines. Seriously wounded, continuously under fire since first engaged by the enemy, and still out in front of and leading his fellow Marines, he once again enabled his unit to accomplish their mission.

"By his outstanding display of decisive leadership, unlimited courage in the face of heavy enemy fire, and utmost devotion to duty, Lance Corporal Perez reflected great credit upon himself and upheld the highest traditions of the Marine Corps and the United States Naval Service."

At any point in this incredible sequence of action, Lance Corporal Perez could have probably let up a bit and let someone else take the point for a bit. Nobody would have questioned his decision given what he had already been through. Yet, he refused to quit. In the face of seemingly impossible odds, he kept on charging forward, making a difference in his life and in the lives of those around him. He led his fellow Marines in intense combat as a junior rifleman, he was the constant target of intense enemy fire, and he was deeply devoted to his Marines and carrying out his mission.

The highest traditions of the Marine Corps and the United States Naval Service were clearly upheld by another of America's newest heroes, Joseph B. Perez.

FOLLOWING THE Navy Cross award ceremonies, the Houston-born Perez commented, "It is unreal. It is not what I expected. It is unbelievable."

LCpl. Joseph B. Perez, USMC, shown on right, receiving the 2004 Latino Heroes and Heritage Award at the annual National Council of La Raza conference in Phoenix in June 2004. (U.S. Marine Corps / Sgt. Jimmie Perkins)

The following July, Vice President Dick Cheney spoke at a rally for the troops at Camp Pendleton. His remarks included the many deeds of bravery shown by Marines who daily fought enemy insurgents in Iraq. Noting specific heroic actions, he said, "We see the spirit of the Corps in men like LCpl. Joseph Perez who sustained multiple wounds in a fight outside Baghdad, yet still directed his platoon's fire to destroy the enemy and seize their position. His actions earned him the Navy Cross. While recovering from his wounds, Corporal Perez expressed one wish: 'to get back to my unit and back to training.'"[3]

On 25 November 2004 correspondent Casey Wian of CNN's "Lou Dobbs Tonight" program reported from Camp Pendleton, where she talked to many Marines about their experiences in Iraq and Afghanistan. She cited the awards the men received and brought Corporal Perez on camera, mentioning his heroic action and his Navy Cross award. Perez responded, "I'm not really big on getting awards and stuff like that. But you know, I just feel like the award . . . reflects the job of all the Marines that serve with me."[4]

ENDNOTES

1. Navy Cross citation for LCpl. Joseph B. Perez, USMC, www.homeofheroes.com/valor/1_Citations/nc_21wot.html.
2. Matthew Dodd, "Upholding the Highest Traditions," *Defense Watch/Soldiers for the Truth* (online magazine), 17 June 2004, www.sftt.org.
3. Vice President's Remarks at a Rally for the Troops, www.whitehouse.gov/news/ releases/2004/07/20 040727-3.html.
4. Joseph B. Perez, interview by Casey Wian on "Lou Dobbs Tonight," CNN, 25 November 2004

Sgt. Anthony L. Viggiani, USMC

Company C, Battalion Landing Team, 1st Battalion, 6th Marines, 22nd Marine Expeditionary Unit

Zabol Province, Afghanistan
3 June 2004

The Navy Cross is presented to Anthony Lester Viggiani, Sergeant, U.S. Marine Corps, for extraordinary heroism in action against Anti-Coalition Force Militia in Zabol Province, Afghanistan, serving as a squad leader for Charlie Company, Battalion Landing Team, First Battalion, Sixth Marines, Twenty-Second Marine Expeditionary Unit, deployed with commander, United States Fifth Fleet during Operation ENDURING FREEDOM 3 June 2004. While leading a company assault against an enemy held ridgeline north of the village of Khabargho, Sergeant Viggiani and his squadron came under heavy and accurate fire from an enemy force well entrenched inside a cave, pinning down one of his teams and wounding two of his Marines. Moving across exposed ground, under observation and fire from an adjacent enemy position, Sergeant Viggiani maneuvered to the cave opening, but achieving no effect on the enemy. Braving enemy fire from the adjacent enemy position, he went back to retrieve a fragmentation grenade. Again, under a hail of fire, he moved to within feet of the cave opening and employed the grenade to eliminate the enemy position, which was actively firing upon friendly forces. Killing three enemy fighters, Sergeant Viggiani destroyed the enemy strongpoint and allowed his company to continue their advance up to the ridgeline, solidly defeating the enemy by killing a total of fourteen Anti-Coalition fighters. In the process, he was wounded by rifle fire from the adjacent enemy position, yet he continued to lead his Marines in the attack. By his outstanding display of decisive leadership, unlimited courage in the face of enemy fire and utmost dedication to duty, Sergeant Viggiani reflected great credit upon himself and upheld the highest traditions of the Marine Corps and the United States Naval Service.[1]

Excerpt from Navy Cross citation for Sgt. Anthony L. Viggiani, USMC

THE "BOOTS" OF INDIA COMPANY, 3rd Recruit Training Battalion, Marine Corps Recruit Depot, Parris Island, South Carolina, stand at rigid attention as their drill instructor stands in front of their ranks, his posture erect. Shoulders back, chest out. Eyes locked forward. For SSgt. Anthony Viggiani, looking forward is a way of life. He spends his days preparing "his boys" for the future. He looks back only to use what he has experienced in combat to teach new Marines the hard lessons he learned on the battlefield. His focus is always forward.

But Viggiani recalls the events of 3 June 2004, when fate put him in the position of combat leadership as his small squad of twelve Marines pursued a force of anti-coalition force militia (ACM) on foot into the difficult terrain of a steep mountain pass in south-central Afghanistan. Viggiani recalled it as "very rocky, rough, jagged edges. Beautiful, but rough and steep. Unforgiving."[2] His actions under fire would earn him the Navy Cross–the first, and to date only, award of that medal to a Marine for actions in Afghanistan.

As Viggiani stands in front of his recruits, he also thinks back to eight years earlier, on 9 June 1998, when he first "stepped on the footprints" at Parris Island as a new recruit. It was the fulfillment of a boyhood dream. Born and raised in Strongsville, Ohio, he admitted, "I wanted to be a Marine since I was a kid." His mother did a two-year hitch with the Marines, and his brother is in the Navy. "Dad's the only civilian, and we kid him about it."

After twelve weeks of basic training and six weeks of infantry training, Viggiani was sent to the Marine Security Forces School at Chesapeake, Virginia. Marines assigned to security force duties guard naval installations within the United States and around the world, protecting those installations from terrorism and other hostile elements. Marines assigned to these duties are required to be eligible for, and maintain, a top secret clearance. Following completion of the school, early in 1999, Viggianni was assigned to Marine Headquarters, Eighth & I streets, in Washington, D.C., to await his clearance. He spent eleven months performing sentry duty until his top-secret clearance came through.[3]

Viggiani was granted the top secret clearance after clearing a "Yankee white" background check, which is required for personnel assigned to work with the president. It requires, among other things, that the applicant be native-born, not to be or have been married to a person of foreign descent, and never to have traveled to any country considered unfriendly to the United States. In October 1999 Viggiani was assigned to the Marine detachment at Camp David, the presidential retreat, where he remained for two and a half years.

In February 2002 Viggiani was transferred to C Company, BLT (Battalion Landing Team), 1st Battalion, 6th Marine Regiment (1/6), at Camp Lejeune, North Carolina. He arrived just as the unit was departing for a combined arms exercise (CAX) in California, where it trained with small arms, crew-served weapons, and mortars, as well as in shoot-and-maneuver drills and small-unit deployment, under live fire. The unit was then deployed in a unit deployment program (UDP) to Okinawa for six months (June–December 2002), where the troops tested new gear designed for military operations in urbanized terrain (MOUT). The 6th Marines then returned to Camp Lejeune, where they continued to train in marksmanship and field exercises.

The unit was scheduled for another UDP to Okinawa, but the new regimental commander arranged instead for it to be sent to Afghanistan. "We were happy," Viggiani recalled. "We didn't want to go back to Okinawa." The unit left from Norfolk, Virginia, on 18 February 2004 aboard the USS *Wasp* (LHD-1), and "floated over to Afghanistan," arriving a month later.

One of the Navy's newest amphibious warships, the primary mission of the *Wasp* is to support Marine landing forces. The ship is specifically designed to accommodate the new LCAC (landing craft, air cushion) for fast troop movement over the beach and Harrier II (AV-8B) vertical/short take-off and landing (V/STOL) jets, which provide close air support for an assault force. The *Wasp* can also accommodate a full range of Navy and Marine Corps helicopters, conventional landing craft, and amphibious vehicles.

Upon arriving in Afghanistan, the unit flew in C-130s to Kandahar Air Field, where the troops spent several weeks getting acclimatized, which involved getting used to temperatures that reached 134° Farenheit in the shade. "We went to the range, did P.T., and liaisoned with the Army guys, getting the latest intell before starting our mission on what to expect to see out there," recalled Viggiani.

As part of the 22nd Marine Expeditionary Unit (MEU) Special Operations Capable (SOC), a large part of that mission involved "cordon and knock" operations in which villages were surrounded and search teams went house to house seeking enemy insurgents, weapons, and ammunition caches. Women Marines accompanied the troops to facilitate searching females in the heavily segregated society. Inserted deep into the remote Oruzgan Province, the 22nd MEU established Forward Operating Base-Ripley, but despite five combat operations prowling the villages, mountains, and deserts searching for the Taliban, the BLT 1/6 had had little combat experience by late May.[4]

On 1 June 2004, Charlie Company and other elements of BLT 1/6 initiated Operation ASBURY PARK in a Taliban stronghold near the village of Dey Chopan. The troops' baptism of fire occurred the following day when their convoy was ambushed by anti-coalition militia (ACM) forces outside the village of Siah Chub Kalay. The unit engaged in a seven-hour battle that included air strikes by jets and helicopters to suppress machine-gun and RPG fire from the insurgents. By nightfall, the Marines of 1/6 were combat veterans. Viggiani admitted it was hard to tell the good guys from the bad guys. "It was hard. Real hard! Because one minute, they'd have their weapons. They'd be shooting at you. Then they'd run over the top of a hillside and pick up a rake. It was hard to tell."

The next day started like every other. "We got up at daybreak," Viggiani said. "We got into a convoy of four to six gun trucks and ten Humvees. We were totally mechanized and we headed out. We got intell from our interpreters and locals that some high risk areas were coming up." That morning, the Marines pushed forward and entered the village of Khabargho. As allied Afghan militia and the battalion's combined anti-armor team (CAAT) provided overwatch, Charlie Company's 2nd and 3rd Platoons dismounted and worked their way through the village.

Sergeant Viggiani was squad leader of the 1st Squad, 2nd Platoon. "We'd worked our way through our area, and had set up security while waiting word from the company commander, when we saw fourteen to twenty insurgents rolling through the valley. This data was confirmed by Apaches on overwatch." Two Army AH-64 Apache attack helicopters reported twenty heavily armed insurgents fleeing into the hills, and the Charlie Company commander, Capt. Paul Merida, ordered his men to push forward in pursuit.[5]

In the energy-sapping heat, the heavily laden Marines worked their way across the rocky, boulder-strewn terrain. Those familiar with the terrain of Afghanistan compare it to the American southwest desert, only rockier and hotter. A group of insurgents took up positions to delay the pursuing Marines. The rest withdrew deeper into the mountains but found their retreat blocked by Humvees equipped with machine guns and TOW antitank missiles, which had maneuvered behind. Opening fire, and assisted by 30-mm cannon fire from strafing Apache helicopters, the Marines killed at least three ACM fighters.

In the meantime, 2nd Platoon moved up a valley bordered by steep walls on either side. "We linked up with 3rd Squad and pushed up the valley, with 1st squad taking point and 3rd squad taking 'tail end Charlie,'" Viggiani recalled. Second squad was farther up on the left flank, with two M240G belt-fed 7.62 machine guns attached. They'd pushed forward to an overwatch position, but lost radio contact in the mountain pass. "We pushed through, and we started hearing machine-gun fire. We all hit the deck, and I told my boys to get up and to push on because I recognized them [the shots] as 240s. It makes a distinct sound. So we got up and we started pushing. We heard 2nd squad was pinned down."

The Marines pushed forward along the steep terrain. The company's first sergeant, Ernest Hoopii, was with Viggiani and provided radio contact with the rest of the company. When they came to a divide in the terrain, 1st Squad went to the left (west), and 3rd Squad went to the right. Hoopii stayed with 1st Squad. Viggiani's squad was comprised of twelve men: a squad leader, two five-man teams, and a corpsman. As they proceeded along the valley, Corporal George's second team took the left flank of the valley and Corporal Mack's first team, with Viggiani, stayed to the right.

Viggiani later described the action.

"We pushed forward so that we could keep interlocking fields of fire. My second team, Corporal George's team, one of his Marines saw an enemy insurgent with weapons, running. He took off. Two shots took him down. We stopped, halted, and tried to wait for the rest of the company to link up with us, because we were only one squad. We were moving so fast, it would take awhile for them to catch up with us.

"Corporal George's team shifted up, and he put them in places he needed to. Corporal Mack took his team, and I had him place them up on the right side. So we had interlocking fire and were covered on all angles. The fire died down for a second so I had Corporal Mack push his boys up to the top, so we had overwatch and interlocking fields of fire up on top of the right side of the valley. The fire died down, and I patted the first sergeant and told him I had eyes on Corporal George's team and I was going to check on Corporal Mack's team, and he said, 'Very well.' He said he'd contacted the company and told them we were holding our position, waiting for them to come up. I went up to check on Corporal Mack's team, and they were all set. I got a radio transmission that said, 'Viggiani, get down here now.' At this time rounds started pouring over everywhere. I started running down the mountainside as fast as I could without killing myself by falling down the steep terrain."[6]

The delaying force of ACM fighters had deployed themselves with three insurgents in a cave on the right (eastern) side of the draw. Another two were deployed in a machine-gun position on the western side, and two insurgents with RPGs were farther up on the western side. As Viggiani rejoined Sergeant Hoopii, rounds were everywhere. Marines returned fire, although no one was certain where the rounds were coming from. Although Viggiani and Hoopii were closest to the cave, they had no idea of its exact location. Intensely aware of incoming fire from both the insurgents and from friendlies on the opposite slope, they inched forward trying to locate the enemy. The echoes of shots off the steep cliffs and the shouts and din of battle added to the confusion.

On the opposite slope, LCpl. James Gould went down with a wound to the right calf. Cpl. Randy Wood, unmindful of rounds kicking up puffs of dirt around him, raced to Gould's position, and both took cover behind a boulder. While working on Gould's wound, Wood discovered that a ricochet had sliced open his own cheek below his left eye. These two Marines were Charlie Company's first casualties since deploying to Afghanistan. Gould recalled, "I raised my head one time and the guy (ACM fighter) hit the rock right in front of us, so we were pinned down pretty good." Hospital Corpsman Brian Imber tried to reach the two Marines, but intense gunfire made progress difficult. "There wasn't enough room for all three of us behind the rock, so we ordered Doc to stay where he was," Gould recalled. With Imber shouting instructions, Wood treated Gould's wound.[7]

Across the valley, Viggiani and others continued to move forward. "I had my M-16A-4 in my right hand, and a frag [fragmentation grenade] in my left. I came running down. I got to my first sergeant. Rounds were flying everywhere. I asked him, 'Where [are] they at? Where they at?' And he said, 'Down there,' and pointed to them. He didn't have any fragmentation grenades on him. I did. I started to move down this side of the valley, looking around, not sure if I'm going to have to go down to the base of the valley. There were holes in the deck that a person might get down if he didn't have any gear, but it was tight. In the opening I saw . . . I'll never forget . . . It was like gray, smoky gray, cloth with red piping on it. It was like in a hole. I fired three or four rounds in it. It moved, I saw skin and fired three or four more rounds, pulled the pin on my frag, dropped the frag in, backed up about two steps and postured myself to the left on the rocks. The frag went off, and everything was coming up every crack and crevice available. By now, the other machine gun position was fixed on my position and was pouring lead on me. The first sergeant came down and covered me so that we could both get out. We came back up, made maybe ten yards, and plastered ourselves against the rocks. By this time rounds were coming everywhere. I mean everywhere!"[8]

With Apaches flying overhead, they marked their position with white smoke, and as Viggiani described it, "The Apaches came screaming in with Gatling guns and neutralized the enemy positions. The firing pretty much died down. We got some casualty reports, and I found out that during a firefight two of my boys on Corporal George's team got hit and were wounded pretty bad. I got wounded when we were moving back."[9]

Viggiani was wounded in the left leg, and the first sergeant called for medevac. But Viggiani refused to be evacuated and told the first sergeant, "I ain't damn going," and the first sergeant told him he'd have to talk to the C.O. [commanding officer]. Viggiani told him, "I'll talk to the C.O., but I ain't leaving my boys." Viggiani met with his captain. "I told him as tactfully as I could that I wasn't f---ing going. He asked if I was fine. I said, 'Sir, I'm fine. I'm going with my boys.' He said, 'Very well, have a corpsman look at it.' I went over, liaisoned with my corpsman. He looked at it real quick, and then we pushed on."

As Charlie Company pushed deeper into the mountains, Sergeant Viggiani stayed with his boys, his wound field-dressed, and helped uncover two arms caches. The 3rd Squad escorted the captured detainees down the hill and provided security, and Hoopii "manpacked" the wounded Gould down the steep incline to a spot where he could be evacuated. "That was the hardest hump of my life," said Hoopii. He was relieved later by 2nd Lt. Michael Keller, the company's forward observer, and Gould finished his journey on the back of a donkey.[10]

In all, fourteen insurgents were killed during the actions at Khabargho on 3 June. The Marines of 1/6 finished their deployment and returned stateside on 15 September 2004. Viggiani heard a rumor that he'd been recommended for an award, but didn't give it much thought. In May 2005 he was assigned as a senior drill instructor at Parris Island.

SSgt. Anthony L. Viggiani, USMC. (U.S. Marine Corps / Cpl. Maryalice Leone)

ON A CRISP, SUNNY MORNING on 24 February 2006, the "boots" of India Company, 3rd Recruit Training Battalion, Marine Corps Recruit Depot, Parris Island, South Carolina, stood at attention as their drill instructor, Sgt. Anthony Viggiani, received the Navy Cross from the base commander, Brig. Gen. Richard Tryon. Viggiani appreciates the honor of the award, but will tell you with no false modesty that he was just doing his job, and keeping his promise. "I told my boys before we left I'd bring them all back. And I brought them all back."[11]

A far greater honor, he will tell you, was when the 22nd MEU (SOC) held a "warriors night" while conducting an end-of-deployment debriefing at the Naval Support Activity, Rota, Spain, on 4 September 2004. Out of each company, the battalion commander, Lt. Col. Asad A. Khan, selected one Marine who had distinguished himself. Viggiani was selected to represent Charlie Company. "That meant more to me [than the Navy Cross]. The boys I brought back were there in the room with me. They were there with me. They understood. I wouldn't trade a one of them."[12]

ENDNOTES

1. Navy Cross Citation for Sgt. Anthony Lester Viggiani, USMC, www.homeofheroes.com/valor/1_citations/nc_21wot.html.

2. Anthony Viggiani, telephone interview by Scott Baron, 5 November 2006.

3. Ibid.

4. Keith A. Milks, "War among the Rocks: Battlefield Standout Wins Navy Cross," *Leatherneck Magazine*, June 2006.

5. Geoff Ziezulewicz, "'There Was Just No Way I Was Leaving my Boys': Shot to the Leg Couldn't Get Marine out of the Fight," *Stars and Stripes*, 14 June 2006.

6. Anthony Viggiani, telephone interview by Scott Baron.

7. Keith A. Milks, "Marines Take Care of One Another in Fierce Afghan Firefight," *Stars and Stripes*, 8 June 2004.

8. Anthony Viggiani, telephone interview by Scott Baron.

9. Ibid.

10. Milks, "Marines Take Care of One Another in Fierce Afghan Firefight."

11. Anthony Viggiani, telephone interview by Scott Baron.

12. Ibid.

The Fallujah Seven

MORE THAN TWO YEARS after U.S. forces assaulted insurgents in Fallujah during Operation PHANTOM FURY in November 2004, the city remains a center of insurgency and a stronghold for anti-occupation Sunni militias and Islamist nationalists. Followers of the late Abu Musab al-Zarqawi and Hussein loyalists find refuge there. U.S. and Iraqi troops and police continue to be the targets of ambushes using rocket-propelled grenades (RPGs) and improvised explosive devices (IEDs). Fallujah has been witness to countless deaths, massive destruction, and selfless acts of valor. Of the twenty Navy Crosses awarded to date in Iraq and Afghanistan, seven have been for acts occurring in Fallujah.

Fallujah is a city in the Iraqi province of Al Anbar, in the notorious "Sunni Triangle." Prior to the invasion it had a population of 350,000. Known as the "City of Mosques," Fallujah lies sixty-nine kilometers (forty-three miles) west of Baghdad and had been a Sunni center of support for the Hussein government and Ba'ath party before the invasion.

Dating back to Babylonian times, Fallujah was the site of the Pumbedita Academy, a center for Jewish learning, from 258 AD to 1038 AD. Of little importance during the Ottoman Empire, it came under the control of the British after the collapse of the empire following the First World War. Lt. Col. Gerard Leachman, a British colonial officer, was killed when he went to Fallujah on 12 August 1920 while trying to put down a rebellion. The British Army crushed the rebellion at the cost of ten thousand Iraqis and one thousand British soldiers.[1]

Iraq gained independence from Great Britain in 1932, but the British retained military bases and transit rights for their forces in the country. In 1941 British forces invaded Al Anbar province when the government of Rashid Ali appeared to ally itself with Nazi Germany. In a battle near Fallujah, the British Army defeated the Iraqi Army, beginning an occupation that lasted until 1947.

Saddam Hussein and the Ba'ath party came to power in 1979, and Fallujah grew into an influential base for the Ba'athist regime. The invasion by the U.S.-led coalition forces of Operation IRAQI FREEDOM on 20 March 2003 had little impact on Fallujah. There was no major fighting there, and Iraqi forces in the area abandoned their positions and deserted. Much of their abandoned equipment fell into the control of various competing militias, and former military and paramilitary personnel found themselves unemployed. One of Saddam Hussein's last official acts was to release all the prisoners at nearby Abu Ghraib prison, flooding the area with political and criminal prisoners.

Although spared destruction from the initial invasion of coalition forces, Fallujah fell victim to the lawlessness and looting that followed the collapse of

Hussein's regime, and the new, nominally pro-American mayor, Taha Bidaywi Hamed, welcomed the 82nd Airborne into the city on 23 April 2003. Troops set up operations at the Ba'ath Party headquarters and al-Qa'id primary school.

A demonstration outside the school on the evening of 28 April by a crowd of approximately two hundred, demanding that the Americans vacate the school so it could be reopened, deteriorated into violence when the rock-throwing crowd, defying a curfew, refused to disperse. After smoke canisters failed to disperse the crowd, shots were fired by American troops. Accounts are in dispute as to whether the American troops were fired upon and fired back in self-defense, or fired first. But the result was fifteen killed and another fifty-three wounded on both sides. The next day, the coalition troops vacated the school.[2]

Two days later, on 30 April 2003, the 2nd Troop (Fox), U.S. 3rd Armored Cavalry Regiment, relieved the 82nd Airborne. A demonstration in front of the former Ba'ath headquarters protesting the earlier shooting led U.S. troops again to fire into the crowd, killing three protesters. The 3rd Cavalry was quickly replaced by the 2nd Brigade of the 3rd Infantry Division. The 3rd Infantry was later replaced by the 3rd Cavalry, which was itself replaced by the 3rd Brigade of the 82nd Airborne in September 2003. After that, the 82nd was responsible for security in Ramaldi and Fallujah, with the 3rd Cavalry responsible for the remainder of the Al Anbar province.

Over the next year, Sunni rebel groups and foreign terrorists aligned to al Qaeda used Fallujah as both a base and a symbol of defiance against coalition forces and the interim Iraqi government. Attacks on U.S. troops were frequent: on 21 May two Iraqis were killed in an RPG attack on an American patrol; on 27 May two Americans were killed and seven wounded in an attack; on 5 June one American died and five were wounded in an RPG attack. Between November 2003 and January 2004, three U.S. helicopters were attacked, resulting in fifteen American fatalities. On 12 February 2004, insurgents fired on a convoy carrying U.S. senior commander Gen. John Abizaid, and two days later they attacked an Iraqi police station in Fallujah, killing twenty-three Iraqis. Almost a year after the invasion, U.S. and Iraqi forces were still unable to restore law and order to Fallujah's streets, and lawlessness prevailed.

In March 2004 the 82nd Airborne transferred authority of the al Anbar province to the I Marine Expeditionary Force (composed of the 1st Marine Division, 3rd Marine Aircraft Wing, and the 1st Marine Logistics Group), but the increasing violence against the American presence in the city resulted in the complete withdrawal of troops from the city, and Fallujah began to fall under the increasing influence of guerilla insurgents.

On 31 March 2004 insurgents ambushed a convoy that included four armed American contractors working for Blackwater USA who were providing security for a food delivery.[3] The Americans were dragged from their car and beaten, then set on fire. Their burned and charred corpses were dragged through the streets, desecrated, and hung from a bridge over the Euphrates River. As one journalist reported, "The bodies were hanging upside down on each side of the bridge. They had no hands, no feet, one had no head. My old Iraqi friend had been driving into Fallujah just after the massacre, the stoning, the burning. He was shaking as he told me what he saw. 'They were hanging upside down above the highway, on the old railway bridge, which is now a road bridge. The people of Fallujah were just driving over the bridge as if nothing was happening, right past the bodies.'" That same day, five U.S. Marines were killed by an IED roadside bomb just outside the city[4]

Photos of the four American civilians' corpses flooded the airwaves and Internet worldwide, and the images of laughing and smiling Iraqis outraged the American public. U.S. military commanders suspended a strategy of foot patrols, humanitarian aid, and cooperation with local leaders, and on 4 April launched Operation VIGILANT RESOLVE, also known as the First Battle of Fallujah, a military operation to reoccupy Fallujah and clear all armed militias and guerillas from the city.

Operation VIGILANT RESOLVE—The First Battle for Fallujah

On 4 April 2004 coalition forces, headed by the 1st Marine Expeditionary Force (2nd Battalion, 1st Marines; 3rd Battalion, 4th Marines; and 1st Battalion, 5th Marines), surrounded Fallujah and executed limited aerial strikes on selected targets. The next morning, roads leading into the city were blockaded. Residents were warned to stay inside and were urged to cooperate with coalition forces and to identify insurgents. A curfew was imposed from 7:00 PM to 6:00 AM, and it was estimated that up to a third of the civilian population evacuated the city.[5]

Efforts by coalition troops to enter the city set off widespread fighting throughout central Iraq and along the lower Euphrates River. On 7 April, U.S. Abrams tanks and AC-130 gunships attacked the outlying districts, and were opposed by guerillas armed with Kalashnikov automatic rifles and RPGs.

In the combat of 7 April, amid countless acts of courage and valor, the heroism of two American Marines—Capt. Brent Morel and Sgt. Willie L. Copeland III— would especially stand out and would merit the Navy Cross.

Capt. Brent Morel, USMC

Al Anbar Province, Iraq
7 April 2004

The Navy Cross is awarded to Captain Brent Morel, United States Marine Corps, for extraordinary heroism as Platoon Commander, 2nd Platoon, Company B, 1st Reconnaissance Battalion, 1st Marine Division, I Marine Expeditionary Force,

U.S. Marine Corps Forces, Central Command in support of Operation IRAQI FREEDOM on 7 April 2004. Captain Morel's platoon escorted a convoy into the Al Anbar Province when 40 to 60 insurgents in well-fortified and concealed positions initiated an ambush. Witnessing a rocket-propelled grenade crippling his lead vehicle and while mortar and machine gun fire erupted, he ordered his remaining two vehicles to secure a flanking position. Captain Morel left his vehicle and led a determined assault across an open field and up a 10-foot berm, in order to maneuver into firing positions. The boldness of this first assault eliminated several insurgents at close range forcing their retreat. Observing his Marines pinned down from enemy fire, Captain Morel left the safety of his position and continued the assault, eliminating the enemy's attack. During this valiant act, he fell mortally wounded by a withering burst of enemy automatic weapons fire. By his outstanding display of decisive leadership, unlimited courage in the face of heavy enemy fire, and utmost devotion to duty, Captain Morel reflected great credit upon himself and upheld the highest traditions of the Marine Corps and the United States Naval Service.[6]

Navy Cross citation for Capt. Brent Morel, USMC

Sgt. Willie L. Copeland III, USMC

Al Anbar Province, Iraq
7 April 2004

The Navy Cross is awarded to Sergeant Willie L. Copeland, III, United States Marine Corps, for extraordinary heroism as Team Leader, 2nd Platoon, Bravo Company, 1st Reconnaissance Battalion, 1st Marine Division, I Marine Expeditionary Force, U.S. Marine Corps Forces, Central Command in support of Operation IRAQI FREEDOM on April 7, 2004. Tasked as the Main Effort to lead a convoy to a Forward Operating Base, Sergeant Copeland's platoon was ambushed by 40–60 insurgents in well-fortified and concealed positions near the province of Al Anbar. After observing a rocket-propelled grenade instantly crippling the lead vehicle and having mortar and machine gun fire disable his own, Sergeant Copeland led five Marines out of the heaviest zone under attack and made an assault across an open field. They continued the assault across a deep and muddy canal, working their way up to firing positions on the far side within hand grenade range of the enemy. The vigor of this first assault eliminated ten insurgents at close range while forcing other enemy positions to flee. During this valiant effort, his commanding officer fell wounded at his side. Unwilling to subject any more Marines to danger, he signaled

Sgt. Willie L. Copeland III, USMC. (U.S. Marine Corps / LCpl. Joseph L. DiGirolamo)

others to remain in covered positions. While placing himself in a position to shield his wounded officer, he applied first aid. Without regard for his own personal safety, Sergeant Copeland stabilized, then evacuated his Captain to a safe area. He then conducted the withdrawal of his team from their covered positions through the use of hand grenades. By his bold leadership, wise judgment, and complete dedication to duty, Sergeant Copeland reflected great credit upon himself and upheld the highest traditions of the Marine Corps and the United States Naval Service.[7]

Navy Cross citation for Sgt. Willie L. Copeland III, USMC

ON THE MORNING OF 7 APRIL 2004, Capt. Brent Morel and Sgt. Willie Copeland were in a convoy en route to a forward operating base along "Route Boston," just outside Fallujah. The first five Humvees were occupied by members of the 2nd Platoon, Bravo Company, 1st Reconnaissance (Recon) Battalion, 1st Marine Division. Copeland, a team leader, and Morel, the platoon commander, were in the second vehicle. Both would earn the Navy Cross that day.[8]

Recon Marines are considered to be among the elite of the Corps, on a par with Navy SEALS, Air Force Pararescuers, and Army Special Forces. Comprised primarily of volunteers from infantry units, they receive intense advanced training in weapons, marksmanship, and small-unit tactics, and attend formal specialized schools (such as airborne and scuba). Their mission usually involves independent small-unit operations in support of larger forces.

That morning, Bravo Company's mission was "to escort a fifteen-vehicle convoy of Humvees and seven-ton trucks on a ten-mile trek to a supply point, where they would hunt for enemy mortar teams."[9] Cpl. James "Eddie" Wright, assistant team leader of Team 1, 2nd Platoon, was in the lead Humvee. He later recalled that they were uneasy as they proceeded through what they knew to be unfriendly territory. "They always had a lot of Improvised Explosive Device (IED) attacks and ambushes in that neighborhood. We knew we were going to get ambushed; we could tell by the people and their actions. But we had to go. We had a mission to accomplish."[10]

The terrain was perfect for an ambush. The road was elevated and exposed, bordered by a series of chest-high berms (earthen walls bordered by ditches) that ran parallel to the road, and there was a canal that acted as a moat. And the ambush did occur. The lead vehicle was hit first when an RPG slammed into the right door, where Cpl. Eddie Wright had mounted an M-249 SAW machine gun. The explosion wounded all five soldiers inside. Wright lost both hands, and took a serious wound to his leg. Where many in Wright's condition would have gone into shock, he calmly directed his Marines in applying his tourniquets while calling out enemy positions. Cpl. Shawn Talbert, behind the roof machine gun, was riddled with shrapnel below the knees. Sgt. Eric Kocher, the team leader, took a hit that tore open his tricep and shattered his right elbow. As a tourniquet was applied, he returned fire with his left hand using the driver's gun. The driver and the soldier behind him were also wounded by shrapnel but were not disabled. The driver replaced Talbert in the turret, returning fire, as Kocher drove the shattered vehicle out of the kill zone.[11]

Approximately forty to sixty insurgents opened up with RPGs, machine guns, and mortars from well-fortified positions and caught the lead vehicles in the kill zone. Captain Morel had ordered his Humvee to take a position between his Marines and the insurgents, and it was hit with machine-gun and mortar fire and disabled.[12] Morel must have remembered his tactical training. Despite the normal instinct to seek cover, Marines are taught to turn into the ambush and assault through it because every second in the kill zone is critical. In a split second, that was

Morel's decision. As Sergeant Copeland would later state, "Nothing's natural about running into bullets."[13]

Morel ordered his troops to stop and dismount, even as he ran toward the enemy positions, followed by Sgt. Michael Mendoza and Sgt. Dan Lalota. Sgt. Willie Copeland provided covering fire, then struggled to catch up as they waded across the canal. In the interim, GySgt. Dan Griego, the platoon sergeant, maneuvered the two trailing Humvees up a dirt road to crest a hill and flank the insurgents. They opened fire, killing several of the enemy and disabling two civilian vehicles that appeared to be shuttling wounded and reinforcements.[14]

Griego had expected Morel's element to set up a base of fire so that his element could roll the flank, but Morel's advance was so rapid that he had to recall a team to prevent a deadly crossfire, and instead laid down a base of fire for Morel. Morel led his Marines through intense small-arms fire, pausing behind the next-to-last berm. "Cover me, we're assaulting through," Morel shouted. "You want to assault through?" Lalota asked, and when Morel said, "Yes," he responded, "Roger."[15]

As they crested the last berm, Morel was struck by automatic-weapons fire under the armpit, puncturing both lungs, and Mendoza was knocked to the ground by an exploding RPG. LCpl. Maurice Scott was the first to reach Morel, and dragged him across open ground to a shallow irrigation culvert. Scott was a former Army Airborne Ranger who enlisted in the Marines following 9/11. Others arrived and stripped off Morel's gear and applied field dressings, all out in the open. Amazingly, no one was hit by enemy fire.[16]

Copeland ordered the others to cover, and he shielded Morel's body with his own until armored Humvees arrived approximately fifteen minutes later. Morel was evacuated, then Copeland used hand grenades to cover the withdrawal of his team.

The Marines of 2nd Platoon killed an estimated thirty enemy fighters, with only one Marine fatality, Captain Morel, who died on the way to the hospital. By his actions, Morel saved every Marine's life but his own.

Sgt. Eric Kocher and SSgt. Dan Lalota were awarded Bronze Star medals in a ceremony at Camp Pendleton in September 2004. SSgt. Mike Mendoza was awarded a Silver Star. Mendoza returned for a second tour in Iraq, where he was wounded on 3 August 2006. Three moths later, he volunteered for a third tour.

Sergeant Copeland was promoted to staff sergeant and assigned to Marine Special Operations at Camp Lejeune, North Carolina. The twenty-six-year-old Utah native was presented the Navy Cross by Assistant Secretary of the Navy Richard Greco in a ceremony at Camp Pendleton on 21 April 2005. Captain Morel's wife, Amy, accepted his posthumous Navy Cross in a ceremony at the Marine Forces Reserve Training Center in Memphis, Tennessee, on 21 April 2005. As his father, Mike Morel, eulogized, "Brent never asked anyone to do anything he wouldn't do himself. He was first in line."

Amy Morel receives Navy Cross (posthumous) for her husband, Capt. Brent Morel, USMC, at a ceremony at the Marine Corps Training Center in Memphis, Tennessee. Captain Morel was killed on 7 April 2004, at Fallujah, Iraq. (U.S. Marine Corps / LCpl. Miguel A. Carrasco Jr.)

On 9 April 2004 Paul Bremer, head of the Coalition Provisional Authority, announced a unilateral cease-fire of coalition forces to facilitate negotiations between the Iraqi Governing Council, insurgents, and local leaders, and to allow humanitarian aid to enter Fallujah. Coalition forces withdrew to the city outskirts, but local insurgents refused to honor the cease-fire and continued to attack, using the cease-fire to resupply and rearm.

Negotiations began on 16 April, and by the 19th a cease-fire agreement was reached, but hostilities continued. On 26 April, two Army Delta Force soldiers, MSgt. Don Hollenbaugh and medic SSgt. Dan Briggs, joined a Marine contingent of about thirty-five men, entered the city on foot, and occupied two houses north and south of an intersection to use as observation posts. Attacked by a superior force of insurgents, they held them off. Both Hollenbaugh and Briggs were awarded the Distinguished Service Cross (the Army's equivalent to the Navy Cross) for "turning the tide of the enemy's ground-force assault on a U.S. Marine Corps platoon" and being "directly responsible for preventing enemy insurgent forces from overrunning the United States Force."[17]

On 28 April, Operation VIGILANT RESOLVE ended when local leaders in Fallujah agreed to keep resistance fighters out of the city. The Fallujah Protection Force composed of local Iraqis was set up to help fight the rising resistance. On 1 May 2004, U.S. forces withdrew from Fallujah, leaving control in the hands of the "Fallujah Brigade." The effort was spectacularly unsuccessful. Over the summer, attacks on U.S. and Iraqi forces continued, as did the kidnapping and execution of foreigners, and both sides prepared for the next offensive. Under leaders such as the Shiite cleric Muqtada al-Sadr and Abu Musab al-Zarqawi, an insurgency leader linked to al Qaeda, the character of the opposition changed from former Saddam loyalists to radical nationalist Islamists.

Operation AL FAJR/Operation PHANTOM FURY—The Second Battle of Fallujah

On 7 November 2004, in what would become the heaviest urban combat that American fighters had seen since the Battle of Hue City in Vietnam, U.S. and Iraqi forces initiated Operation PHANTOM FURY, an offensive against rebel strongholds in the city of Fallujah. Iraqi Prime Minister Ayad Allawi publicly authorized an offensive to "liberate the people" and "clean Fallujah from the terrorists."

Before the attack, American and Iraqi forces established checkpoints around the city, and overhead imagery was used to prepare maps of the city. Iraqi translators accompanied U.S. forces, and after weeks of air strikes and artillery bombardment, the U.S. Marines were ready to return to Fallujah to finish the job they had begun the previous April.

Ground operations began on the evening of 7 November with diversionary attacks in the west and south by the Iraqi 36th Commando Battalion, the Marines 3rd Light Armored Reconnaissance Battalion, and Company B, 1st Battalion, 23rd Marines, capturing Fallujah General Hospital and the Jurf Kas Sukr Bridge over the Euphrates.

Four U.S. Marine light infantry battalions and two Army mechanized cavalry battalions launched a broad attack along numerous fronts. Amnesty was offered to all but major criminals, and a strict shoot-to-kill curfew was put in place. Taking part in a large part of the operations were the Marines of the 3rd Battalion, 1st Marine Regiment, 1st Marine Division, based at Camp Pendleton, California. Veterans of the 2003 invasion, they had redeployed to Iraq in mid-2004 and had been based near Fallujah. Now their mission was to clear significant parts of the city, including the infamous Jolon District.[18]

1st Sgt. Bradley A. Kasal, USMC

Fallujah, Iraq
13 November 2004

The Navy Cross is presented to Bradley A. Kasal, First Sergeant, U.S. Marine Corps, for extraordinary heroism while serving as First Sergeant, Weapons Company, 3d Battalion, 1st Marine Regiment, Regimental Combat Team 1, 1st Marine Division, I Marine Expeditionary Force, U.S. Marine Corps Forces Central Command in support of Operation IRAQI FREEDOM on 13 November 2004. First Sergeant

1st Sgt. Bradley A. Kasal, USMC. (Kasal collection)

Kasal was assisting 1st Section, Combined Anti-Armor Platoon as they provided a traveling over watch for 3d Platoon when he heard a large volume of fire erupt to his immediate front, shortly followed by Marines rapidly exiting a structure. When First Sergeant Kasal learned that Marines were pinned down inside the house by an unknown number of enemy personnel, he joined a squad making entry to clear the structure and rescue the Marines inside. He made entry into the first room, immediately encountering and eliminating an enemy insurgent, as he spotted a wounded Marine in the next room. While moving towards the wounded Marine, First Sergeant Kasal and another Marine came under heavy rifle fire from an elevated enemy firing position and were both severely wounded in the legs, immobilizing them. When insurgents threw grenades in an attempt to eliminate the wounded Marines, he rolled on top of his fellow Marine and absorbed the shrapnel with his own body. When First Sergeant Kasal was offered medical attention and extraction, he refused until the other Marines were given medical attention. Although severely wounded himself, he shouted encouragement to his fellow Marines as they continued to clear the structure. By his bold leadership, wise judgment, and complete dedication to duty, First Sergeant Kasal reflected great credit upon himself and upheld the highest traditions of the Marine Corps and the United States Naval Service.[19]

Navy Cross citation for Sgt. Bradley A. Kasal, USMC

Cpl. Robert J. Mitchell Jr., USMC

Fallujah, Iraq
13 November 2004

The Navy Cross is presented to Robert J. Mitchell, Jr., Corporal, U.S. Marine Corps, for extraordinary heroism while serving as Squad Leader, Company K, 3d Battalion, 1st Marine Regiment, Regimental Combat Team 1, 1st Marine Division, I Marine Expeditionary Force, U.S. Marine Corps Forces, Central, in support of Operation IRAQI FREEDOM on 13 November 2004. During a ferocious firefight with six insurgents fighting inside a heavily fortified house, Corporal Mitchell courageously attacked the enemy strongpoint to rescue five wounded Marines trapped inside the house. Locating the enemy positions and completely disregarding his own safety, he gallantly charged through enemy AK-47 fire and hand grenades, in order to assist a critically wounded Marine in an isolated room. Ignoring his own wounds, he began the immediate first aid treatment of the Marine's severely wounded leg. Assessing that the Marine needed immediate intravenous fluids to survive, he suppressed the enemy, enabling a Corpsman to cross the impact zone. Once the Corpsman arrived, he moved to the next room to assist other casualties. While running across the impact zone a second time, he was hit in the left leg with a ricochet off of his weapon and with grenade shrapnel to the legs and face. While applying first aid, he noticed a wounded insurgent reach for his weapon. With his rifle inoperable, he drew his combat knife, stabbed the insurgent, and eliminated him instantly. Demonstrating great presence of mind, he then coordinated the casualties' evacuation. Limping from his own wounds, Corporal Mitchell assisted in the evacuation of the last casualty through the impact zone under enemy fire, ultimately saving the lives of multiple Marines. By his bold leadership, wise judgment, and complete dedication to duty, Corporal Mitchell reflected great credit upon himself and upheld the highest traditions of the Marine Corps and the United States Naval Service.[20]

Navy Cross citation for Cpl. Robert J. Mitchell Jr., USMC

THE 3/1 WAS INVOLVED IN house-to-house operations in Fallujah, often involving close combat as pockets of resistance were located and eliminated. On 13 November, five days into the battle, Weapons Company 1st Sgt. Bradley Kasal was operating with the 1st section of his anti-armor platoon, providing overwatch for the 3rd Platoon.

Unknown to the Marines, insurgents had set up an ambush within a cinder block house, a death trap that came to be known as the "House of Hell." According to Marine Maj. Gen. Michael Lehnert, it was "set up with one purpose: to kill United States Marines."[21] Inside the house, the insurgents were ready in fortified positions when Marines entered, and the ensuing gunfight left Marines and insurgents dead, dying, and wounded. Some Marines escaped, but three were left pinned down inside. The insurgents were using the trapped Marines, who were either dead or wounded, as bait.[22]

Sergeant Kasal had joined Cpl. Robert Mitchell's squad when the call for help came, and the two Iowa Marine NCOs came to the same decision. "I wasn't going to leave Marines behind in the hands of insurgents at any cost," Kasal recalled in an interview. "I was told they were wounded. I was afraid of them ending up on television being beheaded later. I knew we had to get in there fast, we had to get in and get them."[23]

Sgt. Robert J. Mitchel Jr., USMC. (U.S. Marine Corps / SSgt. Nathaniel Garcia)

Corporal Mitchell felt the same. "When the call came, we knew we had to get them out. That became the mission—the only mission." They quickly established a casualty collection point and assembled for the assault. Mitchell, who had been shot through the right triceps the previous day, had ignored the wound and helped destroy a fortified position, then refused medical evacuation. Now, with Kasal and his squad, they charged through insurgent fire to assault the building and took up firing positions. The insurgents were in fortified positions on the roof, with a skylight providing a field of fire between the Marines outside and the trapped Marines within.

Inside, Cpl. Jose Sanchez was treating LCpl. Cory Carlisle while holding off the insurgents when the Marines began laying down suppressive fire, and Mitchell raced through intense small-arms fire and grenades to reach them. Although wounded himself by shrapnel in the rear of both legs, Mitchell took over treatment of Carlisle's leg wound while Sanchez focused on suppressing the insurgents.

Meanwhile, Kasal positioned his Marines inside to cover insurgent positions, and entered an uncleared room. With LCpl. Alex Nicoll to the rear, he immediately came face to face with an armed insurgent. The two exchanged hurried shots, but Kasal's shots hit their target. "I stuck my barrel right in his chest, we were that close," said Kasal. "I kept pulling the trigger until he went down . . . then I shot him two more times in the forehead to make sure he was dead."[24]

Insurgents on a staircase opened fire, and both Kasal and Nicoll were struck by several rounds of AK-47 fire. Kasal saw Nicoll bleeding severely from the midsection and left leg, and braved additional fire to crawl to Nicoll and drag him out of the line of fire into an adjoining room. For his efforts, Kasal took additional wounds in the buttocks. He began applying field dressing to Nicoll's wounds to stop the bleeding. When insurgents dropped a grenade within two feet, Kasal unhesitatingly sheltered Nicoll's body with his own, suffering forty shrapnel wounds in addition to the seven gunshot wounds he'd already endured. Seriously wounded (some estimates placed his blood loss at 60 percent), the nineteen-year veteran of three tours in Iraq and Afghanistan wasn't through fighting.[25]

Across the kill zone, Mitchell left the wounded Marines in the care of a corpsman and then crossed under enemy fire to come to the aid of Kasal and Nicoll. One enemy round ricocheted off his M16A4 assault rifle into his right leg, and shrapnel struck his face and legs, but he remained on his feet and made it to Kasal and Nicoll.

Despite his wounds, Mitchell began life-saving efforts on Kasal and Nicoll, but when a wounded insurgent went for a weapon, he eliminated the threat with his combat knife, his rifle having been previously disabled by enemy fire. He then communicated the situation to the Marines outside who took up positions on adjacent roofs and laid down suppressing fire on the insurgents as, one by one, the wounded Marines were safely extracted.[26]

Kasal had refused treatment until the other wounded Marines were treated. He left his rifle in the doorway as a sign to others that Marines were inside the room, and covered Mitchell with his 9-mm Beretta pistol. A photo of Kasal by Associated Press photographer Lucian Reed has become an iconic image of the Iraq War. It shows Kasal being carried out of the house by two lance corporals, Chris Marquez and Dan Shaffer, Kasal still gripping his Beretta and ready to cover the two Marines.

Mitchell was one of the last to leave, assisting another wounded Marine as they exited. With the house clear of Marines, demolition charges were flung inside. The explosion reduced the house to rubble, killing the remaining insurgents.

Mitchell, who left the Corps as a sergeant in March 2005, was presented the Navy Cross by Lt. Gen. John F. Sattler, commander of I Marine Expeditionary Force (MEF), at a ceremony at Camp Pendleton on 28 July 2006. Lance Corporal Nicoll was evacuated to Landstuhl, Germany, where his left leg was amputated below the knee. Best friends with Mitchell, Nicoll now lives with Mitchell and his wife in Arizona, where both are studying to be motorcycle mechanics. Cpl. Jose Sanchez was awarded the Bronze Star for valor.

Doctors told Kasal that he'd likely also lose his leg because four inches of bone had been shot away and surgery would be painful and not likely to succeed. Kasal knew that amputation would mean the end of his Marine career. He opted to "gut it out." Twenty operations later, Kasal is still a Marine. Promoted to sergeant major, the highest enlisted rank in the Marines, he was presented the Navy Cross on 1 May 2006. He is assigned as a recruiter as he recovers from his wounds. He hopes to return to the infantry and to Iraq, but he acknowledges that it's unlikely he'll ever fully recover. "I have a lot of issues I'll have to deal with for the rest of my life."[27]

Both Mitchell and Kasal are genuinely modest about their awards, and they doubt their actions were other than what any Marine would do. Kasal declines interviews and doesn't want his acclaim to overshadow the actions of his Marines. "That house was full of heroes," he said.

"I wouldn't want to do it again," Mitchell said of his charge across the insurgents' field of fire. "I'd do it, though. I'd do it for them," he said pointing to a group of Marines. "I'd do it for you."

Although major combat operations ended in Fallujah on 13 November 2004, sporadic fighting continued inside and outside the city as pockets of resistance were identified and eliminated, often involving house-to-house operations.

Sgt. Jeremiah W. Workman, USMC. (U.S. Marine Corps / LCpl. Troy Loveless)

Cpl. Jeremiah W. Workman, USMC

Fallujah, Iraq
23 December 2004

The Navy Cross is presented to Jeremiah W. Workman, Corporal, U.S. Marine Corps, for extraordinary heroism while serving as Squad Leader, Mortar Platoon, Weapons Company, 3d Battalion, 5th Marine Regiment, Regimental Combat Team 1, 1st Marine Division, U.S. Marine Corps Forces, Central Command in support of Operation IRAQI FREEDOM on 23 December 2004. During clearing operations in Al Fallujah, Iraq, Corporal Workman displayed exceptional situational awareness while organizing his squad to enter a building to retrieve isolated Marines inside. Despite heavy resistance from enemy automatic weapons fire, and a barrage of grenades, Corporal Workman fearlessly exposed himself and laid down a base of fire that allowed the isolated Marines to escape. Outside the house, he rallied the rescued Marines and directed fire onto insurgent positions as he aided wounded Marines in a neighboring yard. After seeing these Marines to safety, he led another assault force into the building to eliminate insurgents and extract more Marines. Corporal Workman again exposed himself to enemy fire while providing cover fire for the team when an enemy grenade exploded directly in front of him causing shrapnel wounds to his arms and legs. Corporal Workman continued to provide intense fire long enough to recover additional wounded Marines and extract them from the besieged building.

Although injured, he led a third assault into the building, rallying his team one last time to extract isolated Marines before M1A1 tanks arrived to support the battle. Throughout this fight, Corporal Workman's heroic actions contributed to the elimination of 24 insurgents. By his bold leadership, wise judgment, and complete dedication to duty, Corporal Workman reflected great credit upon himself and upheld the highest traditions of the Marine Corps and the United States Naval Service.[28]

Navy Cross citation for Cpl. Jeremiah W. Workman, USMC

Sgt. Jarrett A. Kraft, USMC

Fallujah, Iraq
23 December 2004

The Navy Cross is presented to Jarrett A. Kraft, Sergeant, U.S. Marine Corps, for extraordinary heroism while serving as Squad Leader, 81-millimeter Mortar Platoon, Weapons Company, 3d Battalion, 5th Marine Regiment, Regimental Combat Team 1, 1st Marine Division, I Marine Expeditionary Force, U.S. Marine Corps Forces, Central, in support of Operation IRAQI FREEDOM on 23 December 2004. As numerically superior insurgent forces attacked Sergeant Kraft and the Marines in Al Fallujah, Iraq, he quickly organized and fearlessly led three assault forces on three separate attacks to repel the insurgents and ensure the successful advance of the battalion. With complete disregard for his own life, he placed himself between intense enemy fire and the men during each attack providing suppressive fire and leadership to sustain the fight and eliminate the enemy. Although grenades thrown by the insurgents rendered him momentarily unconscious during one assault, this did not dampen his spirit or determination. Undeterred, Sergeant Kraft continued to lead from the front, despite being wounded himself. On two more occasions, he was knocked down stairwells by enemy grenade blasts and finally while emplacing a sniper in a critical location, Sergeant Kraft was knocked down by the blast from a friendly M1A1 tank main gun. He demonstrated courageous leadership with a complete disregard for his own safety, during this desperate two-hour battle as he personally braved multiple enemy small arms kill zones to render assistance and guidance to his Marines. By his outstanding display of decisive leadership, unlimited courage in the face of heavy enemy fire, and utmost devotion to duty, Sergeant Kraft reflected great credit upon himself and upheld the highest traditions of the Marine Corps and the United States Naval Service."[29]

Navy Cross citation for Sgt. Jarrett A. Kraft, USMC

ON 23 DECEMBER 2004, as American troops prepared for their second Christmas in the desert, Marines with the 81-mm mortar platoon, Weapons Company, 3rd Battalion, 5th Marine Regiment, 1st Marine Division, were engaged in "clearing insurgents from densely packed homes along a residential street." Already veterans of Iraq, the 3/5 Marines had served a tour of duty as part of Task Force Bruno during the invasion of Iraq in 2003.[30]

Sgt. Jarrett A. Kraft, USMC, with sunglasses, standing next to Sgt. Jeremiah Workman, USMC, in Fallujah, Iraq. (Workman collection)

At 9:15 AM, Sgt. Jarrett Kraft and Cpl. Jeremiah Workman and their Marines were on foot clearing a street. Kraft was to the left, Workman on the right, as they cleared the first two houses. Kraft was outside the second house speaking with his commander by radio, when gunfire erupted inside the third house on the left. Workman recalled, "I was across the street, on the second story of another house, and I heard automatic fire. I wasn't alarmed. A lot of times when we'd go through a house, we'd spray into closets, under beds to be sure. . . . Then I heard AK-47s open up. It has a distinct sound. I grabbed my guys and ran across the street to link up with Sergeant Kraft."[31]

The platoon's second section had been engaged in a firefight the previous evening, so the Marines knew there were insurgents in the neighborhood and expected an ambush. Some of Workman's Marines were carrying "found" AK-47 assault rifles in anticipation of trouble.[32]

Kraft and Workman, both squad leaders in the mortar platoon, ran inside the house to assess. "The wall going up the staircase was being chewed up by rounds impacting it," Workman recalled. "The stairway went up, with a small landing halfway up, then the opposite direction to the top. At the top, there was another small alcove connecting to three bedrooms, with a rooftop patio straight ahead. There was nothing the two of us could do so we ran back outside." They gathered and organized the Marines, then led them inside to rescue the trapped and isolated Marines. "There was nobody in charge. Whoever was standing around got snatched up. We said, 'There's Marines in there. We need to go in and get them.'"

They entered and cleared the first floor, then moved to the stairs. Upstairs they saw six Marines on the second floor, pinned against the wall. They indicated by sign that insurgents, later to be estimated at more than forty in number, were located inside an adjacent room armed with grenades, RPK machine guns, and AK-47s. Other insurgents were on the rooftops of adjacent buildings, firing on the Marines inside the house, as well as outside.

Kraft, Workman, and the other Marines stacked at the base of the stairs. "Somehow, I managed to be the number one man going up the stairs each time, with Lt. [Sam] Rosales behind me, and Kraft behind him. Rosales said, 'On three, we're going up.' And I said, 'Roger that.' I got to the platform and turned around and saw that nobody had gone with me. I was on the landing by myself. They're all yelling for me to come down, so I popped a couple of rounds into one of the bedrooms. There was a lot of fire coming out of it. I'd drawn a lot of attention. I literally jumped down the stairs, which was a good thing because there was a lot of firepower coming my way."[33]

"There was heavy machine gun fire coming through that door. And grenades flying both ways," Kraft would later recall. "Then a grenade went off. I don't know if it was thrown from inside, or one of ours that they threw back at us, but when it exploded, it killed one of my Marines and threw me backwards down a staircase."[34]

Workman's memory is more specific. He remembered that they stacked themselves at the bottom of the stairs, Workman in front, and fired their weapons and threw grenades in preparation for assaulting the room, when, "someone in the stack threw a grenade up the stairs and the damn grenade rolled back down. I remembered looking and people just scattered."[35]

The grenade knocked several Marines off their feet and left them dazed. Kraft, briefly knocked unconscious, would later discover multiple shrapnel wounds that went unnoticed at the time. They carefully crawled down the stairs and regrouped. Again they reached the top of the stairs, firing back and forth and trying to allow the trapped Marines to escape. All of a sudden a grenade rolled out from one of the rooms. Workman remembered, "It was yellow! Something I'd never seen before in my life. It stopped in the middle of the foyer. Unlike an American grenade, which is all shrapnel, this was homemade, a hollowed out metal ball filled with gasoline. It went off and kinda knocked us down the stairs. Everybody got peppered with shrapnel."

The explosion killed two Marines and wounded others, including Workman. "It went off, and I just remember a lot of fire came out of it. It felt like someone had taken a baseball bat to my legs." Two of the wounded jumped from the second floor to find cover in an adjacent yard.[36]

As suppressing fire during a third assault tied down the insurgents, other Marines crossed over from an adjacent rooftop to recover the two mortally wounded Marines. Cpl. Raleigh C. Smith and LCpl. James R. Phillips were passed man-to-man across the rooftop to cover. "The Marines have a code that we don't leave anyone behind, even if they are dead," Kraft said later. "The insurgents . . . will do anything possible to not only kill a Marine, but to take his body and drag it around."[37]

An M1A1 Abrams tank arrived on the scene, accompanied by a quick-reaction force, and it began firing into the house, expending six rounds. Workman recalled that the insurgents continued to fire even as tank rounds slammed their position. A fire team came forward to assist in extracting the remaining Marines. One team member, LCpl. Eric Hillenburg, was killed by sniper fire as the team advanced. Unable to clear the house after two hours, the Marines called in an airstrike that leveled the entire block.[38]

In the confusion of battle, accounts differ as to the exact sequence of events. What is beyond dispute is that Kraft and Workman, as well as their Marines, repeatedly braved intense small-arms fire and grenades, even after being wounded, to launch three assaults on the insurgents to retrieve their wounded and recover their dead. The cost of clearing the house was three dead and eleven wounded Marines. The bodies of forty-seven insurgents were found inside the rubble. Task Force Bruno would continue clearing operations in Fallujah for another week.

Workman, who enlisted in August 2001, was promoted to sergeant and was presented with the Navy Cross on 12 May 2006, during a graduation ceremony at the Marine Corps Recruit Depot, Parris Island, South Carolina, where Workman was assigned as a drill instructor with Delta Company, 1st Recruit Training Battalion. He is currently assigned to the Marine Museum at Quantico, awaiting reassignment. He hopes to start a career in federal law enforcement once he completes his active duty September 2009. "There have been some difficult adjustments," he admitted. "Every day's a struggle, but I'm working on it."

A day earlier in Clovis, California, Kraft was presented his Navy Cross by Maj. Gen. Richard Natonski, commander of the 1st Marine Division. Kraft, who left the Marines in July 2005, went to work for the Fresno, California, Police Department. To him, the real heroes are his three lost comrades. Although Kraft was nominated for the Medal of Honor, he requested the nomination be withdrawn. "I lost Marines that day. I didn't feel I deserved that medal."[39]

There is a genuine modesty about these men, a disinclination to accept praise for actions they considered their duty. "I did what Marines have been doing for several hundred years, taking care of my fellow Marines," Kraft will tell you. Workman says, "I don't look at myself as being any different. I did what any other Marine would have done." Neither man is comfortable with the title "hero."

Another modest but heroic Marine is Cpl. Dominic Esquibel, who was awarded the Navy Cross for his actions in Fallujah on 25 November 2004.

LCpl. Dominic D. Esquibel, USMC

Fallujah, Iraq
25 November 2004

For extraordinary heroism while serving as Scout Sniper, Company B, 1st Battalion, 8th Marine Regiment, Regimental Combat Team 7, 1st Marine Division, I Marine Expeditionary Force, U.S. Marine Corps Forces, Central, in support of Operation IRAQI FREEDOM on 25 November 2004. After an enemy ambush on 3d Platoon nearby, Lance Corporal Esquibel quickly moved to an overwatch position and spotted five wounded Marines in a building courtyard. He courageously low-crawled close to the enemy stronghold to gain intelligence and then ran through the rooftops under intense enemy fire to relay the intelligence to the 3d Platoon Commander. With total disregard for his own safety, he re-occupied his position and threw a grenade, destroying several enemy insurgents and silencing one of the enemy's machine guns. After eliminating part of the threat, he low-crawled to another area and dropped a grenade through a hole in the roof, eliminating several more enemy personnel and silencing another enemy machine gun. As a tank breached the courtyard wall, 3d Platoon began suppressing the target building. He seized this opportunity and quickly moved to the courtyard while under enemy machine gun fire, dragging out a wounded Marine. He re-entered the courtyard to retrieve a second wounded Marine. Still under enemy fire, he moved through the open area a third time, extinguished a fire that had mortally wounded the third casualty, and swiftly carried out his body. Due to his heroic efforts, two Marines survived the devastating enemy ambush. By his outstanding display of decisive leadership, unlimited courage in the face of heavy enemy fire, and utmost devotion to duty, Lance Corporal Esquibel reflected great credit upon himself and upheld the highest traditions of the Marine Corps and the United States Naval Service.[40]

Navy Cross citation for LCpl. Dominic D. Esquibel, USMC

ON THANKSGIVING DAY 2004, Corporal Esquibel, accompanied by LCpl. David Houck, rescued two Marines, Tom Hodges and Mike Rodriguez, but an explosion killed others before they could be rescued. The following day, Houck was killed in action. Corporal Esquibel declined the award of the Navy Cross for "personal reasons," but reenlisted in the Marines on the voyage home.

As for the city of Fallujah, damage from the two operations in March and November 2004 destroyed approximately 60 percent of the housing, and a report by the U.N. Integrated Regional Information Network in March 2006 estimated that sixty-five thousand residents remained displaced and that fourteen months after the battle "power, water treatment and sewage systems are still not functioning properly and many districts of the city are without potable water."[41] In August 2006 al Qaeda vowed to take back the city, and as this is written, resistance continues in the city, but at a much lower rate than before the offensive.

ENDNOTES

1. N.N.E. Bray, *A Paladin of Arabia: The Biography of Brevet Lieut.-Colonel G. E. Leachman* (U.K.: Unicorn Press, 1936).
2. "Iraqis in Deadly Clash with U.S. Troops," CNN.COM-World, 29 April 2003.
3. The four employees were Scott Henderson, Jerko Zovko, Wesley Batalona, and Michael Teague
4. Robert Fisk, "Atrocity in Fallujah," *The Independent UK*, 1 April 2004.
5. "The Siege of Fallujah," *Guardian Unlimited*, www.guardian.co.uk/flash/0,5860,1193510,00.html.
6. Navy Citation for Capt. Brent Morel, USMC, www.homeofheroes.com/valor/1_Citations/nc_21wot.html.
7. Navy Cross Citation for Sgt. Willie L. Copeland III, www.homeofheroes.com/ valor/1_Citations/ nc_21wot.html.
8. Oren Dorell and Greg Zoroya, "Battle for Fallujah Forged Many Heroes," *USA Today*, 9 November 2006.
9. Laura Bailey, "Honored with a bronze star, Cpl. James Wright Sets His Sights on Healing," *Marine Corps Times*, June 2004.
10. "In His Own Words: Marine Sergeant James 'Eddie' Wright," www.Blackfive.net, 19 November 2005.
11. Ibid.
12. Dorell and Zoroya, "Battle for Fallujah."
13. Matthew Dodd, "Running into Bullets: A Marine NCO's Valor," www.ptsdsupport.net/willie_copeland.html, 15 August 2005.

14. Owen West, "A Ghost Is Born: Dispatches from Fallujah," *Slate Magazine*, 28 July 2004.

15. Owen West, "Leadership from the Rear: Proof that Combat Leadership Knows No Traditional Boundaries," *Marine Corps Gazette*, 1 September 2005.

16. Jess Lenens, "Marine Thrives on Army roots: Military Experience Leads Former Soldier to Top Honors in Recruit Training," Marine Corps Recruit Depot Newsletter, San Diego, 7 November 2003.

17. Dorell and Zoroya, "Battle for Fallujah."

18. "3rd Battlion, 1st Marines," http://en.wikipedia.org/wiki/3rd_Battalion_1st_Marines.

19. Navy Cross Citation for 1st Sgt. Bradley A. Kasal, USMC, www.homeofheroes.com/valor/1_Citations/nc_21wot.html.

20. Navy Cross Citation for Cpl. Robert J. Mitchell Jr., www.homeofheroes.com/valor/1_Citations/nc_21wot.html.

21. Patrick J. Floto, "Wounded Marine Photographed in Fallujah Awarded Navy Cross," *Leatherneck Magazine*, July 2006.

22. D. Clare, "Honoring the Brave–Marine Sgt. Maj. Bradley A. Kasal," *DAV: Magazine*, November/December 2006.

23. Bradley Kasal, interview on KETV, Omaha, Nebraska.

24. Tony Perry, "Marine Hero to Be Decorated for His Bravery," *Marine Corps Times*, 1 May 2006.

25. Keith A. Milks, "Second House of Hell Survivor Awarded Navy Cross for Iraqi Action," *Leatherneck Magazine*, October 2006.

26. Clare, "Honoring the Brave."

27. Bradley Kasal, interview on KETV, Omaha, Nebraska.

28. Navy Cross Citation for Cpl. Jeremiah Workman, USMC, www.homeofheroes.com/valor/1_Citations/nc_21wot.html.

29. Navy Cross Citation for Sgt. Jarrett A. Kraft, www.homeofheroes.com/valor/1_Citations/nc_21wot.html.

30. Denny Boyles, "A Marine's Bravery Earns Him Navy's Second-highest Medal," *The Fresno Bee*, 4 May 2006.

31. Jeremiah Workman, interview with Scott Baron, 20 January 2007.

32. R. R. Keene, "In the Highest Tradition," *Leatherneck Magazine*, August 2006.

33. Jeremiah Workman, interview with Scott Baron.

34. Keene, "In the Highest Tradition."

35. Gidget Fuentes and John Hoellwarth, "Intense Firefight: Two Marines Earn Navy Cross during Fallujah Battle," *Marine Corps Times*, 23 May 2006.

36. Ibid.

37. Boyles, "A Marine's Bravery."

38. Fuentes and Hoellwarth, "Intense Firefight."

39. Boyles, "A Marine's Bravery."

40. Navy Cross Citation for LCpl. Dominic D. Esquibel, USMC, www.homeofheroes.com/valor/1_Citations/nc_21wot.html.

41. Integrated Regional Information Network (IRIN), U.N. Office for the Coordination of Humanitarian Affairs, *IRAQ: Fallujah Situation Improving Slowly*, report dated 21 March 2006.

VIETNAM WAR (1959–1975)

Conflict in Vietnam can be dated as far back as 208 BC, when the Chinese Qin Dynasty invaded and established the state of Nam Viet. This area, comprised of southern China and the Red River Delta, remained under China's rule until its defeat at the Bach Dang River in the early tenth century. Eight centuries of national autonomy for Vietnam followed, ending in the mid-nineteenth century when France colonized Indo-China. Despite a call for its independence in the fledgling League of Nations, Vietnam remained firmly under French control until invasion by the Japanese Army during World War II.

During the Japanese occupation, Vietnamese communist nationalists, called the Viet Minh and led by Ho Chi Minh, created an insurgent force that engaged in guerilla warfare against the Japanese. Following the end of the war, the Viet Minh concentrated on achieving independence from France. The French Indochina War, also called the First Indochina War (1946–1954), climaxed with the defeat of the French forces at the Battle of Dien Bien Phu (13 March–7 May 1954) and resulted in the partitioning of Vietnam into two separate countries: the Democratic Republic of Vietnam in the north, with its capital at Hanoi, and the Republic of Vietnam, or South Vietnam, with its capital at Saigon.

Through the first decade following World War II, the United States was not directly involved in the military affairs of Indo-China, although in 1950 the Truman Administration pledged $15 million in military and economic aid, including a military mission and advisers, to the French during the French Indochina War.[1] With the abdication of the French as a power in Southeast Asia, and in response to fears of a "domino effect" that would result in Communist dominance in the region, in 1956 the United States formed the Military Assistance Advisor Group (MAAG), which assumed responsibility for training South Vietnamese forces, replacing the withdrawing French forces.

In 1959 North Vietnam began infiltrating weapons and cadres into South Vietnam along the Ho Chi Minh trail. This path to the south consisted of existing mountain trails that ran south along the mountains of the Chaine Annamitque through the Laotian panhandle and the eastern border regions of Cambodia. Ultimately, these trails were expanded and improved into a major road network.

Also in 1959, the first American servicemen killed in Vietnam, Army Maj. Dale R. Buis and MSgt. Chester M. Ovnand, died in a guerilla attack at Bien Hoa. During the Eisenhower administration the United States sent military advisers to Vietnam, beginning what would become the longest, and possibly the most unpopular, military conflict in American history. The war escalated through the 1960s as the number of U.S. troops grew. America's military involvement would continue until the last Marines scrambled aboard helicopters as they evacuated the roof of the U.S. Embassy in Saigon following South Vietnam's collapse on 30 April 1975.

Although there is no consensus on the actual numbers of American casualties, *The Vietnam War Almanac* estimates that a total of 57,690 Americans were killed in action, died of wounds, died of other causes, or were missing and declared dead during the Vietnam War and that 243,748 South Vietnamese military were killed. There were also 4,407 Korean and 469 Australian and New Zealand (combined) troops killed in combat. The *Almanac* also estimates that 660,000 members of the Vietnamese Peoples Army and National Liberation Front (NFL) were killed and that 65,000 North Vietnamese and 300,000 South Vietnamese civilians also died in the conflict.[2]

Although the Vietnam War did not result in victory for the United States, American servicemen and servicewomen frequently performed heroically in Vietnam. The Congressional Medal of Honor was awarded to 245 individuals, including 13 of the newly established Air Force Medal of Honor, as well as 159 Army and 73 Navy Medals of Honor.[3]

There were 489 Navy Crosses awarded for extraordinary heroism in Vietnam, to 487 individuals. Two Marines, Capt. Martin L. Brandtner and 1st Lt. Joseph P. Donovan, were awarded the Navy Cross twice.

A large number of the awards for valor in Vietnam went to individuals who placed themselves in jeopardy to rescue others. At least thirty-two Navy corpsmen were awarded the Navy Cross, twenty-one of those posthumously. In fact, it was a rescue mission in Vietnam that led to the most-decorated aircrew in Naval and Marine aviation.

ENDNOTES

1. Vietnam Online, companion to "Vietnam: A Television History," PBS American Experience, http://www.pbs.org/wgbh/amex/Vietnam.
2. Harry G. Summers, *The Vietnam War Almanac* (Novato, Calif.: Presidio Press, 1985). These figures do not include the members of South Vietnamese forces killed in the final campaign in 1975.
3. Medal of Honor Statistics, http://www.homeofheroes.com/moh/history/history_statistics.html.

"Death on Skids"
The Most Decorated Aircrew in Marine Aviation History

Capt. Stephen W. Pless, USMC
Capt. Rupert E. Fairfield Jr., USMC
LCpl. John G. Phelps, USMC
GySgt. Leroy N. Poulson, USMC

While conducting a regularly assigned mission, [the crew] monitored a transmission giving the approximate location of four soldiers from a downed Army helicopter. The UH-1E diverted to the site and arrived to find the Army personnel in the midst of an estimated 30 to 40 frenzied Viet Cong, who were bayoneting and beating them with rifle butts. As the UH-IE began a series of low level attacks, the Viet Cong scattered and withdrew to a tree line, firing frantically at the helicopter. Making another low level pass, they observed one soldier raise his hand in a gesture for help. Unhesitatingly, the UH-IE landed on the beach between the wounded men and the Viet Cong, who were now firing furiously at the aircraft.[1]

Excerpt from the Navy Cross citation for Capt. Rupert E. Fairfield Jr., USMC,
LCpl. John G. Phelps, USMC, and GySgt. Leroy N. Poulson, USMC

IT WAS A TYPICAL SATURDAY afternoon in Vietnam on 19 August 1967 for the four-man crew of the UH-1E helicopter gunship (WB-15), known as "Death on Skids." As part of Marine Observation Squadron Six (VMO-6), they spent their days providing cover for Sikorsky H-34 Choctaws performing medical evacuation missions. They were assigned to the Cochise II operational area, and during a pick-up at Nui Loc Son, the H-34 they were escorting sustained damage to the tail wheel, and they returned to Ky Ha to exchange aircraft. "As the MedEvac crew was switching aircraft, we received an emergency MedEvac in an unsecure landing zone," recalled Capt. Stephen W. Pless. "Rather than wait for the H-34, we decided to proceed to the zone independently [to] have it secured upon arrival."[2]

As they approached the MedEvac zone, they received a transmission over the "Guard" (emergency) channel: "My aircraft is all shot up and I have a lot of

Crew of VMO-6 Marine helicopter "Death on Skids." Left to right: GySgt. Leroy Poulson, LCpl. John "Gordo" Phelps, Capt. Rupert Fairfield, Capt. Stephen Pless. (Phelps collection)

the ground. The V.C. [Viet Cong] are trying to take them prisoners or kill them; God, can somebody help them?"[3] As the pilot, Captain Pless, directed the copilot, Capt. Rupert Fairfield, to check on the status of their medevac to see if it could be postponed, he continued to fly toward the distress area while monitoring the UHF. They determined that the H-34 could proceed unescorted, so they continued on toward the area to see if they could assist. Fairfield later recalled: "We radioed back, 'We are a fully armed UH-1E gunship and are in the area. Can we give assistance?' but our call went unanswered. We proceeded to the area, about a mile or so north of the mouth of the Song Tra Kruc River."[4]

LCpl. John "Gordo" Phelps, the crew chief, recalled that they were only ten or fifteen minutes away, and they were familiar with the area. It was a known "hot spot," heavy with enemy activity and close to the village of My Lai. As they approached, they observed a number of explosions on the beach, approximately a mile north of the mouth of the river. "We got in the area, going full steam," Phelps said in a later interview. "We saw Vietnamese all over the beach, beating three Americans."[5]

In the excitement and confusion of combat, memories often differ as to details and recollections can seem contradictory, but the whole crew is fairly consistent in recalling what occurred next. As Fairfield recalled, "Pless said, 'What do you think, can we get them out?' I turned to the others. 'Gordo' gave a thumbs up, and

STEPHEN W. PLESS

Major (then Captain), U.S. Marine Corps VMO-6, Mag-36, 1st Marine Aircraft Wing

Near Quang Nai, Republic of Vietnam
19 August 1967
Entered service at: Atlanta, Georgia
Born: 6 September 1939, Newnan, Georgia

Citation for Medal of Honor:

FOR CONSPICUOUS GALLANTRY and intrepidity at the risk of his life above and beyond the call of duty while serving as a helicopter gunship pilot attached to Marine Observation Squadron Six in action against enemy forces.

During an escort mission Maj. Pless monitored an emergency call that four American soldiers stranded on a nearby beach were being overwhelmed by a large Viet Cong force. Maj. Pless flew to the scene and found 30 to 50 enemy soldiers in the open. Some of the enemy were bayoneting and beating the downed Americans.

Maj. Pless displayed exceptional airmanship as he launched a devastating attack against the enemy force, killing or wounding many of the enemy and driving the remainder back into a tree line. His rocket and machine gun attacks were made at such low levels that the aircraft flew through debris created by explosions from its rockets.

Seeing one of the wounded soldiers gesture for assistance, he maneuvered his helicopter into a position between the wounded men and the enemy, providing a shield which permitted his crew to retrieve the wounded. During the rescue the enemy directed intense fire at the helicopter and rushed the aircraft again and again, closing to within a few feet before being beaten back.

When the wounded men were aboard, Maj. Pless maneuvered the helicopter out to sea. Before it became safely airborne, the overloaded aircraft settled four times into the water. Displaying superb airmanship, he finally got the helicopter aloft.

Major Pless' extraordinary heroism coupled with his outstanding flying skill prevented the annihilation of the tiny force. His courageous actions reflect great credit upon himself and uphold the highest traditions of the Marine Corps and the U.S. Naval Service.

I looked at 'Top' Poulson, and he gave a thumbs up too, but his eyes said 'we're not coming back.' I turned to Steve and said 'OK, let's go.'"[6] It was a decision that changed the lives of the four Marine crewmen who all came from radically different backgrounds.

The pilot, Stephen Wesley Pless, was born in Newnan, Georgia, on 6 September 1939. He attended Decatur High School at Decatur, Georgia, then attended Georgia Military Academy, College Park, Georgia, graduating in 1957. While still a cadet, he enlisted in the U.S. Marine Corps Reserves on 6 September 1956. Assigned to the 1st Motor Transport Battalion in Atlanta, Georgia, he was sent to Parris Island, South Carolina, for recruit training and advanced combat training. He graduated in October 1957, and was assigned as an artillery surveyor with the 10th Marine Regiment, 2d Marine Division, where he served until September 1958.[7]

Pless attended flight training at Pensacola Naval Air Station in Florida, was commissioned a second lieutenant on 16 September 1959, and was promoted to first lieutenant and was awarded his gold aviator wings upon his graduation from flight school on 20 April 1960. There followed a succession of assignments as a squadron pilot with Marine Aircraft Group 26 (MAG-26) at New River, North Carolina, as well as at sea aboard the USS *Wasp* (CV-18) and USS *Shadwell* (LSD-15).

In June 1962, Pless deployed on his first Far East tour of duty, assigned as assistant administrative officer of HMM-162, MAG-16, serving in Thailand and at Da Nang in Vietnam. He returned to Pensacola in June 1963 as a flight instructor, then became a brigade platoon commander at the Marine Corps Air Station (MCAS) Kaneohe, Hawaii, in April 1966. In August 1966 Pless, now a captain, became officer in charge, ROK Detachment, and later brigade air officer, 1st Anglico, Sub-Unit 1, with the 2nd Brigade, Korean Marine Corps, at Chu Lai, in the Republic of Vietnam. For his service in this capacity, he was awarded a Bronze Star and the Korean Order of Military Merit.

On 20 March 1967, Pless was assigned as assistant operations officer, VMO-6, Marine Aircraft Group 36, 1st Marine Aircraft Wing, in the Republic of Vietnam. By the time of the rescue mission that August afternoon, he had already flown over 750 missions.

Unlike Pless, the copilot, Capt. Rupert Fairfield, was new to Vietnam at the time of the rescue. He received his orders in July 1967, and arrived in early August. He had not flown before with any of the others, and was still flying orientation flights as copilot. It would be his first, and only, flight with Pless, and his last flight as copilot.

Born on 8 November 1939 in Lake Charles, Louisiana, a rural hamlet of fifteen families, Fairfield was the oldest of three children. His father worked as a timekeeper on construction projects, but there was little extra money. When he was offered an NROTC scholarship following his graduation from La Grange High School in

1958, Fairfield accepted eagerly. "I liked the people and the food [of Louisiana] but there was little opportunity."[8]

After graduating from "Ole Miss" (University of Mississippi) in June 1962, he fulfilled his four-year military obligation by enlisting in the Marines. "I went down to the Courthouse, and I was gonna go in the Navy, and some crusty old Marine sergeant stuck his head out the door and said 'What's the matter? You chicken?' or something like that, and that was just enough of a dare, you know, to want to be a Marine. So although I won a Navy Scholarship, when I had to make a choice, I chose the Marines."

He went through the Training and Test Regiment at Quantico, Virginia, during his junior year at "Ole Miss," then attended the platoon leaders course after graduating in June 1962. Commissioned a second lieutenant in the artillery, his first tour was overseas at Okinawa with A Battery, 1st Battalion, 12th Marines, serving with Barney Barnum, a recipient of the Medal of Honor. He returned in 1964 for flight training at Pensacola. "They sent about eight of us who were former ground officers from Okinawa, and sent us directly into flight training. The Marine Corps kinda saw the Vietnam War heating up, knew that it had to train more helicopter pilots, and that's how I came to Flight School."

He had had no previous desire to fly. But, he said, "In those days, if you were a Marine and you were given something to do, you didn't whine about it, and you didn't fail. You did it. Eventually as the years went on, I learned to love to fly." While at flight school, he met and married a local girl, Jean Elliott. He graduated training in 1965, then was sent to New River, North Carolina, to learn to fly UH-1 helicopters. He was retained as squadron supply officer as other students were sent to Vietnam.

His feelings about the war were ambiguous. "I had to wait awhile before I could get into combat. . . . I don't know that anyone really wanted to go . . . except maybe Steve Pless, or 'Gordo,' but by this time, I was a professional Marine, and I wanted to practice my profession." In July 1967 orders arrived assigning him to VMO-6, Chu Lai, Republic of Vietnam.[9]

The rescue mission was also GySgt. Leroy Poulson's first flight with Pless. Assigned as the gunner aboard "Death on Skids" that August morning, his regular assignment was as operations chief of VMO-6. "When I arrived, Colonel Maloney, the squadron commander, asked me, 'When are you gonna start flying?' I said I didn't know I was. He replied 'In this squadron, everyone flies.' I guess I flew about eighty-two missions in eleven months."[10]

Leroy "Top" Poulson was born in Newell, Iowa, on 6 March 1932, into a very poor family. His father, a badly wounded World War I veteran, had a stroke, believed to be war-related, in 1939. Poulson was seven at the time, and he began working the next year to help support the family. Growing up he wanted to be a ballplayer, and was scouted by Phil McDermott for the New York Yankees in his junior year at

President Lyndon Johnson pins the Navy Cross medal on GySgt. Leroy Poulson, USMC, at Cam Ranh Bay, a major U.S. base in South Vietnam, 19 August 1967. (Poulson collection)

Newell Consolidated High School. He played company ball in Minnesota before enlisting for a three-year hitch in the Marines on 3 October 1951. "It was the best choice I ever made. I actually went to join the Navy, but the recruiter was not there. And I saw this guy with his blues on, and he asked me if I wanted to join the Marine Corps. I interviewed, and I liked what I heard, and my brother was already in the Marines . . . so I enlisted."

Poulson arrived at San Diego for boot camp, then was assigned as an operations clerk for an F4-U squadron at El Toro Marine Air Station in California in December 1951. After cold-weather training, Poulson was certain he was being sent to Korea, but instead was sent to HQ and Maintenance Section-36 (H&MS) at Kaneohe, Hawaii, in June 1952. He volunteered several times for Korea but was never sent into combat. He returned to El Toro in January 1954, then trained reserves in St. Louis in 1954. In January 1958, he served with Medium Helicopter Squadron HMM-363 in Santa Ana, California. Poulson was then assigned as the assistant group operations chief at Fatema, Okinawa, in January 1960 and as airfield operations chief at Yuma MCAS in Arizona in May 1961. "After two years at Yuma, they gave me a choice, D.I. [drill instructor] or Recruiter School. I don't like to yell, so I picked recruiter." Following a three-year tour as a recruiter in Des Moines and later Mason City, Iowa (1964–1966), Poulson received orders for Vietnam. He arrived on 28 January 1967. "We flew into Da Nang. I was assigned to VMO-6 in the Chu Lai area. It was pouring down rain, and it was cold! I'd heard Vietnam was hot, but not in the wintertime!" He began flying missions his first week.[11]

While the pilots, copilots, and gunners rotated through many different aircraft, the UH-1E (WB-15), Navy Bureau Number 154760, nicknamed "Death on Skids," was the permanent responsibility of LCpl. John "Gordo" Phelps, the crew chief. By the morning of 19 August Phelps had flown over 750 combat missions, approximately 150 of them with Pless, and of those, a number were Special Operations Support missions, operating with Army Special Forces in Laos. Phelps liked working with Pless. "Steve was the best damn pilot I ever flew with," he recalled. "He was hard on my aircraft, but he would always bring us home." At the age of twenty, Phelps was the youngest of the crew, but was "Gung-Ho." Fairfield described him as "filled with the warrior ethic, always looking for a fight."

John "Gordo" Phelps was born the oldest of three in Beaver Dam, Kentucky, on 13 January 1947. He first developed an interest in the military "watching old John Wayne movies like 'Flying Leathernecks.' When a Marine recruiter visited his high school, he knew the military was what he wanted to do with his life. In love with adventure and excitement, he dropped out of school to enlist in the Marines on 20 February 1964, at the age of seventeen. "I'd worked since I was a kid, and in school I felt like a grown man in a room of kids, so I left home, and looked to the Marines to give me adventure and 'three hots and a cot.'" [12]

Phelps' father was a Navy veteran who'd served aboard a minesweeper during World War II. As Phelps later explained, "I was going to go in the Navy, sort of a family tradition. I wanted to see the world. I talked to the Navy recruiter, but he told me to come back after I finished high school. The Marine recruiter across the hall heard, and he said 'C'mere son,' and we talked."

The next thing Phelps knew, he was at Parris Island, South Carolina, in Platoon 121, 1st Marine Recruit Battalion. He enlisted in the Marines under the guaranteed aviation program and scored high on his tests, so following twelve weeks of boot camp and four to six weeks of infantry training, he was sent to Millington Naval Air Station, outside Memphis, Tennessee, for two weeks of aircraft fundamentals and six weeks of jet engine school. He was among the top 10 percent of his class and was therefore sent on to helicopter school for an additional six weeks of training. "I had always wanted to fly, but I'd never been in a helicopter before. The third week of helicopter school, I went up in a Sikorsky CH-19 (Transport) helicopter. It was my first familiarization flight, and it crashed. I thought 'there's my crash,' and I knew I'd be O.K." [13]

His first assignment was at MCAS New River, North Carolina, where he got his first real experience flying and working on helicopters. After a short time he became bored with the routine of stateside flight operations and volunteered for a six-month Mediterranean cruise aboard the USS *Fort Mandan*, (LSD-21). A few months after returning from the cruise, Phelps volunteered to take the orders of a recently married Marine buddy to deploy to Vietnam. He arrived in-country on 12 April 1966, and was assigned to Marine Gunship Squadron VMO-6. After his first thirteen-month combat tour, he volunteered for an additional six-month extension of duty in Vietnam.

The morning of 19 August had promised to be no different from the hundreds before it. "We went out on a couple of routine flights," Phelps recalls. "We were high cover for MedEvac pick-ups, usually CH-34s. Best as I remember, it was about one o'clock. We had an escort, and we made contact, but it was going to a secure facility at Chu Lai, and didn't need us. We were just up in the air. We never saw it, just kept radio contact. During this time, we heard on the 'guard' channel that an aircraft was taking fire. The pilot was screaming that they'd landed on a beach, and he gave the coordinates. There were mechanical problems, and they'd left four [men] on the beach. Fairfield got out the maps, and Pless worked the radio, but never made contact. We knew the area. It was only ten or fifteen minutes away, and definitely not an area you wanted to land in."[14]

The aircraft in distress was an Army CH-47 Chinook helicopter from the 167th Aviation Battalion, returning to Da Nang. Aboard as passengers were a USO troupe, some wounded G.I.s, and Army SSgt. Lawrence H. Allen, assigned to the 167th for base security. The Chinook was flying off the coast when it took a hit from ground fire. The pilot decided to set the aircraft down on what he believed to be an uninhabited beach to check for damage. "They opened the ramp door and the crew chief got off to check for damage, and two other guys and I got off to provide security. We moved to the front of the helicopter, and there was little damage, just a hole in the Plexiglas. Then a grenade exploded near the front of the aircraft."[15]

The ramp was at the rear, but before they could reach it the pilot was lifting off. The crew chief, still attached to the aircraft via an intercom cable was lifted off the ground, snapping his neck. "Looking back now, I understand the pilot had no choice, but at the time I was damn pissed," said Allen.[16]

Tactically, their position was precarious. Allen was armed only with a .38-caliber pistol, the other two with M-16s but no extra ammo. They held off the Viet Cong for fifteen minutes. "We then ran back to our position behind a sand dune," Allen recalled. "We began to receive a barrage of grenades; we returned fire, but soon ran out of ammo. The Viet Cong then moved in close and threw more grenades. Everyone was wounded by this time when one Viet Cong appeared on our flank with an automatic weapon."[17]

The Viet Cong soldier opened fire with his machine gun. Allen believes his position between the other two saved his life, for he was only wounded once, in the left arm. "A bunch of them ran up, and I pretended I was dead. They began stripping off my gear, and they cut the throat of the crew chief. I heard two explosions, and there was this Huey gunship making strafing runs on the Viet Cong."[18]

Phelps stated, "When we approached the area, Captain Pless asked the crew 'You all with me?' He knew the answer would be yes. As we flew on, we saw four U.S. personnel laying on the beach, and around them not less than forty to fifty armed V.C. They . . . were beating the helpless personnel. As we flew over the group of people, one of the men laying on the beach waved to us, and for his effort got a rifle butt in the face."[19]

Fairfield recalled, "Once we broke off, Steve dropped to about a hundred feet, skimming the rice paddies. When we popped over the tree line, just before the beach, we saw the V.C. had four prisoners. They'd already stripped them to the waist, and had them staked out on the beach. They were beating them with rifle butts and stabbing them with bayonets. Steve ordered 'Top' to open fire, and 'Top' was hesitant, not knowing if Steve saw the prisoners or not, but he opened fire. That's where the V.C. made their first mistake, and ran into the tree line and left the guys on the beach."[20]

Phelps recalled, "Captain Pless told Poulson to put down fire. I saw that there were Americans in the group and yelled for Poulson to 'hold fire.' Pless told me to 'shut up' and told Poulson to continue firing. Poulson continued firing and the V.C. broke and ran from the beach. It did the job and scared 'em off. We rolled in on a gun run, so close we picked up body parts on the aircraft windscreen. We were shooting out the side with both door guns and throwing hand grenades. We made five to six passes, with Captain Fairfield switching between guns and rockets. . . .We destroyed those people. We hovered back to the wounded and set down, guns toward the enemy." Pless had landed his aircraft between the enemy in the jungle and the men on the beach. Before sitting the aircraft down, he hovered the helicopter over the beach and unloaded the remaining outboard machine gun ammunition in the direction of the retreating V.C.

Poulson stated, "After several gun runs, we landed on the beach. I unplugged my headset, unhooked my gunner's belt and jumped out of the aircraft to get the wounded. . . . Phelps immediately began to lay down fire on the left door gun and covered me as I went over to check on the medevacs. . . . Phelps did an outstanding job of cover fire and I owe my life to his accurate fire."[21]

Poulson assisted the first man, Sergeant Allen, who was already moving toward the aircraft, and helped him aboard, then went for the second man. Pless ordered Fairfield out to help Poulson, who was having difficulty with the second man due to the soft sand and the size of the man. Phelps remained in the aircraft providing cover fire, but saw they were having difficulty. "I looked at Allen and asked, 'Can you fire this machine gun?' I set him behind my M-60 door gun, loaded a fresh 100-round ammunition belt, and jumped out to help. They were big guys, at least 225 pounds, and unconscious. They were still breathing, but in bad shape."

Poulson stated, "Captain Fairfield and I went out to get the third man. He was heavier than the second man, so Lance Corporal Phelps came out to help us. Phelps and Fairfield were at each arm, and I had the man by his legs. At the same time they were carrying the man, they were firing at the enemy with their revolvers. At one point, Phelps dropped the man we were carrying and shot a Viet Cong that was ten or fifteen feet from us." [22]

As they neared the copter, they heard "lots of incoming, but no outgoing," and Fairfield grabbed the right door gun off the mount and fired the M-60 from the hip, killing three of the nearest V.C., then helped Phelps and Poulson load the last man aboard. Poulson had already determined the fourth man was dead. Fairfield jumped in and Phelps pulled Poulson inside as Pless began to lift off and the V.C. charged the aircraft. [23]

The recommendation letter for the Medal of Honor for Captain Pless states: "With the Americans safely aboard, Captain Pless, encircled on three sides by the frantic Viet Cong, had but one route of departure open to him. Forcing his aircraft, which was now nearly 500 pounds over safe take-off weight, into the air, Captain Pless turned out to sea. Jettisoning his empty rocket pods and ordering his crew to throw all excess gear overboard, Captain Pless skipped over the water. On four separate occasions [the] aircraft settled on the waves, and four times, in an unbelievable display of airmanship, [he] brought it back into the air." [24]

"We had really low engine and rotor RPMs," Phelps remembers. "All sorts of aircraft emergency alarms were going off, and we were taking fire. We were very overloaded, and had a full fuel load. Steve dropped the expended rocket pods, and we threw everything we could overboard: ammo, spare barrels, armor plate, tool boxes, hand tools, a box of grenades. A few times the skids hit the water. Once we got enough forward airspeed, we lifted off." [25]

Fairfield stated, "While Captain Pless continued forcing the aircraft to fly, Gunnery Sergeant Poulson and Lance Corporal Phelps rendered first aid to the three wounded men, I contacted our controlling agencies, told them our position, and requested they cancel any artillery between our position and the First Hospital at Chu Lai. We landed at First Hospital a few minutes later." [26]

Poulson gives credit to two circling Army helicopters for facilitating their escape. As they were loading the last wounded man, "an Army Huey began to strafe the tree lines to keep the enemy away from us. Without their support, we would have been unable to complete the mission." [27]

Two of the three rescued men later died at the hospital. The third man, Sergeant Allen, was awarded the Silver Star. He remained in the Army and retired as a major.

The crew was credited with twenty confirmed kills and another thirty-eight probables. Poulson remembered being called in right after the mission to make an official statement. "We were called in, and originally, I thought we were in trouble over the aborted mission. I asked Captain Pless 'What do I say?' and he said, 'Tell them what happened.'" Phelps also remembered being called in. "Pless had been in trouble a number of times before this with the CO for unauthorized combat actions. I had been with him on a few of these occasions. We were not supposed to land and go into close combat with the enemy."

For actions that their commander described as a "willingness to expose [themselves] to almost certain death to help comrades-in-arms," Pless was awarded the Medal of Honor, and Fairfield, Poulson, and Phelps were presented with Navy Crosses, making them the most decorated aircrew in Marine Aviation history, and Pless the only Marine aviator to be awarded the Medal of Honor in Vietnam.

Pless left Vietnam on 22 September 1967, after flying 780 combat helicopter missions, and was presented the Medal of Honor by President Lyndon Johnson in a White House ceremony on 16 January 1969. He was promoted to major on 7 November 1967, the youngest Marine to hold that rank. Assigned as an administrative assistant at Officer Candidate School, NAS Pensacola, he was killed on 20 July 1969, when his motorcycle plunged off an open drawbridge into Santa Rosa Sound, near Pensacola.

Fairfield came home in 1968 with plans to get out of the Marines. But he ended up staying in for twenty-two years, persuaded by the opportunity to fly A-4 Skyhawks and later F4 Phantoms. He retired as a lieutenant colonel on 1 September 1983. In addition to the Navy Cross, he was awarded two Distinguished Flying Crosses, numerous Air Medals, and the Legion of Merit.

Poulson stayed on in Vietnam, assigned in Da Nang, and was presented the Navy Cross by President Johnson at Cam Ranh Bay on 23 December 1967. He departed Vietnam on 26 January 1968, but returned in November 1970, assigned to HMM-263 until June 1971. He retired as a master gunnery sergeant on 31 July 1978. He taught NROTC and Texas history in Beaumont, Texas, until his second retirement in 1993. In addition to the Navy Cross, he was awarded four Air Medals and the Good Conduct Medal. "It took me three years to earn the Good Conduct Medal, but the Navy Cross was awarded for ten minutes of work."

Phelps departed Vietnam on 12 December 1967, took leave, and spent his remaining time doing what he described as the scariest duty he ever undertook— teaching new second lieutenant pilots about flying helicopter gunships in combat, while assigned to VMO-1 at New River, North Carolina. He was honorably discharged as a corporal on 20 February 1968. In addition to the Navy Cross, he was awarded forty-seven Air Medals, a Navy Commendation Medal with a "V" for valor, the Purple Heart and Navy/Marine Corps Combat Aircrew Wings. He married his high school sweetheart on Halloween 1969, and worked for Louisville Gas & Electric Company for thirty-two years before retiring in 2001 as a station maintenance supervisor.

Fairfield, Poulson, Phelps, and Allen were reunited with Pless when he was presented the Medal of Honor in Washington, D.C., in 1969. The next time they saw each other was thirty-five years later when they met at the Marine Combat Helicopter Association's 2004 convention in Reno, Nevada. They are all, without exception, modest about their accomplishment. As Fairfield stated, "There was no plan, no leaders. 'Top' never fired a shot. His focus was to get the guys on the copter. He was the bravest man I ever saw. We had a job to do, we did it, and we came back. That's what's important."

The helicopter flown on this mission, "Death on Skids," is on display at the National Museum of the Marine Corps in Quantico, Virginia.

ENDNOTES

1. www.homeofheroes.com
2. Official Statement of Captain Stephen W. Pless (#079156), USMC (Pilot), History and Museums Division of the United States Marine Corps, Quantico, Virginia.
3. Ibid.
4. Rupert E. Fairfield, telephone interview with Scott Baron, 29 November 2006.
5. John G. Phelps, telephone interview with Scott Baron, 25 November 2006.
6. Fairfield, telephone interview.
7. Official Biography of Maj. Stephen W. Pless, USMC. History and Museums Division of the United States Marine Corps.
8. Fairfield, telephone interview.
9. Ibid.
10. Leroy Poulson, telephone interview with Scott Baron, 26 November 2006.
11. Ibid.
12. Phelps, telephone interview.
13. Ibid.
14. Ibid.
15. Lawrence Allen, telephone interview with Scott Baron, 29 November 2006.
16. Ibid.
17. Official Statement of SSgt. Lawrence H. Allen, USA.
18. Allen, telephone interview.
19. Official Statement of Lance Corporal John G. Phelps (#1209285), USMC (Crew Chief), History and Museums Division of the United States Marine Corps, Quantico, Virginia.
20. Fairfield, telephone interview.
21. Official Statement of Gunnery Sergeant Leroy N. Poulson (#2076835), USMC (Gunner), History and Museums Division of the United States Marine Corps, Quantico, Virginia.
22. Ibid.
23. Gary Telfer, Keith Fleming, and Lane Rogers, *U.S. Marines in Vietnam: Fighting the North Vietnamese 1967* (Washington, D.C.: Government. Printing Office, 1984).
24. Recommendation letter for the Medal of Honor dated 26 August 1967, by Lt. Col. Joe Nelson, Commanding Officer, Marine Observation Squadron 6, Marine Group 36, 1st Marine Air Wing.
25. Phelps, telephone interview.
26. Official Statement of Captain Rupert E. Fairfield (#085242), USMC (Co-pilot), History and Museums Division of the United States Marine Corps, Quantico, Virginia.
27. Official Statement of Gunnery Sergeant Leroy N. Poulson (#2076835), USMC (Gunner), History and Museums Division of the United States Marine Corps, Quantico, Virginia.

PO3 Nguyen Van Kiet

L.L.D.B. (SEAL), Navy of the Republic of Vietnam

Quang Tri Province
13 April 1972

The Navy Cross is awarded to Petty Officer Third Class Nguyen Van Kiet, Vietnamese Navy (SEAL), for extraordinary heroism while serving with friendly forces engaged in armed conflict against the North Vietnamese and Viet Cong communist aggressors in the Republic of Vietnam. On 13 April 1972, Petty Officer Kiet participated in an unprecedented recovery operation for a downed United States aviator behind enemy lines in Quang Tri Province, Republic of Vietnam. He courageously volunteered to accompany a United States SEAL Advisor in an extremely hazardous attempt to reach the aviator, who was physically unable to move forward toward friendly positions. Using a sampan and traveling throughout the night, they silently made their way deep into enemy territory, past numerous major enemy positions, locating the pilot at dawn. Once, after being spotted by a North Vietnamese patrol, he calmly continued to keep the enemy confused as the small party successfully evaded the patrol. Later, they were suddenly taken under heavy machine gun fire. Thinking first of the pilot, he quickly pulled the sampan to safety behind a bank and camouflaged it while air strikes were called on the enemy position. Due to Petty Officer Kiet's coolness under extremely dangerous conditions and his outstanding courage and professionalism, an American aviator was recovered after an eleven-day ordeal behind enemy lines. His self-discipline, personal courage, and dynamic fighting spirit were an inspiration to all; thereby reflecting great credit upon himself and the Naval Service.

Navy Cross citation for PO3 Nguyen Van Kiet, RVN

THE RESCUE OF BAT 21 Bravo is one of the most remarkable stories of "leave no one behind" to be recorded in any of our nation's wars. This tradition came into force during the Vietnam War. There were cases in earlier conflicts of recovering bodies, but most of those who fell on the battlefield remained there. And prior to World War I, when dog tags began to be issued, it wasn't possible to identify many of the fallen soldiers. The exceptions were the Marines who battled their way out of the frozen mountains of the Chosin Reservoir and brought all their dead and wounded with them. How many times have we witnessed our wounded and dead being evacuated by their fellow soldiers during fierce warfare? It is the noblest of traditions, and one that makes the American military different from any other.

This incident took place in the northern part of South Vietnam in the spring of 1972. After years of a massive U.S. presence in the country, only two infantry brigades were still in the country, and their mission was only to defend their own bases. The U.S. policy was then "Vietnamization"—placing the responsibility for the defense of South Vietnam in the hands of that country's military forces with the support of American air power. With this change in American policy, the North Vietnamese decided to administer a devastating and final blow to their enemy in the south. Some thirty thousand North Vietnamese hardcore troops (NVA) were sent south to invade South Vietnam through the demilitarized zone (DMZ). At the same time, two divisions were positioned to attack from bases in Laos, and several more divisions were poised to attack Kontum in II Corps in the central highlands and An Loc in III Corps north of Saigon.

At this late stage in the war, North Vietnamese divisions openly traveled the roads running south, supported by Soviet-supplied tanks and heavy artillery. In order to counter any American air support, a massive air-defense system had been established with surface-to-air missile sites and a vast array of conventional antiaircraft weapons, including radar-controlled 100-mm guns. The South Vietnamese ground and air forces (ARVN) fought fiercely during this Easter invasion from the North, but they were not prepared to face such a massive onslaught. The United States countered with a major air campaign to support their out-gunned allies. Among the many aircraft involved were B-52 bombers that struck NVA troop concentrations. "Tiny Tim" EB-66 electronic warfare aircraft of the 42nd Tactical Electronic Warfare squadron (TEWS) accompanied the bombers to pinpoint the missile sites and jam their guidance-system radars.

On 2 April 1972 an American bomber strike force flew from Thailand to attack NVA troops streaming across the DMZ. One of the two E-66s was shot from the air by a SAM, and only one of the six crewmen was able to eject safely; the others perished when the crippled aircraft exploded. As fifty-three-year-old Lt. Col. Iceal "Gene" Hamilton descended through a cloud bank to the earth below, he saw a massive enemy force before he dropped to the ground less than a mile from the Cam Lo bridge. The force he had seen consisted of thousands of NVA soldiers supported by tanks and other vehicles of war. He landed smack in the middle of the southward and western pincer thrust of the enemy.

The subsequent attempt to rescue Hamilton was called the biggest U.S. air-rescue effort of the war, involving every branch of the American military service. Critics of the massive effort have charged that in trying to save Hamilton, an entire ARVN division was put in jeopardy.

All U.S. aircraft squadrons had a coded call sign to identify themselves to other operational units on the ground and in the air, especially search and rescue (SAR) aircraft. Additionally, each crew member was given an alpha identifier. Thus a TEWS aircraft pilot was coded BAT 21 Alpha, the next crewmen positioned behind him, in this case Lieutenant Colonel Hamilton, was BAT 21 Bravo, and so on. Veterans of that air war vividly remember their call signs to this day.

Two SAR army helicopters flew in to recover Hamilton, but they were quickly shot down. One was destroyed with the loss of four crewmen; the other made a crash landing in a safe area, and the crew was rescued by a "Jolly Green," a Sikorsky-made HH-3E helicopter. The following morning a Coast Guard pilot flew into the area to attempt a rescue but was driven off by a curtain of fire that literally shredded Jolly Green 65. The crippled aircraft made it back to base due to the flying skill and courage of the pilot, Lt. Cdr. Jay Crowe. Next, Jolly Green 66 broke through the clouds and came within one hundred yards of Hamilton before being turned back by withering enemy fire that riddled his aircraft and shattered the cockpit. Like 65, the pilot was able to gain altitude and return to base. Toward evening an OV-10 Forward Air Controller (FAC) was shot down but both occupants were able to eject safely, pilot Capt. William Henderson and spotter Lt. Mark Clark, grandson of Gen. Mark Clark of World War II fame.

At this point there were three Americans on the ground—Hamilton, Henderson, and Clark. Rescue attempts had amounted to three aircraft downed, five more severely damaged, three Americans dead, and a fourth captured. (Captain Henderson was subsequently captured by the NVA during the night of 3 April.)

When the Air Force learned that one of the downed EB-66 officers was Hamilton, the urgency for rescue intensified. Hamilton had served with the Strategic Air Command. If the information he remembered about U.S. missiles and their targets could be extracted from him, the damage to American strategic capabilities could prove catastrophic, especially if he was turned over to the Soviets. Faced with this problem, the Air Force initiated an all-out rescue effort by sending A-1 Sandys to strike the Cam Lo bridge area. The NVA air defenses were ready for the dive bombers, downing one aircraft and sending the rest back to their bases badly damaged. American aircraft continued to bomb and strafe the area during the following days, and it became apparent that the enemy was using Hamilton as bait to destroy his would-be rescuers.

On 6 April the area was attacked by a wave of fighters and four B-52s. As Hamilton and Clark watched the aircraft wreak havoc on enemy positions, another Jolly Green (67) took off to pluck the men from their hiding places. Because Hamilton was still in contact with overhead units using his hand-held radio, his approximate position was known and tracked as he moved across the terrain. As the helicopter approached the area and began to maneuver for a pickup, the NVA ripped the craft apart and sent it reeling back into the air. Smoking badly, 67 floundered and rolled on its side and exploded as it hit the ground. Six airmen died in the crash.

The next day, an OV-10 was shot down. The two men managed to survive the shoot down. One of them, Air Force 1st Lt. Bruce Walker, transmitted from the ground as he evaded the enemy (he was later killed by a Viet Cong pursuer) The other, Marine Corps 1st Lt. Larry Potts, was reported to have died in captivity. He is still considered to be missing in action because his remains have never been recovered.

The Air Force had to decide whether to continue on with an air rescue operation. By 9 April, five aircraft had been lost, nine airmen were dead, two had been captured, and the fate of Walker and Potts was unknown. It was decided that rescue by a ground force was the only way to extract the downed men. A commando team prepared immediately. However, this operation would require a specially trained team of Navy SEALs. Lt. (jg.) Thomas Norris, a SEAL on his second tour, prepared to set out with a team to rescue Clark and Hamilton. Clark was to be rescued first. He was hidden near the Cam Lo River, which flowed into the Cua Viet. Clark was instructed to move to the water on 10 April and wait for further instructions. Because Hamilton was hiding a mile away from the river, a clever plan was devised to guide him to the river. Hamilton was an avid golfer who had a vivid memory of the many courses he played. Instructed by his squadron mates and others familiar with golf courses Hamilton had played, the downed airman was able to successfully make it to his destination by imagining a series of familiar holes, each representing a specific heading and distance. For over two days he played "nine holes" transiting through fields and villages while avoiding enemy patrols until he reached the river and went into hiding.

Norris and his team were briefed on their mission by Lt. Col. William C. "Andy" Anderson, USMC, commander of the Joint Personnel Recovery Center in Saigon, who had come to the South Vietnamese outpost less than a mile from the survivors. The team members were to proceed to a friendly position along the Cam Lo River, set up an observation post, and wait for Clark and Hamilton to float down the river to them. Norris was used to getting the job done his own way, and although he would follow the briefed plan, he would do what had to be done to accomplish the mission, then tell the planners what they wanted to hear. Norris was the real thing—a tough, experienced SEAL who had a stubborn streak, but a pro when it came to such operations.

Clark was contacted and told to move to the southern shore of the river. At the same time, Norris and his team were directed to begin patrolling to the east. Norris acknowledged the order, turned off his radio, and began to move with his team of five South Vietnamese "frogmen," personnel equipped for extensive underwater reconnaissance and demolition. Leaving the South Vietnamese outpost, Norris and his group made their way up the Cam Lo River, first to rescue Clark, and then to find and bring Hamilton to safety. The team had planned to swim upriver, but the current was too swift, so they stayed on land and moved west along the side of the river, passing by enemy patrols, tanks, and trucks. Although they were ordered not to go more than one kilometer into enemy territory, from past experience Norris knew that he and his men would have to move closer. So he led the team another kilometer and waited.

A forward air controller (FAC) aircraft flying overhead instructed Clark to slip into the river and float down so he could be rescued by the Norris team. In the early morning hours of 10 April, Norris saw Clark out in the river and, waiting until an enemy patrol passed, he entered the chilly river waters and floated downstream after Clark. He soon lost track of the pilot, emerged from the river, and searched back along the banks until he reached his hidden team. They then left their position, leaving Norris to once again float down the river while the team moved eastward searching the shoreline. Norris found Clark hiding along the river bank. With Clark now in hand, the team evaded enemy patrols and brought the exhausted pilot to safety. Clark was transported by armored personnel carrier (APC) to the last outpost on the Cua Viet River at Dong Ha and flown to Da Nang. Norris and his South Vietnamese frogmen remained at the upriver outpost. They still had to retrieve Hamilton.

Before they could attempt their second rescue, spotters sighted NVA tanks and trucks crossing the Cam Lo bridge. Colonel Anderson ordered the air strikes on the bridge, and three tanks and several enemy trucks were destroyed. In response, NVA artillery shells, B-40 rockets, and mortars rained down on the outpost, killing and wounding several soldiers. Among the wounded were two of Norris' frogmen. The wounded were MedEvaced in APCs.

After he went down, Hamilton remained in contact with SAR personnel and was able to direct air attacks against the massive enemy force. But he had been on the ground for nine days, and was weak. Norris contacted him and said that they were about to come for him. Hamilton had made slow but good progress to the river, but he couldn't hold out much longer.

On the night of 11 April the SEAL team, now down to four men, began their trek and took a bunker position three-and-a-half kilometers northwest to wait for Hamilton to reach them. Hamilton contacted a circling FAC and informed the pilot that he was too weak and exhausted to go on. Though Hamilton attempted to give his position, the information was garbled, and Norris knew that he would have to leave the bunker and search for him. Norris crept along the shore, but he could not make contact and returned to the bunker. At this point he let two of the frogmen leave because they had voiced their reluctance to put themselves in further danger by following an American to save another American. One of the frogmen, Petty Officer Nguyen Van Kiet, the ranking South Vietnamese commando, volunteered to stay with Norris.

In darkness the two dressed themselves as fishermen, found a sampan that was intact, and paddled upstream. As they made their way they could hear the voices of enemy soldiers on both sides of the river. The FAC aircraft, piloted by Capt. Harold Icke, monitored their position, and Norris was able to pass along significant enemy targets for subsequent air strikes. As they rounded a bend in the river, they heard the roar of tanks starting their engines—they had stumbled onto the assembly area of an enemy armor battalion. As they progressed westward they ran into a fog bank, which gave them good cover; when they emerged from the fog, however, they found themselves under the Cam Lo bridge. As enemy troops marched across the bridge, Norris and Kiet quickly turned the sampan around and started downstream. As they moved down the river, they searched the shoreline, finally finding Hamilton in a clump of bushes. After he was checked over for injuries (there were only some cuts and bruises), Hamilton was placed in the sampan and covered with bamboo.

Norris notified Icke that they had found Hamilton and were coming out. The sky began to lighten as dawn approached, creating a sense of urgency for Norris and Kiet. They knew they had to move downriver as quickly as possible before being detected by enemy soldiers patrolling the shoreline. Norris told Icke to have air strike aircraft available—he might need them! The two SEALs eventually slipped into the water to avoid being spotted by the enemy, but it was not long before a patrol began to shout and run after them. They got lucky when, upon reaching a bend in the river with heavy foliage along the shoreline, they were able to hide the sampan and elude the enemy soldiers. Further on down the river they were fired on by a heavy machine gun.

Norris called FAC for an air strike, but none was available. On the emergency frequency, however, he was contacted by a flight of five A-4 attack aircraft from the carrier USS *Hancock*. The aircraft bombed the village from which the enemy fire originated and obliterated the entire area.

The FAC was able to bring in two A-1 Sandys to work over the north shoreline. When the Sandys had done their work, Norris and Kiet climbed back into the sampan to try to reach their friendly outpost. As they beached their boat, they began taking fire from NVA soldiers on the northern shore. ARVN soldiers at the outpost returned fire, and some of the soldiers rushed down to help bring Hamilton up the hill to a bunker.

Hamilton, Norris, and Kiet were taken to Dong Ha, and Hamilton was then delivered by helicopter to Da Nang. Later, when Norris was asked by a reporter if he would do it again, he replied, "An American was down in enemy territory. Of course I would do it again!"

For their heroic action, Lt. Tom Norris received the Medal of Honor, and Petty Officer Nguyen Van Kiet was awarded the Navy Cross. Colonel Hamilton is retired and living in Arizona. Both Lieutenant Norris, now medically retired, and Nguyen Van Kiet live in the Pacific Northwest.

Retired Col. William C. Anderson, USAF, wrote a book about the rescue of BAT 21 Bravo in 1982. Unfortunately, at that time much relevant information was still classified, which limited him from providing a full account of the incident.

ENDNOTES

Two main sources were used to write this chapter. The most definitive book on the subject, *The Rescue of BAT 21*, was written by Darrel D. Whitcomb in 1998. Because all the material that was classified when Colonel Anderson wrote his account had since been declassified, Whitcomb was able not only to tell the complete story of the rescue, but also to keep the reader abreast of the overall war as it was progressing at that time, and to deal with some of the controversy that folowed the SAR operation. Whitcomb is a fine author and is probably the best individual to tell the BAT 21 story. From 1972 to 1974 he was a forward air controller (FAC) in Southeast Asia, directing air strikes in support of friendly forces in Vietnam, Laos, and Cambodia. He was awarded the Silver Star medal for gallantry in action, two Distinguished Flying Crosses, and sixteen Air medals for his service.

The other source was the Home of Heroes website (www.homeofheroes.com/brotherhood/seals.html), which is a treasure trove of information for military historians. The story, "The Brotherhood of Soldiers at War," offers a well-written, compelling narrative of the BAT 21 rescue with color illustrations. It contains the only photograph these authors have been able to find showing Lieutenant Norris with PO Nguyen Van Kiet wearing his Navy Cross medal.

Lt. Cdr. Jesse Junior Taylor, USN

Quang Tri Province
17 November 1965

For extraordinary heroism in aerial flight as a pilot in Carrier Air Wing SIXTEEN, embarked in the USS ORISKANY (CVA-34), during a rescue combat air patrol over hostile territory in North Vietnam on 17 November 1965. Although his aircraft was severely damaged by heavy enemy ground fire while he was attempting to locate a downed pilot, Lieutenant Commander Taylor persisted in his efforts until he had definitely ascertained the location of his fellow airman. He then proceeded to attack enemy gun sites which threatened the approach of the rescue helicopter. Only after his own aircraft caught fire and a crash was imminent did Lieutenant Commander Taylor cease his efforts. With his aircraft burning and heavily damaged, he succeeded in reaching the coast of the Gulf of Tonkin in an attempt to ditch but did not survive the crash of his crippled aircraft. In sacrificing his life in an effort to save the life of a fellow airman, Lieutenant Commander Taylor displayed the highest degree of courage and self-sacrifice. His actions were in keeping with the finest traditions of the United States Naval Service.[1]

Navy Cross citation for Lt. Cdr. Jesse Junior Taylor, USN

ON 17 NOVEMBER 1965, Lt. Cdr. Jesse Junior Taylor, USN, was engaged in attacking a key bridge near the North Vietnam port of Haiphong while flying a propeller-driven Skyraider (nicknamed the "Spad"). The Spad was a mainstay of the American air arsenal during the war, capable of carrying out a wide range of combat missions. Intense antiaircraft fire had downed one of the American aircraft, and its pilot had ejected from his doomed plane into a densely populated and heavily defended area. Taylor overheard the radio transmission about the pilot's plight. Although it was not his assigned mission, he realized that time was of the essence in any attempt to rescue the downed pilot, and he made a courageous decision. Having discovered that other rescue aircraft were occupied elsewhere, he took command of the rescue effort.

Lt. Cdr. Jesse Junior Taylor, USN. (U.S. Naval Institute Photo Archives)

Despite heavy antiaircraft fire, Taylor flew to the scene and found the downed pilot still in his parachute harness in shallow water. To cover the approach of a rescue helicopter, he attacked the antiaircraft sites with 20-mm machine-gun fire, despite the fact that his own plane had sustained severe damage. The storm of enemy flak soon made it obvious that the helicopter would not be able to extricate the man on the ground. And because of fire in his own aircraft, Taylor was forced to break off his own persistent attacks. Rather than abandon his plane in enemy territory, he elected to try and ditch it in the Gulf of Tonkin. However, fire burned through the wing of his aircraft, and it crashed into the sea before he had time to eject, and he died. Other pilots on the scene observed North Vietnamese boats with soldiers leave the beach and head for the wreckage. For his extraordinary determination to save a fellow pilot, even at the ultimate risk, Lieutenant Commander Taylor was posthumously awarded the Navy Cross.[2]

Jesse Taylor was born in Wichita, Kansas, on 16 January 1925. He enlisted in the Navy in October 1942 and served as a Douglas Dauntless SB2C-3 aviation radioman and rear gunner with Bombing Squadron VB-11 aboard the carrier USS *Hornet* (CV-12) in the South Pacific until the end of World War II.[3]

On 17 November 1965, Lt. Cdr. Jesse Junior Taylor, flying a Fighter Squadron One Fifty Two (VF-152) A-1 Skyraider, was shot down and killed by intense enemy antiaircraft fire over North Vietnam while trying to protect the rescue of a downed fellow aviator. (U.S. Naval Institute Photo Archives)

During the Korean conflict Taylor returned to the Navy for training as an aviator, and in May 1952 he won his wings of gold and was commissioned an ensign. He was ordered to report to Composite Squadron Four, which was home-based at the Naval Air Station, Atlantic City, New Jersey. The squadron had several types of aircraft, and in 1953 Taylor was assigned to a team of five F2H-2N Banshee pilots whose primary mission was special-weapons delivery. They were also considered to be night fighters. The following year, the team deployed to the Mediterranean aboard the USS *Lake Champlain* (CV-39). Jesse was considered to be an outstanding, aggressive pilot.[4] Following the end of his tour with VC-4, he served as an NROTC instructor at the University of California at Los Angeles. He then underwent further flight training and completed a tour with the staff of the chief of naval air training at Pensacola, Florida. After this tour he journeyed to England, where he attended the Empire Test Pilot School at Farmborough. He then rejoined the U.S. fleet, serving as a replacement pilot in Fighter Squadron VF-174, and was promoted to lieutenant commander. He subsequently was transferred to Fighter Squadron 62, where he flew F-8 Crusaders until July 1962.[5] And he then underwent instruction at the Naval War College in Newport, Rhode Island. He completed the course in 1963 and was next assigned as director of the Flight Test Division, Office of the Bureau of Naval Weapons Representative, St. Louis, Missouri.

In July 1965, Taylor was assigned to Air Wing 16 aboard the attack carrier *Oriskany* (CVA-34), which was operating in the Gulf of Tonkin. He flew sixteen missions between September and November of that year. He was promoted to the rank of commander on 1 September 1965; at the time of his death, however, he had

USS *Oriskany* (CVA-34) with VF-152 A-1 Skyraiders on afterdeck off North Vietnam, June 1967. (U.S. Naval Institute Photo Archives)

not been officially given the rank. In addition to being awarded the Navy Cross, Taylor earned an Air Medal and a Gold Star in lieu of a second award; the Navy Commendation Medal with Combat "V"; the Purple Heart; the Vietnam Service Medal with bronze star; the Vietnamese National Order Fifth Class; the Vietnamese Gallantry Cross with Palm; and the Philippine Republic Presidential Unit Citation Badge. His remains were returned by the North Vietnamese in 1975.[6]

On 1 December 1984 the guided missile frigate USS *Taylor* (FFG-50) was commissioned during ceremonies at Bath Iron Works, Bath, Maine. Present at the commissioning ceremony were Mrs. Barbara A. Taylor, wife of Commander Taylor, and her children, Jeffery Taylor, Diane Taylor Oeland, and Greg Taylor. The ship was subsequently home-ported at Charleston, South Carolina.[7]

The USS *Taylor* has operated extensively in the western Atlantic, the Caribbean Sea, the Mediterranean Sea, and ocean areas in southwest Asia. The ship has made six extended deployments: with NATO's standing Naval Force Atlantic in 1987, in

USS *Taylor* (FFG-50) under way. (U.S. Naval Institute Photo Archives)

the Arabian Gulf in 1988, in 1990 as part of Operation Desert Shield, in 1992 as part of Operation Southern Watch, in 1994 to the Mediterranean Sea and Red Sea, and in 1997 and 2002 with NATO's Standing Naval Force Mediterranean.[8]

ENDNOTES

1. Paul Drew Stevens, *The Navy Cross: Vietnam, Citations of Awards to Men of the United States Navy and the United States Marine Corps 1964–1973* (Forest Ranch, Calif.: Sharp & Dunnigan Publications, 1987), 318.
2. Official U. S. Navy Biography of Lieutenant Commander Jesse Junior Taylor, USN, 8 November 1971. (Operational Archives, Naval Historical Center, Washington, D.C.)
3. Ibid.
4. Interview with Capt. E. T. Wooldridge, USN (Ret.), 5 December 2006. Captain Wooldridge was a team member in Jesse's "Banshee" VC-4 group and deployed with him on the *Lake Champlain*.
5. Captain Wooldridge again associated with Jesse while their two squadrons (Jesse in VF-62, Wooldridge a Phantom pilot in VF-102) were aboard the USS *Enterprise* during a shakedown cruise in the Caribbean.
6. In the late 1970s, Captain Wooldridge was driving home from the Pentagon one evening and heard over the radio that the North Vietnamese had returned the remains of American pilots, among them Lt. Cdr. Jesse Junior Taylor. Wooldridge contacted Taylor's widow, who was thankful for the information. During their conversation she mentioned to Captain Wooldridge that if he happened to watch the upcoming Rose Bowl game, her son was playing tackle on the UCLA team.
7. Official U.S. Navy Biography of Lieutenant Commander Jesse Jr. Taylor, USN, 8 November 1971. (Operation Archives, Naval Historical Center, Washington, D.C.)
8. "Launching of the Guided Frigate *Taylor* (FFG 50) 5 November 1983, at Bath, Maine," Bath Iron Works Corporation brochure.

KOREAN WAR (1950–1953)

Following the end of World War II, the alliance of convenience that had existed between the Soviet Union and the Western allies disintegrated into a competition for influence in the postwar world. International tension was further complicated by the emergence of a second communist nation, the People's Republic of China, in 1949.

This competition, which became known as the Cold War, led to a military confrontation in Korea. Occupied by the Japanese for thirty-five years, Korea had been promised independence at the Cairo Conference in 1943. Instead, following its liberation in 1945, it was provisionally divided at the 38th parallel. In the north, a Communist government emerged, the Democratic People's Republic of Korea, under the control of Kim Il Sung. In the south, the Republic of Korea, led by Syngman Rhee, created a right-wing, marginally democratic, republic. Both governments claimed to be the legitimate government of all of Korea.

On 25 June 1950 North Korean forces crossed the 38th parallel into South Korea with the intention of unifying the country by force. North Korea was supported by China and to a limited degree by the Soviet Union, which provided advisers and military equipment. Two days later, on the 27th, the United Nations passed a resolution in support of South Korea, and sixteen countries committed combat troops to repel the Communist aggression.

In order to avoid the necessity of having Congress declare war, President Harry S. Truman termed his intervention a "police action." He deployed the 7th Fleet to the Sea of Japan and named General of the Army Douglas MacArthur as commander of all American forces. MacArthur was later named commander in chief of all U.N. forces in Korea.

Fighting in Korea lasted from 25 June 1950 until a cease-fire agreement was reached on 27 July 1953. Approximately 1,789,000 Americans served in Korea during the war. As is common with figures on war casualties, sources disagree as to the exact number, but Department of Defense statistics list 33,742 Americans killed in combat, including 4,735 individuals presumed dead under the definition of the Missing Persons Act. Of the total American fatalities, 23,615 were killed in action, 2,459 died from their wounds, 4,821 were missing in action, and 2,847 died while prisoners of war. An additional 2,830 died from accidents and illnesses not related to combat.[1]

Two hundred sixty-eight Navy Crosses were awarded during the Korean conflict to 266 individuals; two men earned two Navy Crosses. Of the 268 medals awarded, 94 were awarded posthumously. The majority of the medals (224) went to Marines, with another 41 awarded to the Navy and three to Army personnel. One soldier, Lt. Col. John Page, earned both the Medal of Honor and the Navy Cross. The legendary Marine Lewis "Chesty" Puller earned his fifth Navy Cross as well as the Distinguished Service Cross in Korea, and four recipients from World War II earned a second award.[2]

The exact number is uncertain, but the Navy Cross was awarded to at least twenty-eight Navy corpsmen, eight posthumously, and nine Navy Crosses were awarded to pilots, among them Maj. Jack Bolt, the only Marine ace of the Korean War.

ENDNOTES

1. Department of Defense, U.S. Military Korean War statistics.
2. www.homeofheroes.com.

Maj. John F. Bolt, USMC

Republic of Korea
11 July 1953

The Navy Cross is presented to John F. Bolt (O-13522), Major, U.S. Marine Corps, for extraordinary heroism in connection with military operations against an armed enemy of the United Nations while attached to the First Marine Aircraft Wing and serving as Pilot of a Plane in the THIRTY-NINTH Fighter-Interceptor Squadron, Fifth Air Force, in action against enemy aggressor forces in the Republic of Korea on 11 July 1953. Sighting four hostile jet interceptors immediately after the second section of his four-plane flight was forced to retire from the area because of a low fuel supply during a reconnaissance mission deep in enemy territory, Major Bolt quickly maneuvered his aircraft and that of his wingman into attack position and deliberately engaged the numerically superior enemy in a head-on firing run, destroying one of the hostile planes with his initial burst of fire. Although his fuel supply was dangerously low, he initiated repeated attacks on the remaining enemy aircraft and severely damaging the engine section of the lead interceptor, resolutely pressed his attack against the crippled plane until the enemy pilot was forced to bail out. By his exceptional courage and superb airmanship in destroying the two aircraft, Major Bolt raised his total of enemy jet planes destroyed during the Korean conflict to six, thereby becoming the first jet ace in the history of Marine Corps aviation. His inspiring leadership and great personal valor reflect the highest credit upon himself and was in keeping with the highest traditions of the United States Naval Service.[1]

Navy Cross citation for Maj. John F. Bolt, USMC

In the brotherhood of military aviators, only a small percentage of pilots ever engage in actual air-to-air combat. And only a few of the pilots who do see combat earn the title of "ace" by downing five enemy aircraft. Only seven men earned the distinction of being aces in both World War II and Korea, and only one of those seven was a naval aviator—Maj. John "Jack" Bolt.[2]

The weather was marginal on the morning of 11 July 1953 as Major Bolt strapped into his F-86F Sabre, "Darling Dottie," and took off with three other Sabres from Suwon Airfield, Republic of Korea, en route to what was called "MiG Alley," a strip of territory along the Yalu River. "We flew with a minimum of four aircraft. That's a 'division' in the Marines, but a 'flight' to the Air Force. Our F-86

Maj. John F. "Jack" Bolt, USMC, in his F-86 Sabre jet fighter, "Darling Dottie." He was the only Marine ace of the Korean War. (U.S. Naval Institute Photo Archive)

Sabres took off in twos. . . .We would normally set up a patrol along the Yalu River. The MiGs were at Chinese airfields like Antung, right across the river."[3]

Bolt was a Marine aviator serving as an exchange officer with the 39th Fighter Interceptor Squadron (FIS) Cobras, 51st Fighter Interceptor Wing, U.S. Fifth Air Force, and already had four MiGs to his credit. The 51st hosted Australian, Canadian, and British flyers, as well as other Marine pilots. One Marine pilot who flew with the 51st was John Glenn, the future astronaut and senator, who flew twenty-seven missions and downed three MiGs to earn the nickname "MiG Mad Marine" while serving with the 25th Fighter Interceptor Squadron.[4] Like Glenn, this was not Bolt's first war.

Fuel was always a concern for American fliers. "A mission was an hour and twenty minutes," Bolt stated. "If we became engaged, we had to drop our [fuel] tanks. That limited our time in the area. . . .The enemy didn't have to think about fuel starvation. He didn't have to worry about handling a long flight at high altitude. He was always fighting over his own territory." At times, fuel would be so low that American pilots would depend on tailwinds out of Manchuria to glide part of the way back to Suwon, then hope there was enough fuel to restart the engine for a power landing.

Just as the second section of Bolt's four-aircraft flight had been forced to leave the area due to low fuel, Bolt and his wingman, Air Force 1st Lt. Jerry Carlile, sighted four hostiles.[5] Although low on fuel themselves, Bolt and Carlile initiated an attack.[6]

Born on 19 May 1921 in Laurens, South Carolina, Bolt dreamed of becoming a pilot while growing up in Sanford, Florida, and left the University of Florida after two years, in the summer of 1941, to enlist in the Marine Corps Reserve to train as a pilot and earn money for college. He was an aviation cadet at the Naval Air Station (NAS) at Pensacola, Florida, when the Japanese attacked Pearl Harbor on 7 December 1941.

Bolt earned his wings and a second lieutenant's commission upon his graduation in July 1942 and was so proficient as a pilot that his first assignment was as an instructor pilot at Jacksonville's Lee Field. He was then assigned to advanced training in the F-4F Wildcat and became carrier-qualified, after which he was ordered to the Solomon Islands in June 1943, where he joined a pool of replacement pilots at Turtle Bay, Espiritu Santo. This pool was organized into a squadron, VMF-214, under the command of Maj. Greg "Pappy" Boyington, a Marine veteran of the American Volunteer Group (the "Flying Tigers") in China.[7]

VMF-214, which became known as the famed "Black Sheep" squadron, fought above the Northern Solomons and Rabaul from August 1943 through January 1944. The squadron flew the Chance-Vought F4U-1 Corsair (nicknamed the "Bent-Winged Bird"), a single-seat fighter with a maximum speed of 417 miles per hour, a service ceiling of 36,900 feet, and a range of 1,015 miles. Its Pratt & Whitney R-2800-8 power plant generated two thousand horsepower, and its inverted gull wings gave it lift. Its six .50-caliber machine guns made it a formidable warplane, and it remained in use into the Korean War. The Black Sheep accounted for ninety-four Japanese planes, and produced eight aces, including Bolt, who flew ninety-four missions to down six enemy fighters.

On one occasion, on 16 October 1943, Bolt earned Boyington's ire. As Boyington led a fighter sweep over Kahili's Tonolei Harbor, he observed that the harbor was filled with Japanese barges but ordered his flight of eight not to attack. When Boyington returned to Munda, Bolt refueled on Vella Lavella and, alone and without orders, returned to Tonolei to sink a barge filled with troops, an empty barge, a tugboat, and a small cargo vessel. As a fellow pilot had warned Bolt, Boyington was "pissed," but a congratulatory telegram from Admiral Halsey praising Bolt as "a one-man war" and the award of a Distinguished Flying Cross served to limit any consequences Boyington may have considered.[8]

After a brief break from combat in 1944, Bolt returned to fly in 1945 with VMF-472 from an escort carrier, the USS *Block Island* (CVE-106), and as part of the Marines' first carrier-based fighter squadron, he took part in the Battle of

Okinawa. He also set an endurance record for single-engine aircraft when he flew a fourteen-hour mission in a Corsair.

Bolt remained in the Marines following VJ Day and learned to fly the F-86 Sabre jet while participating in an exchange program with the Oregon Air National Guard. In 1952 he was sent to Korea for a combat tour in the F-9F Panther.[9]

Arriving in Korea in mid-1952, Bolt was assigned to VMF-115 (the "Able Eagles") at the K-3 airfield at Pohang, where he flew ninety-four ground-support missions in an F9F-2 Panther jet. Because of his familiarity with the F-86 and his friendship with Lt. Col. George Ruddell, USAF, commander of the 39th Fighter Interceptor Squadron (FIS), Bolt was accepted by the Air Force for a ninety-day exchange program. He flew as part of "D" or "Dog" Flight under Cpt. Joseph McConnell, the ranking ace of the war, then took over as flight leader when McConnell returned stateside in May 1953.

Bolt's first kill came on 16 May, followed by a second and third on the 22nd and 25th. On 30 June Bolt and Ruddell crossed the Yalu to bag Ruddell one last MiG before he returned stateside, but it was Bolt who got the kill. He later took a lot of ribbing for "stealing the colonel's MiG." It was Bolt's fourth MiG.[10]

Bolt requested, and was granted, a three-month extension. He had already flown thirty-four missions when he and his wingman found themselves facing a numerically superior enemy on the morning of 11 July. Bolt recalled the MiGs as being "sitting ducks," and felt his only danger would be accidentally crossing into his wingman's stream of bullets.[11]

The official version is less modest. "Major Bolt quickly maneuvered his aircraft and that of his wingman into attack position and deliberately engaged the numerically superior enemy in a head-on firing run, destroying one of the hostile planes with his initial burst of fire. Although his fuel supply was dangerously low, he initiated repeated attacks on the remaining enemy aircraft and severely damaging the engine section of the lead interceptor, resolutely pressed his attack against the crippled plane until the enemy pilot was forced to bail out."[12]

With his fifth and sixth shoot-downs, Bolt became a double-ace, the thirty-seventh ace of the Korean War, and the first jet ace in the history of Marine Corps aviation. Sixteen days later, on 27 July 1953, the armistice was signed, ending hostilities in Korea.

Following Korea, Bolt held a number of staff and flying positions, including command of his old unit, VMF-214, for two years, and working at the Pentagon as an analyst of Marine tactics. In 1958 he led the first flights of single-engine fighters from Hawaii to California, using unit aircraft to refuel one another. He retired in 1962 with the rank of lieutenant colonel. In addition to the Navy Cross, Bolt was awarded three Distinguished Flying Crosses.[13]

After retiring from the Marine Corps, Bolt returned to school at the age of forty-seven and graduated from the University of Florida law school, which he attended with his son. He spent over twenty years in private practice before retiring in 1992. He died in Tampa, Florida, on 8 September 2004, at the age of 83.

James MacAlpine, a pilot who flew with Bolt, remembered him: "He was a hell of a flier. He just made the airplane do what he wanted it to do. . . . He would go all the way to the Great Wall of China to shoot down a MiG."

ENDNOTES

1. Navy Cross Citation for Maj. John F. Bolt, USMC, www.homeofheroes.com/valor/1_Citations/05_Korea-nc/nc_08korea_usmc.html#A.
2. Robert F. Dorr, *Marine Air: The History of the Flying Leathernecks in Words and Pictures* (New York: Berkeley Publishing Group, 2005).
3. Ibid.
4. Official biography. John Glenn Archives, Ohio State University, www.osu.edu.
5. Some sources, such as Dorr, state that Bolt and his wingman only fought two MiGs on 11 July, but the official Navy Cross citation and the Air Force credit them with engaging four hostile jet interceptors.
6. Dorr, *Marine Air*.
7. John F. "Jack" Bolt Official Biography. USAF Air University, Maxwell-Gunter AFB, Montgomery, Alabama, www.au.af.mil/au/goe/eaglebios/97bios/bolt97.htm.
8. Bruce Gamble, *The Black Sheep* (New York: Presidio Press, 1998).
9. John F. "Jack" Bolt Official Biography.
10. Eric Hammel, *Aces at War: The American Aces Speak*, vol. 4 (New York: Presidio Press, 1997).
11. Dorr, *Marine Air*.
12. Navy Cross citation for Maj. John F. Bolt, USMC, 6 January 1954.
13. "John 'Jack' Bolt, 83; Double Ace Fought in WWII, Korean War," obituary, *New York Times*, 14 September 2004.

Lt. Col. John U. D. Page, USA

Sudong-ni, Korea
10 December 1950

The Navy Cross is presented to John Upshur Dennis Page (O-29085), Lieutenant Colonel, U.S. Army, for extraordinary heroism in connection with military operations against an enemy of the United Nations while attached to the 52nd Transportation Truck Battalion . . . X Corps Artillery, in action against enemy aggressor forces near Sudong-ni, Korea, on 10 December 1950. When numerically superior enemy forces ambushed a Marine regimental convoy with which he was traveling, Lieutenant Colonel Page repeatedly exposed himself to intense hostile machine gun, mortar and small arms fire to move forward in an effort to organize friendly elements and reduce the roadblock. Realizing the extreme danger to the stationary convoy while under the relentless fire of enemy forces commanding high ground on both sides of the road, he bravely fought his way to the head of the column accompanied by a Marine private and, undaunted by point-blank machine gun fire, continued directly into the hostile strong-point, taking 30 of the enemy completely by surprise and inflicting severe casualties among them. With the Marine private wounded by a hand-grenade fragment, Lieutenant Colonel Page ordered him to withdraw and provided him with covering fire fiercely continuing to engage the enemy single-handedly and killing 12 of them before he himself was mortally wounded. By his valiant and aggressive fighting spirit in the face of overwhelming odds during this self-imposed mission, he was directly responsible in disrupting the hostile attack, thereby allowing the members of the convoy to regroup, re-deploy and fight off succeeding attacks. His outstanding courage, self-sacrificing efforts and unswerving devotion to duty reflect the highest credit upon Lieutenant Colonel Page and the United States Armed Forces. He gallantly gave his life for his country.[1]

Navy Cross citation for Lt. Col. John U. D. Page, USA

By the end of November 1950, U.S. Army and Marine Corps units had pressed north to the Yalu River and the Manchurian border following successful landings at Inchon and Iwon. At the same time, Chinese troops infiltrated down from the high ridges and flowed out into the countryside in the north, raiding villages, attacking outposts of U.N. troops, and striking at supply lines far to the south. No U.S. vehicles could move on the main supply route during hours of darkness due to the increasing guerilla activity and destruction of bridges. The situation had deteriorated in the rear as well, to the extent that some means had to be found for regulating, controlling, and reporting on convoys en route to and from the front.

Lt. Col. John U. D. Page, USA, assigned to X Corps Artillery, was attached to the 52nd Transportation Battalion to help get the job done. After establishing traffic regulating points, the plan was for him to make daily inspections—a round trip of 120 miles over icy, narrow, corkscrew mountain roads from the city of Hamhung through the cities of Chinhung-ni and Koto-ri and north to Hargaru-ri.

Colonel Page and his convoy of jeeps left Hamhung before dawn on 29 November as the first step toward establishing traffic control and communication links along the main supply route to 1st Marine Division positions in the north and to those of some Army troops in the Chosin Reservoir Plateau. Officers and enlisted men were dropped off at check points along the route. Finding the road to the north blocked when he reached Koto-ri, Colonel Page, his mission accomplished, decided to return to Hamhung with his driver, Cpl. David E. Klepsig. After traveling less than a mile on the return trip, Page learned from Military Police on the road that some North Koreans had been forced out of their house by Chinese troops. Deciding to investigate, he and a few men started up the side of a mountain. Soon they sighted about thirty or forty of the enemy at a point not far from the 96th Field Artillery radio relay unit station on the mountain top. Learning from an officer assigned to the radio outfit that the 96th needed ammunition badly, and fearful that the Chinese would attack the station once it became dark, Colonel Page and his driver headed back to Koto-ri for help. Just as they started, Chinese machine gunners opened up on Page and his driver at close range. Both men jumped out of the jeep and ran for the protection of a ditch.

"It was beginning to get dark and the Colonel began to get worried," Corporal Klepsig said later in recalling the incident. "He said, 'Well we can't stay here.' He told me, 'Corporal, go get the jeep and I'll cover you and meet you where you turn back on the road.'. . . I went through a creek which was about ten feet deep and nine feet wide, and ice and everything. I went through and jumped in the jeep. I looked up then and there was Colonel Page standing in the middle of the road firing at the enemy with his M-2 carbine. He was drawing attention away from me, standing up in full view. He sprayed the hill, and I guess it took the Chinese by surprise."[2] The Chinese soldiers, somewhat confused by the turn of events, fled their positions.

On reaching Koto-ri, Page immediately started gathering ammunition, intending to return to the radio relay post that same night. Just before leaving, however, he learned that personnel of the outfit had escaped from being cut off by the Chinese at the mountain-top station and had reached a point of comparative safety on the plateau below.

By now the Chinese troops coming down from the north had consolidated their positions. Colonel Page, ready again for a return trip to Hamhung, learned

Lt. Col. John U. D. Page, USA, at Koto-ri, North Korea. Colonel Page was killed while performing heroically in disrupting enemy attacks. (Princeton University Education Department)

the worst from Col. Lewis B. Puller, then commanding at Koto-ri. The entire plateau had been surrounded by the enemy.

Quickly sizing up the situation, Colonel Page went to work forming Army troops, most of them separated from their parent organizations, into some kind of a fighting force that could be placed at the disposal of the Marines. On his own initiative, he organized an infantry company of three rifle platoons, supported by an additional weapons platoon made up of men from an antiaircraft artillery unit. Still not satisfied that he was doing everything possible under adverse circumstances, he drew up offensive and defensive battle plans and had them approved by the Marines.

Meanwhile, the enemy was not content to wait out a long siege. Chinese snipers and infiltrating troops took a heavy toll on U.N. personnel in the besieged Koto-ri area. Navy medical corpsmen with the Marines were pressed harder and harder for hospital space and medical supplies. Helicopters that were evacuating the wounded were inadequate in number and made excellent targets for snipers in the hills during takeoffs and landings.

Early in December Colonel Page won approval for a plan calling for construction of an airstrip where small planes could be brought in to evacuate the wounded. Under his supervision a strip 100 feet wide and 2,000 feet long was constructed; while the airstrip was in operation about 750 wounded U.N. soldiers were evacuated from the area. Colonel Page's idea of the landing field was directly responsible for saving the lives of many of them.

Soon after the airstrip, dubbed the "Panicky Pocket" by U.N. troops, was finished, Colonel Page persuaded the pilot of an L-16 to take him on a tour of the perimeter defenses. Sighting enemy foxholes, he had the pilot fly as low as possible and dropped grenades on the Chinese positions. Later, he began firing at them from the air with his carbine, with devastating effect.

When enemy forces coming down from the hills attempted to raid the airstrip where evacuees were being loaded into planes, he commandeered a friendly tank, manning a .50-caliber machine gun on the turret. Standing fully exposed to enemy fire, he pursued the retreating enemy into a no-man's land beyond the support of U.N. forces. On another occasion, when behavior of an approaching enemy force indicated that it might surrender, he personally assumed command of a patrol and moved out beyond the perimeter to bring in approximately ten prisoners of war.

After ten days of constant fighting, the Army and Marines had blasted their way to the edge of the plateau. Colonel Page realized that the beleaguered troops were going to have to fight their way fifty miles back to the sea. He flew to Hamhung to arrange for additional artillery support for the retrograde movement. None of his men expected that he would return to Koto-ri. When Page again landed on the airstrip, Corporal Kelsig greeted him and asked, "Colonel, why didn't you stay there at Hamhung where you had a good thing?" "He grinned that funny smile of his," Klepsig recalled later. "And he said, 'Corporal, you didn't think I was going to leave the men, did you?' Well, we thought he was crazy to come back but we sort of knew he would."

On 20 December 1950 elements of the 1st Marine Division and the 7th Infantry Division, both of which had been trapped at Hagaru-ri, passed through Koto-ri on their way to Hungnam. Troops at Koto-ri were assigned the mission of fighting a rear-guard action.

As the men moved south during the early stages of withdrawal from Koto-ri, the enemy halted Colonel Page's section of the convoy at the critical Funchilin Pass. Realizing how desperate the situation was and disregarding his own safety, he immediately mounted a tank and from an exposed position manned a .50-caliber machine gun against enemy positions until his ammunition was expended and the convoy had resumed its movement. Later, at a railroad cable-car overpass, when enemy machine gun and rifle fire halted the column, he assumed command, firing a machine gun to keep the enemy down. Meanwhile, he directed the action of moving and towing heavily loaded trucks through a mudhole area.

American troops depart Koto-ri in bitterly cold weather, traversing mountainous terrain while under attack by Chinese soldiers. (National Archives)

During a still later assault by Chinese forces at Sudong-ni, the enemy overran, ransacked, and destroyed vehicles at the head of the column. Realizing the movement had become disorganized and halted as a result of this assault, Colonel Page left his position near the rear of the column and fought his way to the head of the convoy, accompanied by only one enlisted Marine, Pvt. Marvin Wasson.

Surprising enemy troops ransacking a supply truck, and although greatly outnumbered, he and his companion immediately attacked, pursuing a score of Chinese soldiers who were running toward several houses on a nearby slope. During the firefight the enemy began throwing grenades, and Wasson was wounded. Page shouted to the Marine to make a run for it, saying that he would cover his withdrawal with point-blank fire. Within minutes a furious burst of gunfire from the hillside engulfed Page, throwing him from his feet and killing him. Late that night, 10 December 1950, the Marine column, moving once more, came upon the body of John Page—and the bodies of sixteen enemy soldiers he had taken out. Many Marines knelt beside Page's body and offered prayers.

John Page and many other Americans who were killed on the road from Koto-ri to the seaport at Hungnam were buried in a military cemetery at Hamhung. His remains were eventually returned to the United States, where he was buried at Arlington National Cemetery. Colonel Page was awarded a posthumous Navy Cross by the Marine Corps. In 1956, three years after the statute of limitations had run out, the U.S. Congress enacted a special bill awarding Lt. Col. John U. D. Page, U.S. Army, a posthumous Medal of Honor.[3]

Colonel Page was born on 8 February 1904, on Malahi Island, Luzon, Philippine Islands. His father was a career military officer, and John decided early on that he wanted to follow in his father's footsteps. But weak eyes denied him entry to West Point, and he attended Princeton University to become an engineer. He graduated from Princeton in 1926 and was commissioned in the Army Reserve that same year. He became an exceptional engineer, but soldiering remained his dream. He took numerous military courses, learned how to fly, became a crack shot, and attended every summer camp during the 1920s and 1930s. Called to active duty in 1942, he served in Europe as commanding officer of a field artillery battalion. Following the end of the war, he was accepted into the Regular Army with the rank of major, and later served as a National Guard senior instructor at New Orleans, Louisiana. As he was about to be transferred to the Command and General Staff School at Fort Benning, Georgia, a step that would enhance his chances of promotion, the Korean War broke out, and his orders were changed. He was to go to war in Korea. In twelve incredible days of combat (29 November–10 December 1950) he fiercely engaged the enemy heedless of his own safety until he was mortally wounded.[4]

ENDNOTES

1. Full Text Citations for Award of the Navy Cross to U.S. Army Personnel, Korea 1950–1953, www.homeofheroes.com/valor/1_Citations/05_korea-nc/nc_08korea_army.html.
2. Department of Defense, "Army Awards Medal of Honor to Officer for Action in Korean Fighting," news release, 19 December 1956.
3. Ibid.
4. Ibid.

Lt. Gen. Lewis B. Puller, USMC

Nicaragua (two), Guadalcanal,
Cape Gloucester, Korea

NO STORY OF THE NAVY CROSS would be complete without the inclusion of "Chesty" Puller. When Gen. Oliver P. Smith presented Marine Col. Lewis B. Puller with the Navy Cross at Camp Pendleton, California, on 2 February 1952, Puller must have had a sense of déjà vu. He had been awarded the Navy Cross on four previous occasions (two for Nicaragua, one for Guadalcanal, and one for Cape Gloucester). Now he was being awarded his fifth Navy Cross, this one for his rear-guard actions during the withdrawal from the Chosin Reservoir in Korea in December 1950, making him the only Marine to amass five Navy Crosses and the most decorated Marine in U.S. history. His thirty-seven-year career placed him at some of the most significant battles of the twentieth century.

Puller was a colorful figure—famous, or infamous, for speaking his mind and turning a catchy phrase. Once, when surrounded by enemy troops, he is purported to have said, "All right men, they're on our left, they're on our right, they're in front of us, they're behind us . . . they can't get away this time!" Chesty was fearless, quick to speak his mind, and, as one correspondent recalled, "good copy." He had both admirers and enemies. There are enough Chesty stories to fill several volumes, but rather than his witticisms, it is his courage and skill as a warrior and tactical combat leader for which he is best remembered. And he looked the part with his bulldog face, square jaw, barrel chest, and parade-ground voice. He was a Marine's Marine.

Lewis Burwell Puller was born in West Point, King William County, in eastern Virginia, on 26 June 1898, the first male, and third of four children, born to Matthew and Martha Puller. He grew up in rural Virginia listening to old veterans' tales of the Civil War and reading books on military history and heroes. A good athlete, Puller was only a fair student. Distantly related to George S. Patton (both men had grandfathers who fought for the Confederacy), his boyhood idol was Thomas "Stonewall" Jackson.

His father, a prosperous wholesale grocer, died when Puller was ten, and as the oldest male young Lewis developed a sense of responsibility early. He grew up hunting, trapping, and fishing and dreamed of becoming a soldier. Too young to enlist without his parent's consent, he tried to convince his mother to allow him to join the Richmond Blues, a local militia, to fight in Mexico in 1916, but she refused.[1]

In the spring of 1917 Puller accepted an appointment to the Virginia Military Institute (VMI) at Lexington, Virginia, and on 1 September 1917 he was sworn

Then Col. Lewis "Chesty" Puller, USMC, at Koto-ri, North Korea. Often considered "the Marines' Marine," Lieutenant General Puller was the most decorated Marine in U.S. history. (National Archives)

in as a state cadet. Founded in 1839, VMI was the nation's first state-supported military academy. Its alumni include George Marshall and numerous other noted generals and Medal of Honor recipients. Puller's hero, Stonewall Jackson, once taught at VMI. Following America's entry into World War I, Puller resigned from VMI to enlist as a private in the Marine Corps on 25 July 1918—perhaps inspired by the 4th Marines at Belleau Wood, or possibly because the Marines' minimum commission age was 20. Despite his best efforts, Puller remained stateside and didn't see combat in the war.

Private Puller reported for boot camp at Parris Island. With the Corps expanding, leaders were needed, and promising privates were sent for training as NCOs. On 1 October 1918, Puller began NCO school, and on 10 January 1919 he reported to OTC (Officers Training Course) at Quantico, Virginia. He graduated and was appointed a second lieutenant in the Marine Reserve on 16 June 1919. Ten days later, with the reduction of forces that followed the end of the war, Puller was transferred to inactive status.[2]

Undeterred, Puller reenlisted in the Marine Corps for a four-year term on 28 June, and with a fellow OTC graduate, Sgt. Lawrence Muth, shipped out to Haiti. Enlisted Marines could serve as officers in the Gendarmerie d'Haiti, the Haitian National Police. They arrived in Port-au-Prince on 30 July 1919.

Four years earlier, President Woodrow Wilson had sent 330 Marines to Port-au-Prince after a popular uprising against Haitian dictator Jean Vilbrun Guillaume Sam threatened American interests. Using the justification that Haiti was unstable (there had been seven presidents between 1908 and 1915) and was vulnerable to German influence, as well as the need to protect American interests, the United States gained control of the Haitian government and administered it largely through the U.S. Marines. This control would remain in effect until August 1934.[3]

Opposition to the American occupation began early, and armed rebels, called "Cacos" by the Marines, were in the forefront. The Cacos were loosely knit bandit organizations that hired out to the highest bidder and had played an influential role in the continual transfer of power in Haiti, often forming into mercenary armies to overthrow the incumbent. Now they began to unify against the United States. The first Caco insurrection ended with the capture of their stronghold at Fort Rivière by a force of Marines and Sailors from the USS *Connecticut* under the command of Maj. Smedley Butler, earning Butler his second Medal of Honor. A second Caco insurrection began late on 3 September 1918 when native leader Charlemagne Peralte began a revolt against Marine rule.[4]

Puller spent most of the period between 1919 and 1923 in Haiti, assigned as a lieutenant with the Gendarmerie d'Haiti, a force composed of native Haitian troops and officered by Marine NCOs given officer rank. The mission of the Gendarmerie was varied, including law enforcement, running the jails and courts, overseeing local government, and acting as paymaster to the civilian government. The Gendarmerie regulated education, sanitation, and agriculture, and oversaw the construction and maintenance of roads. Sometimes the projects overseen by the Marines used forced labor, which provoked opposition to American rule. Puller participated in over forty engagements against Caco rebels during his time in Haiti.

On 7 April 1921 "Lieutenant" Puller was promoted to corporal, but he still had ambitions for a commission in the Marines. On 17 June 1921 he sailed for home with orders to report to the Marine Barracks at Eighth and I streets in Washington, D.C. Assigned to Officers Candidate School, he scored too low, and returned to Haiti on 29 March 1922, this time assigned as an adjutant to Maj. Alexander Vandegrift, a future Marine commandant. On 11 May, Puller was promoted to sergeant.

When Puller's enlistment ended on 30 June 1923, he returned to the United States. Shortly after arriving back, Puller reenlisted and was accepted a second time as an officer candidate. This time Puller graduated, ranking fifth of the ten NCOs who passed. On 6 March 1924, Puller was commissioned a second lieutenant in the Marines, and he served at the Marine Barracks, Norfolk Navy Yard, Virginia, while awaiting a vacancy at the Marine Basic School in Philadelphia.

On 2 January 1925, Puller began a five-month course of instruction devoted to academic study, drill, marksmanship, and military law, as well as to practical exercises, physical training, inspections, and examinations. Puller completed the training on 1 July 1925, and was then assigned to the 6th Battery, 10th Marine Artillery Regiment, at Quantico, Virginia. He requested training as an aviator, and in January 1926 was detailed to the 1st Aviation Group for training as a naval aviator at Pensacola Naval Air Station.

Aviation was in its infancy, and extremely hazardous—as many candidates died in accidents as successfully passed the course. Puller was consistently rated as unsatisfactory, and he was reassigned after failing to complete the course. He requested reassignment to Haiti, either with the Gendarmerie or the Marine brigade. Instead, he was ordered to Hawaii.[5]

On 17 July 1926 Puller reported to the Marine Barracks at Pearl Harbor, assigned as a platoon leader with the 92nd Company. He performed the routine duties of guard and ceremonial drill and was officer in charge of the rifle range. In mid-April 1928 he traveled to San Diego with the marksmanship team for the 1928 western division competition. Because he was at the end of his two-year assignment, Puller remained in San Diego after the competition, performing a variety of fill-in assignments.

In 1927 civil wars broke out in both China and Nicaragua, and Marines were deployed to both theaters. In May 1928 Puller requested assignment to the Marine brigade in either country. His request was denied. In October he requested assignment specifically to the Guardia Nacional de Nicaragua, the Nicaraguan National Guard. This time, his request was approved. The situation there was intensifying, and on 5 November 1928 Marine headquarters ordered Puller to Nicaragua. It was in Nicaragua that the young Marine officer would begin to be noticed.

In 1909 the United States had sent warships to Nicaragua to protect U.S. lives and property when conservative-led forces rebelled against President Jose Santos Zelaya. Because Zelaya had attempted to control foreign access to Nicaraguan resources, the United States supported conservative elements in Nicaragua. Zelaya resigned later that year. Except for a brief period in late 1925 and early 1926, U.S. Marines would occupy Nicaragua until 1933.

In August 1925 Carlos Solórzano, a moderate conservative, was elected president of Nicaragua. He purged the liberals from his coalition government, but was forced out of power in November 1925 by a conservative group that proclaimed General Emiliano Chamorro as president in January 1926. Fearing a new round of conservative-liberal violence, the Marines, which had left the country in August 1925, returned in May 1926, again to "protect American interests." The United States mediated a peace agreement between the liberals and the conservatives in October 1926, the Pact of Espino Negro.

A rebel liberal group under the leadership of Augusto César Sandino refused to sign the Pact. Sandino, seen as a "bandit" by U.S. forces, led a six-year armed resistance to the U.S. military presence in Nicaragua and became a popular symbol of resistance to the U.S. domination of Latin America. He successfully evaded capture and would eventually force the withdrawal of U.S. troops from Nicaragua.[6]

Upon Puller's arrival in Managua on 5 December 1928, he was assigned to the Guardia Nacional staff as G-1 (personnel). He performed his duties, as he always did, in an exemplary fashion and accompanied or led patrols as often as he could. On 6 March 1929, Puller was given command of the garrison at Corinto, a major seaport on the west coast, and was soon in action against Sandino rebels.

On 24 May 1929, Puller was promoted to first lieutenant, and concurrently as a captain in the Guardia. After a brief period in command of the penitentiary in Managua, he finally got his wish for a field assignment. He was assigned to the 1st Battalion, headquartered in the town of Jinotega in central Nicaragua. Located in a valley bisected by rivers and surrounded by wooded mountains, Jinotega was a center of guerilla activity. Much to Puller's consternation, he was assigned as quarter-master upon his arrival on 4 June. Despite his staff position, Puller led patrols, and on 30 May, his superiors perhaps surrendering to the inevitable, Puller was placed in command of Company M, the Guardia's sole dedicated field force of two officers and thirty-five enlisted men.

In 1930, according to his first Navy Cross citation, he "led his forces in five successive engagements against superior numbers of armed bandit forces; namely at LaVirgin on 16 February 1930, at Los Cedros on 6 June 1930, at Moncotal on 22 July 1930, at Guapinol on 25 July 1930 and at Malcate on 19 August 1930, with the result that the bandits were in each engagement, completely routed, with losses of nine killed and many wounded. By his intelligent and forceful leadership . . . Lt. Puller surmounted all obstacles."[7]

In July 1931 Puller left Nicaragua for a coveted one-year assignment to the Company Officers Course at Fort Benning, Georgia, where he reported on 11 September 1931. Under the supervision of Lt. Col. George Marshall, Puller learned the basics of company maneuvers, tactics, and operations. His classmates included future generals Walter Beedle Smith, Omar Bradley, Oliver P. Smith, Joseph Stilwell, and Charles Willoughby. After completing the course of instruction, Puller departed Fort Benning on 1 June 1932 and returned to Nicaragua.[8]

Hailed as "The Tiger of Segovia" upon his return in July, Puller found that the situation in Nicaragua was changing. The U.S. public and Congress were becoming increasingly frustrated with the intervention and wanted the Nicaraguans to take responsibility for their own defense. The onset of the Depression in 1929 added finan-cial considerations, and the number of American casualties was causing concerns. When eight Marines were ambushed and killed near Ocotal on 31 December 1930, the United States announced it would withdraw after the Nicaraguan presi-dential election at the end of 1932. Despite requests for delays, President Herbert Hoover announced that the last Marines would be withdrawn by the 1 January 1933 deadline.[9]

By August, Puller was again back in command of Company M. His second in command was Lt. William A. Lee, a Marine gunnery sergeant who would eventually be awarded three Navy Cross medals of his own.[10] Puller was once again tasked with capturing Sandino, who in turn put a price of five thousand pesos on Puller's head.[11]

On 20 September 1932 Puller and his unit departed Jinotega and penetrated the mountainous bandit territory almost one hundred miles north of Jinotega, his nearest base. The patrol was ambushed on 26 September at a point northeast of Mount Kilambe by an insurgent force of 150. The insurgents were in a well-prepared position, armed with not less than seven automatic weapons and various classes of small arms, and well supplied with ammunition. Early in the combat, Gunnery Sergeant Lee, the second in command, was seriously wounded and reported as dead. The Guardia soldier immediately behind Puller in the point was killed by the first burst of fire. Lieutenant Puller displayed great courage, coolness, and military judgment as he directed the fire and movement of his men. The insurgents were driven from the high ground on the right of his position, and then a flanking movement forced them from the high ground to the left. Finally the insurgents scattered in confusion, with a loss of ten killed and many wounded by the persistent and well-directed attack of the patrol. The numerous casualties suffered by the enemy and the Guardia losses of two killed and four wounded are indicative of the severity of the enemy resistance. This signal victory in jungle country, achieved with no lines of communication and one hundred miles from any supporting force, was largely due to the indomitable courage and persistence of the patrol commander, Lieutenant Puller. Returning with the wounded to Jinotega, the patrol was ambushed twice by superior forces on 30 September. On both of the occasions the enemy was dispersed with severe losses.[12] For this patrol Puller received his second Navy Cross, and Sergeant Lee his third.

With the Nicaraguan elections scheduled for November, the constabulary launched a major offensive to keep the rebels from disrupting the voting. But U.S. operations were slowing as the withdrawal approached, and the Marines departed Jinotega by truck on 15 December for Managua, then left by train on 1 January for Corinto, where they boarded ships the following day. The U.S. withdrawal would lead to a weak government, which was overthrown in 1934 by the Guardia and its commander, Anastasio Somoza, initiating a dictatorship that would endure for more than four decades.

Puller's aggressive tactics and two Navy Crosses earned him a reputation as a combat leader. The long patrols he led in the Nicaraguan jungles, cut off from headquarters and supplies, were experiences that would later serve him well in the Pacific. They were also the source of the legend of "Chesty" Puller.

Upon his return stateside, Puller quickly received orders for duty overseas, and he and other officers departed San Francisco on 10 February 1933 bound for China. They arrived in Peiping (Beijing) via Manila and Shanghai on 22 March, and Puller was assigned to Company A of the Legation Guard. The Guard's twenty-six officers and five hundred enlisted men were the elite of the Marines, and spent their time in competition with the guards of the Japanese, French, British, and Italian embassies. China was considered good duty, in part because military pay, reduced fifteen percent by Congress, went further overseas.

When the Japanese invaded and conquered Manchuria in 1932, tension between Japan and the United States increased, and in November 1933 Puller was transferred to Legation headquarters as assistant G-2 (intelligence). The following January, Puller assumed command of the Peiping Horse Marines, a mounted detachment, but continued his duties as assistant G-2.

In August 1934 the commander in chief of the Asiatic Fleet requested that Puller be assigned to command the Marine detachment aboard his flagship, the USS *Augusta* (CA-31), under the command of Capt. Chester W. Nimitz, USN. Puller departed Peiping on 8 September, and reported aboard at Chingwangtao on the 11th.

The *Augusta* was a new heavy cruiser, built under the Washington Naval Treaty of 1922 and finished during the Depression. It was armed with nine 8-inch guns, and would later carry both Franklin Roosevelt and Harry S. Truman during World War II. Puller spent time improving the marksmanship of the crew, achieving 100 percent Marine and 90 percent Sailor qualification. He also spent time learning the seamanship skills of a naval officer, even acting as officer of the deck while under way.[13]

It was while serving aboard the *Augusta* that another Chesty Puller legend was born. On 10 November 1935, while the ship was in Australia, Puller and some other officers were returning by ferry from a rifle match when they observed a car roll off the slip into the water. Without hesitation, Puller jumped in and rescued two of the three women trapped inside. A spectator gave the chilled Puller some medicinal whisky, of which he partook liberally. When he returned to the barracks in his disheveled appearance, smelling of whisky, he was kidded about his "wild liberty," and he just smiled modestly. Only later did they learn of his heroism.[14]

In February 1936, the same month that Puller was promoted to captain, the *Augusta* participated in joint Army-Navy maneuvers in the Philippines. Nearing the end of his tour, Puller requested assignment to a school, and on 25 May 1936 he departed Yokohama, Japan, aboard the SS *President Jackson* with orders to report to the Navy Yard at Philadelphia, where he was assigned as a drill and command officer at the Officer's Basic School. In addition to duties as an instructor, he supervised a platoon of new lieutenants.

Puller served from June 1936 until May 1939 at the Basic School, where he influenced numerous junior officers who would later command companies and battalions during World War II. And during this period he married Virginia Evans. He had again requested a school assignment in 1938, but he was perceived as academically weak by his superiors, and in April 1939 Puller was ordered to the 4th Marines in Shanghai. This event may have soured Puller on schooling, as he was later quoted as declaring, "Service in the camp and in the field is the best military school."

Puller took leave in May, and he and his wife traveled to San Francisco, where they sailed for China. But his orders were changed en route, and he reported back aboard the *Augusta* at Tsingtao on 9 July 1939. The situation in China had changed significantly in his absence. Two years earlier, tensions between Japan and China had erupted into a full-scale war, and Japan now controlled northeastern China, including the ports, with the Western powers restricted to Peiping and Shanghai, and there was increased tension as Japan flexed its military muscle. Even after war broke out in Europe in September 1939, the focus in the Far East was on Japanese aggression.

On 21 May 1940, Puller was again ordered to join the 4th Marines in Shanghai, assigned as both the executive officer and intelligence officer of the 2nd Battalion. The Marines had been in Shanghai since 1927, but the force had recently been reduced to two battalions (each comprised of two infantry companies and a machine-gun company) and was severely understrength. Puller worked to make his Marines combat ready, but being confined to the city, there was little opportunity to train. His duties consisted of guard duty and parades.

Events soon began to accelerate for Puller. The British left Shanghai in August. In October, Puller was promoted to major, effective 29 August. In September, Japan joined as an Axis power with Germany and Italy, resulting in a U.S. embargo on steel and heightening tensions. In November, when U.S. dependents were ordered home, his wife Virginia returned to the United States with their newborn daughter. Puller, aware of how precarious his situation was, expressed his intentions thus: "I don't know what the U.S. Government will do. I don't know what Marine Headquarters will do, and I don't know what the regiment will do. But, no orders to the contrary, I'll take my battalion and fight my way the hell back to Frisco!"

When it came time for Puller to request his next assignment, early in 1941, he declined to ask for a school, instead requesting assignment to an infantry regiment. That summer, he received orders to take command of the 1st Battalion, 7th Marines, and he departed Shanghai on 14 August 1941. He left with grave concerns for the Marines staying behind. He arrived in San Francisco in September, then traveled to Quantico before assuming command of the battalion at New River (Camp Lejeune), North Carolina, in October.

Firm in his belief that a war was coming, Puller began training his Marines for war, building endurance and challenging limits, going so far as arranging for his battalion to train under actual live artillery fire provided by the 11th Artillery. Twelve-mile hikes eventually became fifteen, then twenty. Despite the harshness of the training, Puller had a reputation for fairness—Chesty led from the front, and officers ate after the men. One story has Puller observing a private at rigid attention before a young lieutenant, repeatedly saluting. When Puller inquired as to the reason, the young officer explained that the private had neglected to salute, and so was ordered to salute one hundred times. "You are right, lieutenant. So right," Puller responded. "But you know an officer must return every salute he receives." Puller stood by to see that it was done correctly.[15]

Puller was on leave in Saluda, Virginia, when the Japanese attacked Pearl Harbor on 7 December 1941, and he immediately returned to New River. Training became even more intense as war was now a reality. In mid-March the 1/7 Marines was detached from the 1st Division and joined with the 11th Artillery and the 1st Raider Battalion to form the 3rd Marine Brigade. Rumors began circulating about shipping out, and on Easter Sunday, 5 April 1942, the 1st Battalion began boarding the USS *Fuller* (AP-14) at Norfolk. They had no information about their destination when they sailed on 10 April, but Puller was confident that they would be the first Marines into combat. He was greatly disappointed when he learned their destination was Samoa.

Both of Samoa's islands, Tutuila and Upolu, had good harbors and were suitable for airfields. If the Japanese captured the islands, they could sever the supply lifeline between Australia and the United States. The 2nd Marine Brigade had been on Tutuila since January, and the 3rd Brigade was en route to Upolu to reinforce the small New Zealand garrison there. They arrived and began to disembark on 8 May. Two weeks later, Puller was promoted to the temporary rank of lieutenant colonel.[16]

The men worked long hours in the heat at hard physical labor, building defenses, doing construction projects, and hauling material, all of which toughened their physical conditioning. Puller knew from his experiences in other jungles that his men would need to be tough. For Puller, whose previous combat experience had been in commanding small units, the challenge would be to learn on the job how to command a battalion. His frustration grew as he learned that the 1st Marine Division had landed in the Solomon Islands on 7 August.

In early September, Puller's battalion was alerted, and the 7th Marines landed without incident on Guadalcanal to reinforce the 1st Division on 18 September. But a Japanese naval barrage struck the coconut grove in which the 7th was bivouacked, resulting in the first casualties of the battalion. More casualties were added in the next couple of days as the battalion's troops went on patrols.

Late in September, Maj. Gen. Alexander Vandegrift, the 1st Division commander, decided that he was now sufficiently reinforced to expand his defensive perimeter west across the Matanikau River. Over several days, numerous attempts to cross the Matanikau met with stiff opposition. On 27 September, Vandegrift ordered Lt. Col. Merritt Edson, commander of the 5th Marines, to take command of a combined force consisting of the 1st Battalion, 7th Marines, the 2nd Battalion, 5th Marines, and the 1st Marine Raiders under Lt. Col. Samuel Griffith. The plan to envelop the enemy was to have the Raiders and C Company of the 1/7 move south two thousand yards and cross the Matanikau, then attack north toward the coast. At the same time, in an effort to anchor the enemy in place, the 2/5 would make a direct assault across the mouth of the river, and the remainder of the 1/7 would make an amphibious landing near Point Cruz, on the coast west of Matanikau, to cut off any Japanese retreat.

Both the Raiders and the 5th Marine complements were unsuccessful in achieving their objectives. Maj. Ortho L. Rogers, the 1/7 executive officer, only learned that morning at church that he would be leading A and B Companies, augmented by a few crew-served weapons, in an amphibious assault. Hastily assembled, the 398 Marines embarked from Lunga Point on ten LCPs and LCTs, and landed at a small cove west of Point Cruz. Although the landing was unopposed, they met resistance as they moved inland. The Japanese had been anticipating the maneuver, and were well prepared. Major Rogers was killed early in a mortar barrage that also wounded Capt. Zach Cox, the B Company commander, leaving Capt. Charles W. Kelly, A Company commander, in charge. Simultaneously, Japanese troops overwhelmed the Marines' rear, cutting them off from the beach and encircling them. A second attack by the 2/5 failed to reach the west bank to relieve the pressure on the 1/7.

Kelly belatedly learned he had no radio with which to advise Division that they were surrounded, outnumbered, and under attack. By a stroke of fortune, Marine pilot Lt. Dale Leslie was overhead in a Douglas Dauntless dive bomber and saw that Kelly's men had spelled out "HELP" using their white T-shirts, and he radioed the information to Division. Edson refused to order another useless assault into fortified positions, and authorized the Raiders to withdraw. Puller, livid at the idea of abandoning his men, took unilateral action.

On the beach, Puller had a signalman contact the USS *Monssen* (DD-436) to request that a launch pick him up. It was 2:00 PM. Explaining the situation to the captain, Puller had the *Monssen* steam to the scene while he requested landing craft from Lunga Point. Familiar with naval firepower from his service aboard the *Augusta*, Puller directed the 5-inch guns to lay down a covering fire to cover the Marines' withdrawal, assisted by Sgt. Robert Raysbrook, who stood exposed on a ridge to send semaphore messages to the *Monssen*.

The same Higgins boats that had earlier landed the Marines now returned to extract them under heavy fire, supported by fire from the *Monssen* and Leslie's strafing cover. As the Marines withdrew to the beach, Japanese troops were successful in cutting off part of Company A, and Sgt. Anthony Malanowski was killed when he stayed back to cover the withdrawal.

Signalman 1st Class Douglas Munro, U.S. Coast Guard, was the officer in charge of the boats as they approached the shore, and his actions in supporting the withdrawal would result in the award of the Medal of Honor, the only Coast

Guardsman so honored to date. Munro's posthumous Medal of Honor citation states that "while engaged in the evacuation of a Battalion of Marines trapped by enemy Japanese forces at Point Cruz, Guadalcanal . . . Munro, under constant risk of his life, daringly led five of his small craft toward shore. . . . In order to draw the enemy's fire and protect the heavily loaded boats, he valiantly placed his craft with its two small guns as a shield between the beachhead and the Japanese. When the perilous task of evacuation was nearly completed, Munro was killed by enemy fire, but his crew, two of whom were wounded, carried on until the last boat had loaded and cleared the beach. . . . [Munro] undoubtedly saved the lives of many who would otherwise have perished."

The cost of the fight on 27 September was two killed and eleven wounded for the Raiders, and sixteen killed and sixty-eight wounded over two days for the 2/5. Puller's 1/7 losses were twenty-four dead and thirty-two wounded, including the loss of the battalion executive officer and all three company commanders, proving that Puller's officers followed his example and led from the front. Lieutenant Leslie, Sergeant Raysbrook, Sergeant Malanowski, and two navy coxswains, Walter Bennett and Samuel Roberts Jr., received the Navy Cross for their actions at the Matanikau River.[17]

Despite their losses and the resulting decline in morale, the next day the battalion was ordered to replace 2/7 on the perimeter of Henderson Field, in the southern jungle flatlands, to the right of the 1st Marines. As they had done in Samoa, they again found themselves fortifying defensive positions to protect an airfield, this one critical to their position on Guadalcanal. Early October was spent working to prevent the Japanese from reinforcing their troops and expanding the defensive perimeter around Henderson to keep it out of range of Japanese artillery. A third battle at the Matanikau River, 7–9 October, resulted in 1/7 bloodying a battalion of the newly arrived Japanese 4th Infantry Regiment, which lost 690 men, primarily to the 1/7. After a brief time in reserve, the 1/7 moved back into the line on 20 October.

Division intelligence officers were correct in their prediction that the Japanese were massing for an attack on Henderson, but they incorrectly anticipated that the attack would come from the west, across the Lunga River. Puller's three companies were deployed in a line south of Henderson with the 1st Marine Regiment to the west of B Company, C Company in the center, and A Company to the east, linking with the Army's 164th Infantry, which covered Henderson's eastern flank. From 24 to 26 October the Japanese attacked from the south, and the resulting Battle for Henderson Field earned Puller his third Navy Cross and Sgt. John Basilone the Medal of Honor. (See the chapter on John Basilone.)

On the night of 24–25 October, the Japanese repeatedly attacked along the thinly manned mile-long line in regimental strength, but the Marines doggedly endured, withstanding several "Banzai" charges, massed attacks by large number of troops. By 3:00 AM the unit had sustained six major assaults, and ammunition was running low. One officer called back to advise he was almost out of ammo. "You've got bayonets, haven't you?" Puller answered. Even after reinforcements from the 3rd Battalion arrived, Puller remained in command. His Navy Cross citation notes:

> On the night of 24 to 25 October 1942 . . . Puller's battalion was holding a mile long front in a heavy downpour of rain . . . [when] a Japanese force, superior in number launched a vigorous attack . . . through a dense jungle. Courageously withstanding the enemy's desperate and determined attacks, Lieutenant Colonel Puller not only held his battalion to its position until reinforcements arrived three hours later, but also effectively commanded the augmented force until late in the afternoon of the next day. . . . His tireless devotion to duty and cool judgment under fire prevented a hostile penetration of our lines and was largely responsible for the successful defense of the sector assigned.

Two weeks later, at the Battle of Koli Point, 4–8 November, Puller's luck ran out. After having come through Haiti, Nicaragua, and Guadalcanal unscathed, he was wounded in combat for the first time. During operations to clear Henderson Field's eastern flank, Puller was wounded by Japanese artillery while in his command post just behind the lines. There were twenty other casualties, mostly clerks and medics. Although wounded in the arm and left leg and foot, Puller's response to the corpsmen who suggested his removal to the rear was pure Chesty: "Evacuate me, hell! I will remain in command." It wasn't empty bravado that kept Puller in place. As he later explained, "The situation was far from good. I had no officer of significant experience to take over command."[18]

Relieved at 7:00 AM on 9 November, Puller was evacuated by landing craft to the division hospital at Lunga Point. He returned to command on 18 November, and the 7th remained in the line until relieved by the Army's 35th Infantry on Christmas Eve. The 1/7 bivouacked at Lunga Lagoon until they boarded the SS *President Hayes, President Adams,* and *President Jackson,* the same transports that had brought them to Guadalcanal. The 7th departed for Australia on 5 January 1943, the last of the 1st Division to leave the island, the 1st and 5th Marines and HQ Company having previously departed. But Puller was not among them.

Puller received orders on 31 December to proceed to Washington, D.C., by "first available air transport." He flew out of Henderson the following morning, New Year's Day, arriving in Washington on 9 January. He immediately took leave and traveled home to Saluda and his family. On 18 January, Puller reported to Marine Headquarters, located in the Navy Annex adjacent to Arlington Cemetery. He was to be part of a War Department project to interview Guadalcanal veterans to see what could be learned to improve tactics and equipment. Puller argued for more use of artillery ("[The enemy] hates it," he said), the need for more and better shovels, and the advantages of the M-1 rifle.

Gen. George Marshall, Puller's commanding officer at Benning and now Army Chief of Staff, recalled Puller as a fine officer, and arranged for him and other Guadalcanal vets to tour training facilities across the United States and share their experiences and lessons learned in combat. It was a grinding six-week tour, and after another week of leave in Saluda, Puller returned to the Pacific. In the interim the 1st Division had moved from Brisbane to Melbourne, where Puller rejoined them on 5 April.

Puller returned to find himself no longer in command of the 1st Battalion but serving rather as regimental operations officer, no doubt enjoying the irony of the fact that he had argued for smaller staffs while in Washington. A three-week bout with malaria put him in the hospital, and when he was released for duty on 1 May he found himself assigned as executive officer of the 7th Marines. As replacements arrived and the sick and wounded returned to the regiment, Puller began an intense regimen of training and physical conditioning. He retained an affection for the men of 1/7, whom he proclaimed were "not only the first in the Regiment, but also the first in the Division."

In August 1943 the 1st Division moved to New Guinea, where it was divided into three combat groups, each comprised of an infantry regiment with supporting units. The 7th Marines were designated Combat Team C and sent to Oro Bay, where they practiced landing operations using newly developed amphibious equipment. On 9 December they learned that the forthcoming operation would be the invasion of New Britain, scheduled for a D-day of 26 December. Combat Team C's mission was to capture two airfields at the western end of the island, at Cape Gloucester. They finished loading at Camp Sudest at noon on Christmas Eve and sailed before dawn on Christmas morning. At 7:45 AM on 26 December, the 1/7 and 3/7 stormed ashore at Cape Gloucester but met no resistance to their landing, despite the fact that the Japanese were aware of the impending landing and had even announced it on Radio Tokyo.[19]

After saturation bombing by aircraft and naval batteries, eleven thousand men landed on D-day, and by nightfall the 7th Marines occupied a beachhead nine hundred yards deep and a mile long. On 4 January 1944, Puller took temporary command of the 3/7 after the regimental commander, Colonel Frisbee relieved its commander for lack of aggressiveness. After the commander, executive officer, and five other officers of the 3/5 were wounded on 7 January, Puller was given command of the unit, placing him in simultaneous command of both battalions. His fourth Navy Cross citation states:

As executive officer of the Seventh Marines, First Marine Division, serving with the 6th U.S. Army in combat against enemy Japanese forces at Cape

Gloucester, New Britain, from 26 December 1943 to 19 January 1944. Assigned temporary command of the 3rd Battalion, Seventh Marines from 4 to 9 January . . . Puller quickly reorganized and advanced his unit, effecting the seizure of the objective without delay. Assuming additional duty in command of the 3rd Battalion, Fifth Marines . . . [he] unhesitatingly exposed himself to rifle, machine gun and mortar fire from strongly entrenched Japanese positions to move from company to company in his front lines, reorganizing and maintaining a critical position along a fire-swept ridge. His forceful leadership and gallant fighting spirit under the most hazardous conditions were contributing factors in the defeat of the enemy.

On 18 January the 7th was taken off the line, and by 20 January the Japanese forces were in full retreat toward Rabaul, a Japanese stronghold on the eastern end of the island. On 17 February Puller learned of his temporary promotion to full colonel, effective 1 February, and he was placed in command of the 1st Marines shortly afterward. Conditions slowly improved at Cape Gloucester, and at a divisional parade on 12 April, Puller was presented with his fourth Navy Cross. After leading the 1st Marines for the remainder of the campaign, he sailed with it on 27 April 1944 for Pavuvu, the largest of the Russell Islands, located thirty-five miles northwest of Guadalcanal. The 1st Marines went ashore on 29 April to find that their "rest and rehabilitation area" was totally lacking in facilities.

The Marines built their camp from scratch in conditions of squalor, with a scarcity of food and supplies but an abundance of mud, bad water, rain, and rats. It was on Pavuvu that Puller's reputation for putting the troops first was enhanced as he waited in chow lines and did calisthenics with the troops. On 27 July Puller learned that his brother, Sam, executive officer of the 4th Marines, had been killed in action on Guam. It was also at this time that the division learned of its next objective, the Palaus, a group of islands located at the west end of the Caroline Islands that had been seized by Japan from Germany following World War I. Puller intensified his troop's training, practicing maneuvering and landing assaults along the coast, and sending them on long hikes through rugged terrain. In August, Bob Hope's troupe of entertainers stopped briefly on Pavuvu, but Puller spent his time writing home and preparing for combat.

The plan was to seize three islands in the Palau Islands (Peleliu, Anguar, and Yap) to use as airbases to support the impending invasion of the Philippines, six hundred miles away. Peleliu was the target of the 1st Marine Division. Opposed by ten thousand troops of the never-defeated Manchurian Imperial Guards, the division was ordered to land, three regiments abreast, along the west coast, seize the airfield, and drive a wedge to divide the enemy. Puller's 1st Marines would land to the left, on the north, with the 5th Marines in the center, the 7th Marines to

Lieutenant Colonel Puller (second from left) with the regimental staff of the 7th Marines at Cape Gloucester, 10 January 1944. (U.S. Marine Corps / Sgt. Robert. R. Brenner)

the south, and one battalion of the 7th kept in reserve. Gen. William Rupertus and most of the division staff were optimistic that Peleliu would be easily taken in two days.[20] Puller was not as optimistic, correctly believing that the Japanese, like the Americans, had learned lessons from earlier campaigns, and he expected the resistance to be determined and prolonged. "We won't find little log barricades like they had on Tarawa," he said. "We're going to catch some real fire." His words would prove prophetic. When Puller's Marines landed, they discovered that Japanese engineers had constructed a network of underground defenses that had withstood the initial bombardment.

On 3 September 1944 the slower LSTs departed for Peleliu, followed by the rest of the convoy four days later. Three fast carrier groups arrived and began a three-day bombardment of Peleliu on 6 September. On 12 September, the surface-fire support group, consisting of five battleships, eight cruisers, and fourteen destroyers, arrived and began a full-scale bombardment of Peleliu and Anguar. At 5:30 AM on 15 September, the Navy began the final bombardment prior to the Marines' landing. As Puller readied to depart, the ship's captain asked Puller if he'd be returning for dinner. "Everything's done over there, you'll walk in." Puller, less confident and more realistic, replied, "If you think it's that easy, why don't you come on the beach at five o'clock, have supper with me, and pick up a few souvenirs?"

It was a clear, moonless dawn on 15 September as the 1st Marines boarded the amphibious tractors. The 2nd and 3rd Battalions would go ashore first, with the 1st Battalion held in reserve. Puller, with part of his headquarters staff (he'd divided his staff into three sections) was in the third wave, at approximately 8:30 AM. As they approached the beach, shots pinging on the armor of the boat, he warned his men, "When we beach, get the hell out of here. We'll be a big target." The Japanese were entrenched in fortified positions along a sheer coral ridge. Their fire, both direct and indirect (mortars and artillery), swept the beach, taking a horrific toll.

"I went up and over the side as fast I could scramble, and ran like hell at least twenty-five yards before I hit the beach," said one Marine. "When I looked back to the amtrac, I saw four or five shells hit it all at once. A few men were killed getting out too slow, but most of them were saved because they got out before we stopped moving. . . . I looked down the beach and saw a mess—every damn amtrac in our wave had been destroyed in the water by the enemy, or shot to pieces the moment it landed."[21]

By 9:30 AM Puller, with the 2nd Battalion, had advanced 350 yards to line up with the 5th Marines. Puller characterized the following eight hours as "the most savage fighting in the Pacific War." Everyone went into the line, including mechanics, wiremen, and clerks. By nightfall, they'd advanced a thousand yards and were on the edge of the airfield, but had sustained an estimated five hundred casualties. Firefights and explosions continued through the night.

On the second day, Saturday the 16th, fresh American attacks met stubborn resistance despite the effectiveness of the newly issued M-1 rifles and flamethrowers. Casualties reached one thousand, and only those wounded by bullets or shells were evacuated. A Japanese counterattack was launched at 10:00 PM and continued to 2:00 AM the following morning. The third day saw more severe fighting with slight American gains but high casualties. By nightfall the regiment had a foothold on the first chain of coral ridges, and naval gunfire onto the entrenched Japanese positions continued throughout the night.

With casualties closing in on 50 percent, Puller called back to the division's chief of staff for reinforcements, requesting some of the seventeen thousand "specialist" troops on the beach. Told that he couldn't have them because they weren't trained infantry, Puller replied, "Give 'em to me, and by nightfall tomorrow, they'll be trained infantry." Without reinforcements, Puller attacked the next morning, 18 September, across terrain that was as much an obstacle as the Japanese. So too was the intense heat and lack of fresh water. Position by fortified position, the regiment advanced. By 4:30 PM they rested at the base of Bloody Nose Ridge, where the heart of Japanese resistance was protected by strong fortification. By nightfall the regiment's casualty count was at fifteen hundred. But American planes had begun landing at the captured airfield—fighters for ground support and piper cubs for observation. Now it would be time for the Japanese to suffer.

On the 19th the attacks continued, supported by tanks, flamethrowers, bazookas, mortars, and air support, but they achieved only small gains as the enemy proved extremely difficult to dislodge. On the 20th a dozen machine guns crewed by cooks and clerks were brought forward to bolster the casualty-thinned lines. By the end of the day, the regiment's casualties had risen to 1,878. For the next two days the regiment rested in line with no advance, its posture defensive to ward off counter attacks.

At 2:30 PM on 23 September, troops of the Army's 321st Regiment, 81st Division, relieved the 1st Marines, and its commander's first decision was to move the command post farther behind the line. In nine days of combat, the 1st Marines had killed 3,942 Japanese, with no prisoners taken. The 1st Division had a casualty rate of 54 percent, one of the highest in Marine Corps history, with a casualty rate of 71 percent for the 1st Battalion, 56 percent for the 2nd Battalion, and 55 percent for the 3rd Battalion. The headquarters and weapons section sustained 32 percent casualties.[22]

Gen. O. P. Smith, the 1st Marine Division's executive officer, would later observe, "It seemed impossible that men could move forward against the intricate and mutually-supporting defenses the Japanese had set up. It can only be explained as a reflection of the determination and aggressive leadership of Colonel Puller." On 2 October the 1st Marines boarded ships to return to Pavuvu. Still suffering from the leg wound he'd received at New Britain, Puller had endured the pain throughout the campaign. Now he boarded the hospital ship USS *Pickney* (PH-2) with many of the other wounded, where a navy surgeon removed the shrapnel during a lengthy surgery. Puller spent nearly a week in bed, but he was well enough to march ashore with his troops on 9 October.

The 1st Marine Division lost 1,397 killed at Peleliu, with an additional 5,699 wounded. Three-hundred eleven of those killed or missing were from the 1st Marine Regiment, which also suffered 1,438 wounded out of the 3,251 who had landed. The regiment's estimated 54 percent casualty figure compares with 43 percent for the 5th Marines and 46 percent for the 7th Marines, and Puller took criticism for his high casualty rate. But if Puller asked a lot of his men, it was no more than he gave of himself, and he could always be found in front of his men in combat.

Peleliu would be Puller's last action during World War II. Fatigued and recovering, he and other officers departed the Pacific for the States by air on 4 November, arriving in San Francisco two days later. On arrival, Puller found orders assigning him to New River, North Carolina, with thirty days leave in transit. On 27 December he reported to Camp Lejeune as executive officer and later became commander of the Infantry Training Regiment (ITR). Veteran officers were needed to train troops for combat, and Puller supervised one hundred officers and NCOs supervising the training of as many as fifteen battalions simultaneously.

With the deployment of the atomic bomb in August 1945 and the subsequent Japanese surrender, the Marines began to plan for demobilization. The final ITR class at New River graduated on 14 September, and Puller took over the Specialist Training Regiment (STR) until July 1946, when he was placed in command of the

8th Marine Corps Reserve District, headquartered in New Orleans. The reserve had ceased to exist following the start of the war, and it now needed to be rebuilt. Puller had a staff of two officers and four NCOs to administer an area that stretched from Florida to Texas, and north to Tennessee. In March 1948 Puller was advised that his next assignment would be in command of the Marine Barracks at Pearl Harbor. Still a colonel, he was afraid that his two previous assignments indicated that he was disfavored at headquarters, and he expected that his next assignment, as commander of the 1st Marines at Camp Pendleton to begin in mid-1950, would be his last before retirement. It was not to be.

On 25 June 1950, North Korean forces crossed the 38th parallel and invaded South Korea. On the same day that the first U.S. ground troops landed in Korea, Gen. Douglas MacArthur asked for the Marines. Puller telegraphed Headquarters USMC, advising them of his availability for Korea, stressing his combat experience and requesting early release from his Pearl Harbor assignment. Orders finally arrived, and on 14 July Puller and his family departed by air for Camp Pendleton.

Puller arrived in San Diego to bedlam and sent his family back to Saluda while he reported to General Smith, an old friend and the new division commander. The 1st Marine Division was being rebuilt, and Puller was given command of the division, comprised primarily of World War II veterans. He had considerable challenges: overcoming poor World War II–surplus ordnance (67 percent of the rifles were unserviceable), building cohesive units, and loading supplies piecemeal onto transports in the rush to deploy. Loading was completed on 22 August, but the ships didn't depart until 1 September. Only after docking in Kobe, Japan, did they learn about Operation CHROMITE, a plan for an amphibious landing behind enemy lines at Inchon, a heavily defended city on Korea's western coast. This operation would cut off the invading NKPA (North Korean Peoples Army), recapture Seoul, and take pressure off U.N. forces at Pusan. D-day was scheduled for high tide at 5:30 PM on 15 September.

The force departed Kobe on 12 September, accompanied by four carriers, two cruisers, twenty-five destroyers, and sundry other craft. On the 15th the landing came off on schedule and largely uncontested. Marines used scaling ladders to mount the fifteen-foot Inchon seawall, the first time such ladders had been used in combat since taking the Halls of Montezuma at Chapultepec in 1847.

The resistance was light, the division losing only twenty killed the first day, and by the next day Puller's 1st Marines were only seventeen miles from Seoul. The Marines' performance made an ally of MacArthur, but not President Truman, who referred to them derisively as "nothing but a police force." In response, Marines painted their vehicles with "Truman's Police" and M.P. (military police) on their tanks. The 1st Marines took Hill 118 on 19 September, then withstood a counterattack the following day, the same day the 7th Marines landed to complete the division. By the 25th, Puller was on the outskirts of Seoul, and the fighting for the city was house to house, almost forcing the Marines to destroy the city to save it. And Chesty Puller was in the thick of it, as Sgt. Maj. Bill Ferrigno recalled. "It was like going through hell, passing down that Seoul street. And who should we pass in the middle of it but 'Chesty.' It was so hot I thought the grenades and ammunition we carried would explode. The flames almost met over our heads from the burning house. The colonel didn't seem the least concerned. It gave us an extra push."[23]

MacArthur declared Seoul liberated on 29 September, despite continued fighting. Puller was one of only four Marines invited to the lavish, V.I.P.-filled ceremony. He attended in rumpled fatigues, parking his mud-covered jeep beside gleaming staff cars, then returned to his command, which had sustained 787 casualties, including 92 killed, in the fight for the city. The following day, 30 September, General Smith was ordered to plan for landing his division at Wonson, on Korea's eastern coast, for a drive on Pyongyang in North Korea. The target date was 15 October.

The 1st Marine Division was trucked to Inchon on 6 October, then boarded the USS *Noble* (APA-218) on the 15th. They arrived to find the Wonson harbor mined, beginning what some Marines called "Operation YO-YO" as they sailed back and forth for ten days waiting for the harbor to be cleared. They finally disembarked on 25 October to find Bob Hope and the ROK (Republic of Korea) Army already present to welcome them.

On 26 October the division began its drive toward the Yalu River, with the 5th and 7th Regiments moving northward. Puller's 1st Marines remained in reserve at Wonson, with one battalion, 2/1, detached to Kojo and one battalion, 3/1, to Mayon-ni. The division commander's concern about being dispersed increased when ROK units captured sixteen Chinese "volunteers" at Sudong on 28 October. His concerns were validated on 2 November, when a supply convoy was ambushed and the 3/1 was isolated. Puller was ordered to reopen the road, but an effort by A Company on 4 November was repulsed by a North Korean roadblock. The next morning, they advanced quietly on foot and took the roadblock by surprise as the ambushers listened for trucks. With the scarcity of roads in vastly separated mountain canyons, breaking roadblocks would become a frequent task.

The 7th Marines reached Koto-ri on 10 November, Hagaru-ri on the 15th, and as far north as Yudam-ni on the 25th, supported by the 5th Marines on the western side of the Chosin Reservoir and the 7th Division on the eastern edge. On 23 November the 1st Marines moved north, arriving in Koto-ri on the 25th, its mission to guard the division's rear. Puller left the 1/1 behind to garrison Chinhung-ni.

That same day, Chinese forces, which six days earlier had secretly crossed the Yalu 260,000 strong, counterattacked the Eighth Army in the west, and two days later X Corps in the east. The massive attack by six divisions resulted in a complete envelopment of the 5th and 7th Marines at Yudam-ni, cutting the road to Hagaru-ri. On the 28th, Smith ordered Puller to open the road to Hagaru-ri. Speaking to newspaper reporters that had flown into Koto-ri, Puller made perhaps his most famous quote: "We've been looking for the enemy for several days now. We've finally found them. We're surrounded. That simplifies our problem of getting to these people and killing them."

A company of Puller's Marines was unable to breach the roadblock on the 28th, but the next day Puller formed Task Force Drysdale, consisting of George Company (the division recon unit), Company B of the Army's 31st Infantry Regiment, and 235 British Royal Marines under the command of Lieutenant Colonel Douglas Drysdale, the Royal Marine commander. The unit, supported by four platoons of tanks, left Koto-ri at 9:30 AM on the 29th and was partially successful in breaking through, but enemy artillery destroyed several vehicles, forcing the withdrawal of half the force. The tanks in the rear fought their way back to Koto-ri under unrelenting enemy fire. With the loss of air cover as darkness fell, the decision was made to surrender. More than three hundred Americans, Brits, and Koreans had been killed or captured.[24]

On 30 November, General Almond flew into Hagaru-ri to inform General Smith that the entire Corps would fall back to Hungham. Authorized to destroy equipment and supplies, Smith declined, saying it would be needed for the fight to Hungham. When asked by a reporter about the retreat, Smith's reply was, "Retreat, hell! We're just advancing in a different direction."

What made the fight so severe was that in addition to fighting the North Koreans and Chinese, the Marines were fighting the freezing temperatures of the Korean winter. Short of cold-weather gear—and what there was, was inadequate for subzero temperatures—the intense cold sapped energy, froze fuel lines and weapons, interfered with the treatment and transportation of casualties, froze plasma, and made "digging in" problematical.

Puller won his fifth Navy Cross during the retreat from the Chosin Reservoir by leading one of the most successful withdrawals under fire in Marine Corps lore. The Marines fought their way south, inflicting enormous casualties on the enemy and successfully bringing out their equipment, their wounded, and their dead.

Puller's citation reads:

The Navy Cross (Fourth Gold Star) is presented to Lewis B. Puller (O-3158), Colonel, U.S. Marine Corps, for extraordinary heroism in connection with military operations against an armed enemy of the United Nations while serving as Commanding Officer of the First Marines, First Marine Division (Reinforced), in action against aggressor forces in the vicinity of Koto-ri, Korea, from 5 to 10 December 1950. Fighting continuously in sub-zero weather against a vastly outnumbering hostile force, Colonel Puller drove off repeated and fanatical enemy attacks upon his Regimental defense sector and supply points. Although the area was frequently covered by grazing machine-gun fire and intense artillery and mortar fire, he coolly moved along his troops to insure their correct tactical employment, reinforced the lines as the situation demanded, and successfully defended the perimeter, keeping open the main supply routes for the movement of the Division. During the attack from Koto-ri to Hungham, he expertly utilized his Regiment as the Division rear guard, repelling two fierce enemy assaults which severely threatened the security of the unit, and personally supervised the care and prompt evacuation of all casualties. By his unflagging determination, he served to inspire his men to heroic efforts in defense of their positions and assured the safety of much valuable equipment which would otherwise have been lost to the enemy. His skilled leadership, superb courage and valiant devotion to duty in the face of overwhelming odds reflect the highest credit upon Colonel Puller and the United States Naval Service.[25]

The movement south from Hagaru-ri began on 6 December, and the 1st Marine Division left Koto-ri on the 9th. They were in Hungham two days later. Between 27 November and 11 December, the division's losses were 561 killed, 2,894 wounded, 182 missing, and 3,657 sick and injured.

On 10 January 1951 the 1st Marines moved to Pohang, and on 26 January Puller finally got his star and his promotion to brigadier general, effective 1 January. With a glut of senior officers in Korea, Puller expected to be rotated home. Instead he was appointed assistant commander of the 1st Marine Division, and he left the regiment on 1 February. Puller briefly took command of the 1st Division when General Smith was selected to command IX Corps when its commander died. But by 5 March General Smith was replaced at IX Corps with Army Gen. William Hoge, and Smith returned to resume command of the 1st Marine Division.

In May 1951 Puller was ordered to Camp Pendleton to take command of the 3rd Marine Brigade. Again, in time of war the Corps was expanding. Puller would be commanding the third largest force in the corps, and the only field force that was commanded by a brigadier general. After departing with other officers by air on 20 May, Puller took leave before reporting to the base commander, General Smith, on 7 July. In January 1952, Puller's 3rd Brigade was absorbed into the newly reactivated 3rd Marine Division.

On 2 February 1952, General Smith presented Puller with his fifth Navy Cross, three Air Medals, and the Uichi Medal, Korea's second-highest award, for actions in Korea. Some, like Marine Ace Greg "Pappy" Boyington, lobbied for a Medal of Honor for Chesty, but none was ever awarded. And although the retired sixty-eight-year-old Puller would later request restoration to active status for Vietnam, the remainder of his battles would be fought with the bureaucracy.

In June 1952, Puller took command of Troop Training Unit-Pacific (TTU-P) at Coronado, California, where he was promoted to major general on 28 September 1953. Puller departed California on 1 June 1954 for his new assignment as commanding officer of the 2nd Marine Division at Camp Lejeune, assuming command 1 July. He also assumed the duties of base commander on 11 July. It made national news when Puller was admitted at the Naval Hospital at Camp Lejeune on 27 August for hypertensive cardiovascular disease (high blood pressure), but a medical board found him fit for a return to duty on 29 October. The Bureau of Medicine in Washington reviewed the finding and recommended retirement by reason of physical disability, and Puller was transferred for further tests and evaluation at Bethesda Naval Hospital in Maryland, where he was admitted on 1 December. After two weeks of tests, he took sick leave and returned to Saluda for the holidays.[26]

Puller felt he was being forced into retirement, and prepared to do battle. In January 1955 he returned to Bethesda, where a board of three medical officers ruled that Puller had suffered a mild stroke, and it placed him on limited duty. The decision then went to the commandant, Gen. Lemuel Sheppard, an old friend and godfather of Chesty's only son, Lewis Jr. Both Sheppard and Puller were Virginians, VMI alumni, and veterans of the 1st Marine Division. Sheppard arranged for Puller to assume a five-month position as deputy base commander to permit him time to transition for retirement. He was relieved as 2nd Division Commander on 26 January. Puller felt betrayed by an old friend and continued to fight retirement. On 1 July he was back at Bethesda for further tests, and on 10 August the Physical Evaluation Board found him unfit for full duty and recommended retirement. He appealed the decision all the way to the secretary of the Navy, who on 6 October ordered Puller retired at the end of the month.

On 1 November 1955, in a small ceremony in the base commander's office at Camp Pendleton, Coronado, California, Sgt. Maj. Robert Norrish, who had known Puller since 1926, pinned him with the three stars of a lieutenant general in front of an audience restricted to Puller's aide, his driver, two reporters, and the base commander. Chesty Puller's last official words: "I hate like hell to go." He left the Corps after more than thirty-seven years of service.

Puller stayed active in his retirement, testifying at a court martial, attending reunions, and giving interviews, but his health declined with age, and a series of strokes led to his placement in a long-term care facility, where he died on 11 October 1971. But the death of the man only enhanced his legend.

Adm. Arleigh Burke once wrote, "Men fought under 'Chesty' Puller, and they fought magnificently, because he knew how to fight." Undoubtedly true! But men also fought for Chesty because he knew how to lead—from the front, at the front. He once said that he kept his command post in his pocket. He was loved by his men, and as long as there is a Marine Corps, the legend of Chesty Puller will endure.

ENDNOTES

1. Burke Davis, *Marine! The Life of Chesty Puller* (New York: Bantam Books, 1991).
2. Ibid.
3. Mary A. Renda, *Taking Haiti: Military Occupation and the Culture of U.S. Imperialism, 1915–1940* (Chapel Hill: University of North Carolina Press, 2001).
4. Ramy Abdelsamad and Gavin Hawe, "U.S. Occupation of Haiti, 1915–1934," paper, Naval Historical Center, Washington, D.C., July 18, 2005.
5. Jon T. Hoffman, *Chesty: The Story of Lieutenant General Lewis B. Puller, USMC* (New York: Random House, 2001).
6. Sandino was murdered by Gen. Anastasio Somoza on 21 February 1934. Somoza then seized power in a coup d'etat in 1936 and remained in power until 1979, when he was overthrown by Sandino's political descendants, the Sandinista National Liberation Front.
7. Official Navy Cross citation (Puller's first award).
8. Davis, *Marine! The Life of Chesty Puller*.
9. Hoffman, *Chesty*.
10. Eric Page, "William A. Lee, 98, Marines' Acclaimed Ironman," obituary, *New York Times*, 2 January 1999.
11. SSgt. Kurt Sutton, "Chesty Puller: Everyone Needs a Hero," *Marine Magazine*, August 1998.
12. Official Navy Cross citation (Puller's second award).
13. Hoffman, *Chesty*.
14. Ibid.
15. Davis, *Marine! The Life of Chesty Puller*.
16. Ibid.
17. Ibid.
18. Hoffman, *Chesty*.
19. Ibid.
20. Davis, *Marine! The Life of Chesty Puller*.
21. Ibid.
22. Ibid
23. Ibid
24. Hoffman, *Chesty*.
25. Navy Cross citation, 19 November 1951.
26. Hoffman, *Chesty*.

WORLD WAR II (1939–1945)

On 7 December 1941 Japan launched a surprise attack on the U.S. Pacific Fleet at Pearl Harbor, Hawaii, propelling the United States into World War II. On that same day, attacks were made on American bases at Midway Island and the Philippines. Guam was attacked and occupied, making it the only populated U.S. territory to be occupied by foreign troops. Those were indeed some of the darkest days in U.S. military history.

A total of 3,972 Navy Crosses were awarded for heroism during World War II. Of those, 2,897 went to Sailors, 1,034 went to Marines, 6 to Coast Guardsmen, 6 to members of the Army, 9 to members of the Army Air Force, 19 to members of Foreign Allied Forces, and one was awarded to a U.S. civilian.

Two naval submarine commanders, Cdr. Samuel David Dealy and Cdr. Eugene Bennett Fluckey, earned the Medal of Honor and four Navy Crosses in the war. Another submariner, Lt. Cdr. Richard O'Kane, earned the Medal of Honor and three Navy Crosses. Two other submariners, Cdr. Lawson Ramage and Cdr. Howard W. Gilmore, earned the Medal of Honor and two Navy Crosses. Eleven men earned both the Medal of Honor and one Navy Cross. Capt. Roy M. Davenport won an unmatched *five* Navy Crosses during World War II.

The picture in late 1941 wasn't any brighter for the rest of the world. On 8 December Japanese forces invaded Malaya and Thailand and bombed Singapore. Japanese troops landed on Tarawa and Makin in the Gilbert Islands the following day. Hong Kong and the Dutch East Indies were vulnerable. But in the early, dark days of World War II the nation's eyes and hopes rested on a small atoll east of the Mariana Islands and north of the Marshall Islands—Wake Island.

WAKE ISLAND

Maj. James Patrick Sinnott Devereux, USMC
Cdr. Winfield Scott Cunningham, USN
Maj. Paul A. Putnam, USMC
Dr. Lawton S. Shank, U.S. Civilian

For distinguished and heroic conduct in the line of his profession as Commanding Officer of the Marine Defense Battalion, Naval Air Station, Wake Island, where he was responsible for directing defenses . . . during the Japanese siege from 7–22 December 1941, against impossible odds.

Excerpt from Navy Cross citation for Maj. James Patrick Sinnott Devereux, USMC

For distinguished and heroic conduct . . . as Commanding Officer, Naval Air Station, Wake Island, where he was responsible for directing defenses . . . against impossible odds.

Excerpt from Navy Cross citation for Cdr. Winfield Scott Cunningham, USN

For extraordinary heroism as Commanding Officer of Marine Fighter Squadron Two Hundred Eleven (VMF-211) in action against enemy Japanese forces at Wake Island. . . .When the island was subjected to a relentless attack by carrier-based hostile aircraft . . . proceeded by truck to the airfield . . . embarking in a friendly fighter plane . . . executed an unsupported flight far out to sea in a desperate attempt to locate the Japanese carrier.

Excerpt from Navy Cross citation for Maj. Paul A. Putnam, USMC

For extraordinary heroism against the enemy while associated with the naval defenses on Wake Island on 9 December 1941 . . . during an intensive bombing and strafing attack (on the camp hospital) in the course of which the hospital was completely destroyed . . . supervised the evacuation of the patients . . . with absolute disregard for his own safety . . . Doctor Shank's display of outstanding courage and devotion to duty were in keeping with the highest traditions of the United States Naval Service.

Excerpt from Navy Cross citation for Dr. Lawton S. Shank

ALTHOUGH IN 1941 most Americans believed that a war between the United States and Japan was inevitable, the attack on Pearl Harbor on 7 December caught the nation by surprise, and U.S. forces were woefully unprepared for war.

Within hours of the attack on the Pacific fleet, Japanese bombs began falling on Wake Island, the westernmost of the U.S. bases in the Pacific. The impassioned defense of Wake Island by a small force of Marines, naval personnel, and civilian construction workers against insurmountable enemy forces was a spark of defiance that inspired the nation in the dark, early days of the war.

Located 2,300 miles west of Hawaii, 1,194 miles southwest of Midway, and 1,485 miles northeast of Guam, Wake Island is a remote 2,600-acre atoll of three islands (Wake, Wilkes, and Peale) of sand and coral surrounding a lagoon, with no fresh water and little vegetation. Its inhabitants include rats, crabs, and assorted birds. Measuring six miles by three miles at its widest point, Wake was developed in 1935 as a seaplane refueling base for Pan American Airline flights from Hawaii to Guam, Midway, and the Philippines.[1]

When the war began, Wake became strategically important to the United States because it was two thousand miles closer to Japan than Hawaii and could be used as a base to launch operations against the Japanese-held Marshall Islands. Several construction companies, primarily the Morrison-Knudsen Company of Boise, Idaho, with 1,146 civilian contractors, had been laboring since 9 January 1941 to build roads, an airfield, a submarine base, and other installations to be utilized as a base for amphibious patrol planes, and to dredge the channel between the islands. Their work was scheduled for completion by July 1942.[2]

On 15 October 1941, Marine Maj. James Patrick Sinnott Devereux arrived to take command of Wake's detachment of the 1st Defense Battalion. The advance party had arrived two months earlier. Devereux brought six 5-inch guns salvaged from retired battleships for use in coastal defense, and three batteries of 3-inch anti-aircraft guns, as well as twenty-four .50-caliber machine guns for air defense and thirty .30-caliber machine guns for beach defense. The Marines also brought six searchlights.

James P. S. Devereux was born in Cabana, Cuba, on 20 February 1903. His family later moved to Maryland, where he grew up and attended Loyola College in Baltimore before enlisting as a private in the Marines in July 1923. Commissioned a second lieutenant in February 1925, he saw service at Quantico, Virginia; Guantanamo Bay, Cuba; two tours in Nicaragua; one with the Legation Guard at Peking; and at sea aboard the battleship USS *Utah* (BB-31). In 1933 he was assigned to the Coast Artillery School at Fort Monroe, Virginia, and by 1935, then a captain, Devereux taught at the Base Defense Weapons School, concurrently writing a Marine Corps manual on base defense weapons. He was stationed at the Marine Base, San Diego, California, when he received orders to take command of the Marines on Wake Island.[3]

On 2 November the Marine presence on Wake was bolstered by the arrival of 9 officers and 104 enlisted men aboard the USS *Castor*. On 28 November, Cdr. Winfield Scott Cunningham arrived to take command of the Naval Air Station on Wake, relieving Major Devereux. As yet, there were no aircraft on the island. His orders were to give priority to completing construction of the naval air station over the improvement of island defenses. The advance party of VMF-211 also arrived with Cunningham.

Born on 15 February 1900 in Rockbridge, Wisconsin, Winfield Scott Cunningham was accepted at the age of sixteen to the U.S. Naval Academy, after completing his junior year of high school. America's entry into World War I resulted in his early graduation and his commissioning as an ensign on 6 June 1919. His first assignment was aboard the USS *Martha Washington*, a naval transport tasked with bringing the troops home from France. He later saw service off Turkey's shores and in China, then was trained as a naval aviator in 1925.

On 4 December 1941 Marine Fighter Squadron VMF-211 arrived on Wake with twelve Grumman F-4F Wildcats under the command of Maj. Paul Putnam, an experienced naval aviator who had taken command of the squadron less than a week earlier. Only three of the pilots had any training in flying F-4Fs, and the ordnance available on the island was incompatible with the Wildcat's bomb racks. The planes were therefore obsolete and without armor or radio homing equipment.[4]

Born in Milan, Michigan, in 1903, Paul Albert Putnam attended Iowa State College before enlisting in the Marines as a private. On 3 March 1926, while stationed at Norfolk Navy Yard, he was appointed a second lieutenant. He was sent to Nicaragua, where he was commended for the "suppression of banditry." In 1929, after aviation training in San Diego, Putnam was designated a naval aviator. Later he returned to Nicaragua to assist after the earthquake of 1932. Upon his return from Nicaragua, Putnam served at Pensacola Naval Air Station in Florida, attended officers school at Quantico, and was stationed at San Diego from June 1939 until ordered to Wake Island in late November 1941.[5]

Capt. Henry Wilson of the U.S. Army Signal Corps was on Wake to support the ferrying of a flight of B-17 Flying Fortresses to the Philippines. On 8 December 1941 (which was 7 December in Hawaii), he picked up a message from the Army Air Base at Hickham Field, Hawaii: "SOS – ISLAND OF OAHU UNDER ATTACK. THIS IS NO DRILL. THIS IS THE REAL THING!" Wilson promptly reported the raid to Devereux, who ordered a call to arms.[6]

Major Devereux assembled his officers, advised them of the attack on Pearl Harbor, and warned them to "expect the same thing anytime now." Within half an hour, all Marine positions were manned and ready. Commander Cunningham, the senior officer, was at breakfast in the contractors' mess hall at Camp 2, at the northern end of Wake, when he learned of the attack. He ordered the troops to battle stations, but the civilian contractors continued their construction work.

Cunningham also ordered Pan Am's *Philippine Clipper*, a Martin 130 flying boat, recalled from its flight.

Major Putnam ordered two sections, each with two planes, into the air over Wake; 2nd Lt. John Kinney and TSgt. William Hamilton patrolled the south and southwest at thirteen thousand feet. Capt. Henry T. Elrod, the squadron executive officer, and 2nd Lt. Carl Davidson flew north. Putnam also ordered construction of dugout plane shelters.

On the morning of 8 December there were 449 Marines on Wake Island (15 officers and 373 enlisted of the 1st Defense Battalion, and 12 officers and 49 enlisted of VMF-211 and attached units), 69 naval personnel attached to the Naval Air Station (10 officers and 59 enlisted), an Army Air Corps detachment of 1 officer and 4 enlisted, and 1,146 civilian workers. The Naval and Air Corps personnel and the construction workers were without arms.[7]

Marine Gunner John Hamas, the detachment munitions officer, began unpacking and issuing Browning automatic rifles and Springfield '03 rifles to the sailors and civilian contractors, who had volunteered for combat duty. Many had tried to enlist immediately, but there was no legal way that could be done, so they simply attached themselves as civilians. Devereux asked one volunteer, "Why are you doing this? You're a civilian. You don't have to fight." The man replied, "I'm an American. Isn't that enough?" Devereux nodded, and permitted the issuing of arms.[8]

Among the civilians on Wake was Dr. Lawton S. Shank, a thirty-four-year-old physician from Angola, Indiana. Although a first lieutenant in the U.S. Army Reserve, he was on Wake as a civilian physician at the contractors' hospital at Camp Number 2. Civilians assisted in manning the antiaircraft batteries, serving as observers on watch, digging foxholes, building revetments, filling sandbags, and hauling ammunition.

As the morning wore on and no attack came, many became skeptical that an attack had really occurred at Pearl Harbor. That skepticism disappeared at 11:58 AM, when thirty-six twin-engine Mitsubishi Nell medium bombers broke through the rain clouds at two thousand feet and bombed the island, beginning with the airfield. The war had arrived.

The approach of the Japanese bombers had been obscured by thick clouds from the four Wildcats on air patrol. The remaining eight Wildcats sat fueled and ready, parked near the runway. Two pilots, Lt. Graves and Lt. Conderman, sprinted to their planes as bombs began exploding. A direct hit on one of the Wildcats exploded the plane, killing Graves. Conderman was cut down by the bullets of a strafing Nell and crawled under cover, only to be trapped by the wreckage of another exploding Wildcat.

Wake Island F-4F-3 Wildcat fighters of Marine squadron VMF-211 wrecked by Japanese bombing attacks. (Naval Historical Center)

As the Nells flew off toward their secondary target, they left behind an airfield in ruins. All eight Wildcats were destroyed. Also destroyed were all spare parts, tools, tires, and both gasoline storage tanks. Eighteen of VMF-211's personnel, including most of the mechanics, and twenty-five civilian workers, were killed. Another five pilots and ten enlisted men were wounded.[9]

The bombers attacked their secondary target, the Pan Am station, setting fire to the hotel, the stock room, fuel tanks, and auxiliary buildings. The radio transmitter and the hospital were also hit. Within several minutes four Marines, several corpsmen, and fifty-five civilians lay dead. But miraculously, the Pan Am *Philippine Clipper* lay anchored and undamaged except for twenty-three bullets holes.

Before returning to their bases in the Marshall Islands, the Japanese bombers strafed the camps, killing two sailors and a civilian, then made a last run over the airfield to deploy the last of their bombs and ammunition. They departed at 12:10 PM. As a final, fateful insult, one of the four Wildcats on combat air patrol bent its propeller on bomb debris while landing, reducing the squadron's operational aircraft to three.

Immediately Marines, Sailors, and civilian volunteers went to work to improve defensive positions, mine the runway with explosives, and distribute ammunition and supplies across the islands. The remaining Wildcats refueled and returned to the air. There was no time to bury the dead; instead they were gathered and stored in a large freezer.

The wounded were transported to the contractors' hospital, which was put into use as the island aid station. The battalion surgeon, Lt. (jg) Gustave M. Kahn, USN, and the contract surgeon, Dr. Shank, worked continuously on a steady stream of wounded and injured. They stayed alert throughout the night, uncertain when the Japanese would return, but certain that they would.

The next morning, 9 December, was clear and bright as the three Wildcats took off at dawn. Using spare parts, the fourth Wildcat was also operational, minus a reserve tank, by 9:00 AM.

Twenty-seven Nell bombers attacked at 11:45 AM, dropping from 13,000 feet, but this time they found Wake's defenders prepared. Second Lt. David Kliewer and Sergeant Hamilton, in two of the three airborne Wildcats, downed one bomber, and antiaircraft fire downed another and damaged twelve others. But the remaining bombers wreaked havoc on Camp Number 2 and Peale Island.

The warehouse, barracks, and administration building at Peale were completely destroyed. At Camp Number 2 the machine shop and a warehouse were damaged, and the hospital and adjacent barracks were struck with direct hits, resulting in severe damage and fires. During the attack, while bombs exploded and the hospital was strafed, Dr. Kahn and Dr. Shank, assisted by volunteers, calmly evacuated the wounded, salvaged what equipment they could, and relocated the hospital within magazines 10 and 13, concrete bunkers adjacent to the airfield.

According to his Navy Cross citation, Shank "during an intensive bombing and strafing attack . . . in which the hospital was completely destroyed . . . remained at his post and supervised the evacuation of the patients and equipment. . . . [W]ith absolute disregard for his own safety . . . he was thus enabled to save those still living and establish a new hospital in an empty magazine." Marine Gunner Hamas, trapped by the raid while delivering ammunition to gun positions, witnessed Shank enter burning buildings to carry out the wounded and was so impressed that he later recommended Shank for the Medal of Honor.

The following day at 1:20 AM, the Japanese attacked a third time with twenty-six bombers, concentrating on the airfield and gun emplacements. A strike on Wilkes destroyed 125 tons of dynamite, the explosion damaging a gun position. Gun batteries downed two bombers, and Captain Elrod downed two others.

Shortly after midnight on the morning of the 11th, lookouts spotted blinking lights to the south. Alerted, Devereux scanned the horizon, spotting ships on the horizon. The Japanese Sixth Destroyer Squadron of the Fourth Fleet was offshore of Wake, tasked with the invasion and capture of Wake Island. Under the command of Rear Admiral Sadamichi Kajioka, the Japanese invasion force consisted of three light cruisers (*Yubari, Tatsuta,* and *Tenryu*), six destroyers (*Oite, Hayate, Mutsuki, Kisaragi, Mochizuki,* and *Yayoi*), two patrol boats (32 and 33), two transports (*Kongo Maru* and *Konyru Maru*), and 450 men of Special Naval Landing Force Five. Admiral

Kajioka was confident that three days of bombardment had reduced the island's fighting spirit.

He was wrong.

Commander Cunningham, notified by Gunner Hamas by telephone at about 3:00 AM, ordered all guns to hold their fire and all searchlights to remain dark until the ships closed the distance. Without fire-direction equipment, range-finding apparatus, or radar, he intended to engage the fleet point-blank. At 4:00 AM, Major Putnam and Captain Elrod, Captain Tharin, and Captain Freuler took off in the four remaining Wildcats, a 100-pound bomb under each wing. At 5:22 AM, the three cruisers commenced fire on the island, but the Marine guns remained silent as the cruisers closed the distance and pounded the island. At 6:15 AM, with the *Yubari* less than a mile offshore, Cunningham finally responded to all the requests to open fire. "What are we waiting for, John? Cut loose at them."[10]

Despite their shortcomings, the Marine batteries performed magnificently. In a forty-five-minute engagement, the Marine guns sank a destroyer, the *Hayate*, and severely damaged all three cruisers, three additional destroyers, the *Oite*, *Mochizuki* and *Yayoi*, and Patrol Boat 33. By 7:00 AM Admiral Kajioka ordered the fleet to retire behind a smoke screen. The *Hayate* was the first Japanese surface craft to be sunk during the war.

But the battle wasn't over. Major Putnam's Wildcats weren't through with the Japanese, and hadn't yet used their bombs. In ten sorties, they dropped twenty 100-pound bombs and fired twenty thousand machine-gun bullets, landing to rearm and refuel. For their efforts, they sank the destroyer *Kisaragi*, damaged the *Tenryu*, and strafed the *Kongo Maru*, which ignited barrels of gasoline.

At about 9:15 AM, a flight of seventeen Nells appeared and bombed Peale's gun positions, but with little effect. They were engaged by two Wildcats, piloted by Lieutenant Kinney and Lieutenant Davidson, both of whom "splashed" a bomber. Ground batteries damaged eleven others. But the defenders also sustained losses. Captain Elrod's plane was shot up so badly it crashed upon landing, damaging it beyond repair, and Captain Freuler's plane barely returned with a shot-up engine, also beyond repair. The squadron was now reduced to two operational aircraft. The remainder of the day was spent relocating and reinforcing gun positions. The U.S. contingent at Wake Island had won a tremendous victory, and it was a boost to a sagging national morale following Pearl Harbor. Cunningham's message of victory, sent by radio to Pearl Harbor: "Send us more Japs."

For the next six days, Wake Island was attacked eight times from the air. On the 18th the Japanese mounted a photo-reconnaissance mission over Wake, then resumed air raids on the 19th. The next day, a PBY Catalina (maritime patrol bomber) landed at Wake with news that lifted the defender's spirits—a relief force, Task Force 14, had sailed from Pearl Harbor on the 16th. The PBY departed the next day, taking with it Maj. Walter L. Baylor, who would become known as the "last

American off Wake." Within an hour, twenty-nine Japanese bombers and eighteen fighters flew overhead, attacking the gun positions. Ominously, the men recognized the aircraft as carrier-based aircraft. Later that day, Wake was hit by a second air raid of thirty-three bombers from Roi Island. The constant bombing took its toll and made rest impossible.

Only the creativity and ingenuity of the military and civilian mechanics kept the few Wildcats aloft by scavenging destroyed aircraft, but the enemy took its toll. On the 22nd, Captain Freuler and Lieutenant Davidson went aloft in the last two Wildcats to engage thirty-three "Kate" dive bombers and six "Zero" fighters off the carriers *Soryu* and *Hiryu*, both of which had been present at Pearl Harbor.

Freuler shot down two dive bombers (reputed to be those that sank the USS *Arizona*) but was shot up so badly that he crashed upon landing, destroying the plane and landing him in the hospital. Davidson never returned. Both men would be awarded the Navy Cross, Davidson posthumously. With the loss of the last two aircraft, the remaining twenty officers and men of VMF-211 reported to the 1st Defense Battalion as infantrymen.[11]

While the U.S. command had agonized over the decision of whether to reinforce or evacuate Wake, and as Task Force 14 steamed west at only twelve knots so as not to lose its slow-moving tanker, and paused to refuel on the 22nd, the Japanese acted with greater resolve.

The night of 22 December was moonless. After reinforcing his fleet at Kwajalein, Admiral Kajioka had returned to attempt another landing on Wake. Added to his invasion force were the destroyers *Aoba, Furutaka, Kinugasa,* and *Kako*, the cruisers *Tone* and *Chikuma*, the destroyer *Oboro* with six 5-inch guns, the carriers *Soryu* and *Hiryu*, three submarines, a mine-layer, a floatplane tender, and the two thousand–strong Second Special Landing Force, fresh from its victory on Guam. The two sunken destroyers were replaced by the *Ashagi* and *Yunagi*.[12]

To avoid Wake's deadly seacoast batteries, Kajioka ordered the initial landings to take place shortly before dawn and with no preliminary naval bombardment, so as to maintain surprise. He also ordered the two destroyer-transports, Patrol Boats 32 and 33, to be run aground on the south shore in the vicinity of the airstrip. At least six landing barges, with fifty men each, would land along the south shore —two on Wilkes, two between the end of the airstrip and Camp Number 1, and two just west of Peacock Point. In the event that the Special Landing Force troops, numbering approximately one thousand, were unable to force a decision ashore, a reserve of five hundred men, to be organized from ships' landing forces, would be committed.[13]

Shortly after midnight on 23 December 1941, American lookouts began to note irregular flashes of light in the black, gusty, rainy predawn sky. Devereux was notified, and he ordered his force on alert.

At 4:15 AM a report was received that an enemy landing was in progress at Toki Point, at the tip of Peale. Devereux alerted the battalion, and Cunningham radioed the commandant of the 14th Naval District, reporting "gunfire between ships to northeast of island."

Sometime around 6:00 AM, Cunningham issued the last communication off Wake: "Enemy on Island–Issue in Doubt." Only a few of the Marines on Wake were infantrymen, being mostly artillerymen and the air crews of VMF-211, yet they fought tenaciously and courageously, only reluctantly giving ground to a numerically superior enemy force. One example was Capt. Henry Elrod, the VMF-211's executive officer.

A fourteen-year veteran of the Marines, Elrod had already distinguished himself on 12 December with his downing of two enemy bombers and the sinking of the destroyer *Kisagari*. On the morning of the 23rd he was in command of some of the remaining Marines, which he placed in an improvised line of defense along the beach. It held against repeated attacks. Elrod repeatedly exposed himself to enemy fire in order to cover unarmed ammunition carriers as they rushed forward to replenish dwindling stocks, until he fell mortally wounded.

By 7:00 AM, both Devereux and Cunningham recognized that further resistance would be a temporary holding action at best, and began discussing surrender. There was no word on when the relief force would arrive, and in fact they were unaware it had been recalled. After fifteen days of siege, Cunningham, as ranking officer, made the decision to surrender Wake. "I'll pass the word," Devereux told him.

Devereux first passed the word to surrender to units still in communication with the command post, including Batteries A and E on Wake, and B on Peale, ordering them to destroy everything possible prior to surrender. Then, at about 8:00 AM, Devereux, accompanied by Sgt. Donald Malleck, tied a white flag to a mop handle and went forward into Japanese lines even as small arms fire crackled around them. As he passed Marine positions, he ordered them to cease fire and surrender. Devereux and Malleck were halted just prior to the hospital by Japanese riflemen who disarmed them and led them into the hospital, which had already been captured by the Japanese. They found the patients, wrists bound with telephone wire behind their backs tied to a noose around their necks, lying outside on the ground.

Devereux explained his mission to an English-speaking officer, then Commander Cunningham arrived in his dress blue uniform to arrange the formal surrender. Devereux and Malleck, with a Japanese escort, set out to communicate the surrender to isolated units. By about 1:30 PM, resistance on Wake was at an end. The flag that had flown so heroically for two weeks had become a souvenir of a Japanese soldier.

While sources differ as to the number of casualties and persons taken prisoner on Wake Island, documents of the U.S. Marine Corps Historical Division provide the following figures: out of the 449 Marines present on Wake, 46 were killed in action, 1 died from wounds, and 2 were missing; of the remaining 400 Marines, 32 were wounded. Of the 68 naval personnel, 3 were killed and 5 wounded. All 5 of the Army communications personnel were captured alive. Of the 1,146 civilian contractors, 70 were killed and 12 wounded. In total, of the 1,668 Americans on Wake (522 military and 1,146 civilians), 122 were killed, and the remaining 1,546 were taken prisoner.[14]

Stripped to their underwear, arms bound behind them, pulled high and tied to loops around their necks, the prisoners were marched to the edge of the airfield runway and seated in rows in front of several manned machine guns. Many believed they were to be murdered, and they might have been had it not been for the fortuitous arrival of Admiral Kajioka, who through an interpreter announced, "The Emperor has gracefully presented you with your lives." A voice called out from the crowd of Americans: "Well, thank the son-of-a-bitch." Except for a few senior officers and contractors, the rest of the prisoners were left on the rock-strewn runway, exposed to the elements for three days and two nights, suffering from dysentery and other ailments.[15]

Conditions for the prisoners improved marginally on Christmas day. They were allowed to retrieve clothing and bury their dead, and were fed a decent meal before being marched to the barracks on the northern side of the island, where they remained until a transport, the *Nitta Maru*, arrived on 12 January 1942. All but 360 of the civilians were loaded aboard; all of the military personnel were taken, with the exception of 21 severely wounded Marines. The prisoners believed their destination to be Japan, although their true destination was occupied China.

Before loading, the prisoners were given a long list of regulations, disobedience to which meant death. The rules included "disobeying orders or instructions, showing a motion of antagonism, talking without permission, or raising loud voices, carrying unnecessary baggage, trying to take more meal than given, walking or moving without order, and disordering the regulations by individualism, egoism, thinking only of yourself, and using more than two blankets." Five military prisoners (three Marines, two sailors) were beheaded en route for lying about their military experience.[16] The remainder docked at Shanghai, were marched twelve miles to the Woosung Prison Camp, then moved to Kiangwang War Prisoner Camp, where they were put to work at hard labor.

On 11 May 1943 the remaining military prisoners were taken from the atoll aboard the *Asama Maru*, bound for China. In violation of the Geneva Convention, to which the Japanese government was not a signatory, the remaining civilian prisoners were put to work on war-related projects, such as building fortifications. On 30 September, the remaining civilians were evacuated aboard the *Tachibana Maru*, with the exception of ninety-nine civilian heavy-equipment operators and Dr. Shank, who volunteered to remain behind to provide medical care for the remaining prisoners.[17]

The monotonous routine of Wake Island was increasingly disrupted by American air raids on the island, starting with the first carrier strike from the USS *Enterprise* (CV-6) on 24 February 1942. The first land-based strike of eight Army B-24s from bases on Midway came on 8 July 1943. The raids increased in frequency and intensity. On 6–7 October 1943, a U.S. carrier task force including the USS *Yorktown* (CV-10) launched the largest assault on Wake up to that date, dropping 340 tons of bombs and hammering the island with naval gunfire.

Afraid that the island was in imminent danger of invasion, the island commander, Rear Admiral (then Captain) Shigimatsu Sakaibara, who had arrived from Kwajalein in December 1942, ordered the ninety-eight remaining civilians executed. (Two prisoners had been beheaded by the Japanese earlier, both for stealing food.)

On the evening of 7 October, Lieutenant Commander Soichi Tachibana, headquarters company commander, was ordered by Sakaibara to move the prisoners from their compound to an antitank ditch on the north end of Wake. There they were seated in a row along the edge of the ditch, bound and blindfolded, then mowed down by machine guns. They were buried in a mass grave, but were disinterred when a Japanese sailor thought he saw one man escape. After a body count, one civilian was indeed missing. He was recaptured a week later attempting to steal food, and was personally beheaded by Sakaibara, who would radio his superiors "Riotous conduct among prisoners. Have executed them."[18]

Brig. Gen. Lawson H. Sanderson, commander of the 4th Marine Air Wing, and his party stand at attention as the Japanese formally surrender Wake Island to American military forces on 7 September 1945. Second from the left at his rear is Marine Col. Walter L. Baylor, "the last man off Wake Island," who departed Wake in a PBY patrol bomber during the early Japanese attacks on the island in 1941. (National Archives)

On 7 September 1945, Admiral Sakaibara surrendered Wake Island to Brig. Gen. Lawson Sanderson, USMC. First ashore was Col. Walter Baylor, the "last man off Wake." Questions were asked regarding the fate of the remaining POWs. The Japanese had made an effort to conceal the murders by moving the bodies to a cemetery marked with wooden crosses and concocting a story that the prisoners had been killed in an air raid and in a subsequent uprising. Suspicion was aroused when every Japanese recounted the same story, word for word, and an investigation was initiated. Ultimately, Sakaibara and Tachibana were found guilty by a military commission and sentenced to death by hanging. Tachibana's sentence was subsequently reduced to life in prison. Sakaibara was executed on Guam on 18 June 1947. His final words: "I think my trial was entirely unfair . . . and the sentence too harsh."

Following the war, Dr. Lawton Shank was recommended for a posthumous Medal of Honor for his actions during the defense of Wake. Because he was a civilian, the award was reduced to a posthumous Navy Cross, the only civilian to be so honored during World War II.

Capt. Henry Elrod, posthumously promoted to major, was awarded the Medal of Honor for his heroism at Wake, both in the air and on the ground. His wife, a former commissioned Marine officer, was presented his medal on 8 November 1946. Initially buried on Wake Island, Elrod was reinterred in Arlington National Cemetery in October 1947.

Cdr. Winfield Scott Cunningham endured 1,330 days as a prisoner of the Japanese. He twice attempted to escape, both times accompanied by Dan Teters. The first attempt, from Shanghai on 11 March 1942, was with two others. All four were recaptured the next day, court-martialed, and confined in Shanghai's municipal jail. A second attempt on 6 October 1944 earned Cunmingham a more rigorous confinement in a succession of military prisons in Nantung and Peking before he was liberated on 18 August 1945.

Departing China aboard an Army transport on 24 August 1945, Cunningham arrived in the United States on 7 September 1945, the same day Wake Island was surrendered to American forces. After being examined at the Bethesda Naval Hospital in Maryland, Cunningham was found "fit for duty." He was promoted to captain on 4 December 1945, effective 20 June 1942, and was awarded the Navy Cross for his command of the defense of Wake Island.

In January 1946 Cuningham attended refresher aviation training at the Naval Air Station in Pensacola, Florida, then took command of the USS *Curtiss* (AV-4), a seaplane tender, in May 1946. The *Curtiss*, named after aviation pioneer Glenn Hammond Curtiss, survived both Pearl Harbor and a kamikaze attack. Cunningham retired from the Navy on 30 June 1950 with the rank of rear admiral. In 1961 he wrote *Wake Island Command*, in which he described the historic battle. He died on 3 March 1986 at the age of 86 and is buried in the Memphis National Cemetery.

Maj. Paul A. Putnam was held at the Zentsuji Prison Camp until being moved in June 1945 to Rokuroshi POW camp, where he was liberated in September. He was awarded the Navy Cross, and retired from the Marine Corps as a brigadier general in 1952. He died in 1982.

Lt. Col. James Devereux is shown arriving at Honolulu in 1945, on his way home after he and many of his men were held prisoner by the Japanese until the end of the war. (Naval Historical Center)

Maj. James P. S. Devereux was released from Hokkaido Island Prison Camp on 15 September 1945 and was immediately ordered to Headquarters USMC, personally reporting to the commandant, General Vandegrift, regarding the defense of Wake. Awarded the Navy Cross, he attended the Amphibious Warfare School at Quantico, Virginia, and was detached to the 1st Marine Division at Oceanside, California, before his retirement as a brigadier general on 1 August 1948 after twenty-five years of service.

Devereux served four terms as a U.S. Representative from Maryland from 1951 to 1959, ran unsuccessfully for governor, and served as director of public safety for Baltimore County from 1962 to 1966. He died on 5 August 1988 and is buried in Arlington National Cemetery.

Altogether, nine Navy Crosses were awarded for actions at Wake Island. In addition to Shank, Devereux, Cunningham, Putnam, Davidson, and Freuler, the Navy Cross was awarded to 2nd Lt. Robert M. Hanna, USMC; SSgt. Robert O. Arthur, USMC; and AM1 James F. Hesson.

ENDNOTES

1. Vurlee A. Toomey, "Wake Island, Island of Valor," http://www.geocities.com/ vurleeb/wakeisland. htm (2001).
2. Lydel Sims and W. Scott Cunningham, *Wake Island Command* (Boston: Little Brown & Co., 1961).
3. *Biographical Directory of the United States Congress.*
4. Toomey, "Wake Island."
5. Paul A. Putnam papers. Special Collection #313, Joyner Library, East Carolina University, Greenville, North Carolina.
6. Robert J. Cressman, A *Magnificent Fight: Marines in the Battle for Wake Island*, Marines in WW II Commemorative Series, History and Museum Division, USMC, 2006.
7. R. D. Heinl Jr., *Marines in World War II: The Defense of Wake*, Historical Section, History and Museum Division, USMC, Archive Collection, 1947.
8 . Toomey, "Wake Island."
9. Ibid.
10. Sims and Cunningham, *Wake Island Command.*
11. Robert Sherrod, *History of Marine Corps Aviation in WWII* (Washington, D.C.: Combat Forces Press, 1952).
12. Toomey, "Wake Island."
13. Cressman, A *Magnificent Fight.*
14. Heinl, *Marines in World War II*
15. Gregory J. W. Urwin, *Facing Fearful Odds* (Lincoln: University of Nebraska Press, 1997).
16. They were SN1 John Lambert, SN2 Theodore Franklin, SN2 Roy Gonzales, MSgt. Earl Hannum, and TSgt. William Bailey.
17. Mark E. Hubbs, "Massacre on Wake Island," *Naval History Magazine*, Feb. 2001.
18. Toomey, "Wake Island."

GySgt. John Basilone, USMC

Iwo Jima
19 February 1945

The Navy Cross is presented to John "Manila John" Basilone, Gunnery Sergeant, U.S. Marine Corps, for extraordinary heroism while serving as a Leader of a Machine Gun Section, Company C, 1st Battalion, 27th Marines, 5th Marine Division, in action against enemy Japanese forces on Iwo Jima in the Volcano Islands, 19 February 1945. Shrewdly gauging the tactical situation shortly after landing when his company's advance was held up by the concentrated fire of a heavily fortified Japanese blockhouse, Gunnery Sergeant Basilone boldly defied the smashing bombardment of heavy caliber fire to work his way around the flank and up to a position directly on top of the blockhouse and then, attacking with grenades and demolitions, single-handedly destroyed the entire hostile strong point and its defending garrison. Consistently daring and aggressive as he fought his way over the battle-torn beach and up the sloping, gun-studded terraces toward Airfield Number 1, he repeatedly exposed himself to the blasting fury of exploding shells and later in the day coolly proceeded to the aid of a friendly tank which had been trapped in an enemy mine field under intense mortar and artillery barrages, skillfully guiding the heavy vehicle over the hazardous terrain to safety, despite the overwhelming volume of hostile fire. In the forefront of the assault at all times, he pushed forward with dauntless courage and iron determination until, moving upon the edge of the airfield, he fell, instantly killed by a bursting mortar shell. Stouthearted and indomitable, Gunnery Sergeant Basilone, by his intrepid initiative, outstanding skill, and valiant spirit of self-sacrifice in the face of fanatic opposition, contributed materially to the advance of his company during the early critical period of the assault, and his unwavering devotion to duty throughout the bitter conflict was an inspiration to his comrades and reflects the highest credit upon Gunnery Sergeant Basilone and the United States Naval Service. He gallantly gave his life in the service of his country.[1]

Navy Cross citation for GySgt. John Basilone, USMC

IT WOULD READ LIKE a Hollywood script. Boy of modest means enlists in the Marines, goes to combat, wins the Medal of Honor, and comes home to fame, parades, and dates with beautiful starlets. He's offered a commission and any job in the military he wishes, but all he really wants is to return to his "boys" at the front.

He finds love, marries, leaves before Christmas to return to the battlefield, and dies a heroic death. But rather than fiction, it is the real-life story of John Basilone, the son of an Italian-American tailor, who was the only enlisted Marine in World War II to be awarded the Medal of Honor, Navy Cross, and Purple Heart, the last two posthumously.[2]

After the Japanese attack on Pearl Harbor, the early months of the war in the Pacific did not go well for the United States or her Allies. By July 1942 the Japanese controlled Hong Kong, North Borneo, the Philippines, Malaya, Burma, Siam, French Indo-China, Guam, the Dutch East Indies, and much of New Guinea, and had established bases in the Marshall, Gilbert, Caroline and Solomon islands. The Japanese military seemed invincible.

The first U.S. victories at sea came in late spring 1942. In May the U.S. Navy defeated the Japanese at the Battle of the Coral Sea off the coast of New Guinea, and in June decisively won the Battle of Midway, sinking four Japanese carriers and a cruiser while losing the USS *Yorktown*. But at that point there had not yet been a land offensive against the Japanese.

On 4 July 1942, Allied air reconnaissance discovered a Japanese construction brigade building an airstrip on Guadalcanal, an island ninety miles long and twenty-five miles wide at the southern end of the Solomon Islands, northeast of Australia.[3] If it were to become operative, this airstrip would threaten both the South Pacific and U.S. forces at Espiritu Santo. Adm. Ernest King had already made the decision to occupy the nearby island of Tulagi, and discovery of the new airfield on Guadalcanal only gave impetus to the objective.[4]

As sea transports rushed Army and Marine troops toward the Solomons, plans were made for the first amphibious operation undertaken by U.S. forces since the Spanish-American War. On 7 August, an amphibious force commanded by Rear Adm. R. K. Turner landed elements of Maj. Gen. Alexander Vandegrift's 1st Marine Division on Guadalcanal and Tulagi. The assault on Tulagi met strong opposition from a small Japanese garrison, but on Guadalcanal there was only token opposition to the landings from Japanese construction workers, and the small force of combat troops retreated into the jungle.[5] Among the troops that would fight for six months to take Guadalcanal was Sgt. John Basilone.

John Basilone was born in Buffalo, New York, on 4 November 1916, the sixth of ten children born to Salvatore and Dora Basilone. The family moved to Raritan, New Jersey, where Basilone grew up during the Depression, attending St. Bernhard Parochial School. He was, as one relative put it, "easy-going, popular with the women, and liked good times." But there was another side. "He was strong as an ox, got in lots of fights, and was a high school drop-out with no skills." After leaving school, he obtained his parents' permission to enlist in the Army at the age of seventeen.[6]

GySgt. "Manila John" Basilone, USMC, was the only enlisted Marine in World War II to be awarded the Medal of Honor, Navy Cross, and Purple Heart, the last two posthumously. (U.S. Marine Corps History Division)

It was relatively difficult to enlist in the Army during the Depression, but the recruiter must have sensed a latent strand of martial ability in Basilone, and he was enrolled for a three-year hitch in June 1934. After basic training at Fort Jay, New York, he was sent to the Philippines, where he gained experience with heavy machine guns while assigned to Company D, 16th Infantry. He spent his time in the pursuit of bandits, usually without success. It was also in the Army that he first boxed. Good with his fists, he boxed as a light-heavyweight, remaining undefeated in nineteen bouts, and earned the nickname "Manila John." After his tour of duty ended in June 1937, Basilone was honorably discharged as a private first class, and he returned to civilian life.[7] He returned home and took jobs driving a laundry truck and working as a caddie.

Basilone eventually moved to Reistertown, Maryland, to live with his sister. On 11 July 1940, with war raging in Europe, he went to Baltimore to reenlist, this time in the Marines. "He wasn't happy as a civilian," recalled his nephew. "He was a warrior." After finishing boot camp at Quantico, Virginia, he was sent to Guantanamo Bay, Cuba, where he trained in amphibious operations. He was assigned to the newly reactivated 7th Marine Regiment, in the 1st Battalion (1/7), commanded by Lt. Col. Lewis B. "Chesty" Puller, part of the 1st Marine Brigade. The regiment was moved to New River, North Carolina (present-day Camp Lejeune), where they were training when the Japanese attacked Pearl Harbor on 7 December 1941.

On 10 April 1942, the 7th Marine Regiment (which had merged with the 11th Marine Artillery to form the 3rd Marine Brigade) embarked from Norfolk, Virginia, aboard the USS *Fuller* en route to the Pacific to reinforce units already there. They arrived in the Samoa Islands on 7 May 1942 and trained in jungle warfare until deploying to Guadalcanal as reinforcements in September.[8]

On 7 August 1942 the 1st Marine Division made landings on the islands of Guadalcanal, Tulagi, and Florida at the southern end of the Solomons. The Guadalcanal landing went largely unopposed. Per Operation Order 7-42 (dated 20 July 1942), the 5th Marines landed on Beach Red, with 3rd Battalion moving left (southeast) and 1st Battalion moving right to act as a beachhead defense against a Japanese attack, with the 1st Marines landing three battalions at H-hour plus fifty minutes.[9]

The following day, Marines captured the unfinished airfield on Guadalcanal and named it Henderson Field after Maj. Lofton Henderson, a hero of the victory at Midway. That same day, Rear Adm. Frank Fletcher made the decision to withdraw his three aircraft carriers to protect them from Japanese air attack. It was a fateful decision. That evening and into the next morning off Savo Island, north of Guadalcanal, eight Japanese warships sank three U.S. heavy cruisers, an Australian cruiser, and one U.S. destroyer, all in less than an hour in a night attack. Another U.S. cruiser and two destroyers were damaged. Over fifteen hundred Allied crewmen were lost in the Battle of Savo Island. It was a damaging setback for U.S. forces, verging on disaster.[10]

The warship losses at Savo Island forced the withdrawal of the transports, taking with them three thousand Marines yet to disembark as well as the division's heavy artillery and ammunition, isolating the ten thousand Marines on Guadalcanal from supplies and reinforcements. The "Cactus Air Force," the Army, Navy, and Marine fighter squadrons operating out of Henderson Field, proved vital by providing air cover for resupply during the day and for forcing the Japanese to resupply by fast destroyers at night in what was known as the "Tokyo Express."[11] Between August and November the Japanese attempted several major offensives to retake Tulagi and capture Henderson Field. The 7th Marine Regiment, which had landed on Guadalcanal on 18 September, took part in many of the actions.

On 24 October, in what would become known as the Battle for Henderson Field, Lieutenant General Harukichi Hyakutake felt that his force of twenty thousand troops was sufficient to retake the island, and began a series of major attacks that would extend over three days. As part of the offensive, the Japanese 2nd Division attacked along the Matanikau River, west of Henderson, attempting to overrun the airfield. The 7th Marines, including Basilone, were in a defensive line that stretched twenty five hundred yards to the Lunga River.[12]

During that first night, Japanese forces made at least six major assaults on the line. Sergeant Basilone, commanding two sections of .30-caliber, water-cooled heavy machine guns in the Charlie Company zone, "performed magnificently in keeping his weapons operating."[13]

Pfc. Nash W. Phillips of Fayetteville, North Carolina, a member of Basilone's unit at Guadalcanal, later recalled, "Basilone had a machine gun on the go day and night without sleep, rest or food. He was in a good emplacement and causing the Japs a lot of trouble, not only firing his machine gun, but also using his pistol. They stormed his position time and time again. Each time, he piled up four or five more around his emplacement. Finally he had to move out of there; thirty-eight Jap bodies made it kind of hard to fire over the pile." Only two of Basilone's twelve men survived the battle. Of the estimated 1,462 Japanese dead, 150 of them were near Basilone's position.[14]

His official citation for the Medal of Honor stated: "While the enemy was hammering at the Marine's defensive positions, Sgt. Basilone . . . fought valiantly to check the savage and determined assault. In a fierce frontal attack with the Japanese blasting his guns with grenade and mortar fire, one of [his] sections with its guncrews, was put out of action, leaving only two men to carry on. Moving an extra gun into position, he placed it in action, then, under continual fire, repaired another and personally manned it, gallantly holding his line until reinforcements arrived. A little later, with ammunition critically low and supply lines cut off, Sgt. Basilone, at great risk of his life and in the face of continued enemy attack, battled his way through the hostile lines with urgently needed shells for his gunners, contributing . . . to the virtual annihilation of a Japanese regiment."

On 9 December 1942 the 1st Marine Division was relieved by the Army's Americal and 25th Divisions and the 2nd Marine Division. The battle for the island continued, but attrition and lack of supplies reduced the Japanese capacity for offensive operations. Following the evacuation of the last remaining Japanese troops from Cape Esperance, Guadalcanal was declared secure on 9 February 1943.[15]

After six months of hell, the battle was over. Adm. Samuel Eliot Morison described it this way: "Guadalcanal is not a name, but an emotion, recalling desperate fights in the air, furious naval battles, frantic work at supply or construction, savage fighting in the sodden jungle, nights broken by screaming bombs and deafening explosions."

The United States had won its first ground offensive against the Japanese, and the nation celebrated. The myth of Japanese invincibility was destroyed. After Guadalcanal, the Japanese would fight on the defensive, never again winning on the ground. As Admiral "Bull" Halsey would comment, "Before Guadalcanal, the enemy advanced at his pleasure—after Guadalcanal he retreated at ours." It was a great victory, and the nation both wanted and needed victories and heroes.

The 1st Marine Division arrived in Melbourne, Australia, in early January 1943. The troops were hailed as the "Saviors of Australia" and feted with parties and parades. Suffering from malaria, fatigue, and wounds, the division's troops refitted and trained for the next mission. On 5 February 1943, President Roosevelt presented General Vandegrift with the Medal of Honor in a White House ceremony. On 21 May 1943, General Vandegrift presented the Medal of Honor to Sergeant Basilone and 2nd Lt. Mitchell Paige.

Basilone, one of the nation's first heroes, was ordered home to become part of the Third War Loan Drive, and he traveled across the country attending war bond rallies, appeared in newsreels, and escorted Hollywood starlets. Basilone hated it. Shy, he disliked being in the spotlight and was not comfortable speaking in public. Additionally, he was frustrated because he wanted to return to combat, or at least train Marines and give them the knowledge he'd gained in combat, but he was deemed too valuable as a national symbol. Offered a commission, he replied, "I ain't no officer, and I ain't no museum piece."[16]

After the war bond tour, which raised $1.4 million, had ended, Basilone was assigned as a Marine guard at the Navy Yard in Washington, D.C. He began to drink and engage in minor insubordinations. At a function in New York he met with his old commander, General Vandegrift, and begged, "You've got to help me, sir. I want to be with the fleet. . . .They can't take Manila without 'Manila John.'" Vandegrift replied, "I'll see what I can do." After the battle for Peleliu, Basilone went to his commanding officer and demanded that he be returned to combat, possibly even threatening to go AWOL. Faced with the possibility of being forced to court-martial a national hero, orders were cut transferring Basilone to Camp Pendleton, California.[17]

Newly promoted to platoon sergeant, Basilone left for Pendleton on 27 December 1943. He was assigned to C Company, 1st Battalion, 27th Marine Regiment, 5th Marine Division. He began training "boots" and finally felt back in his element. While at Pendleton, Basilone met Marine Sgt. Lena Riggi, an Italian-Catholic girl from Portland, Oregon. They were married on 10 July 1944 in Oceanside, California. The 5th Marines received orders to ship out on 1 August, destination unknown.[18]

The 5th Division boarded the USS *Baxter* (APA-94) and sailed to Hawaii, arriving at Hilo Harbor on 18 August. Four days later they took a train to Camp Tarawa, where they trained in new tactics for taking fortified positions, using a new weapon, the flamethrower. While in Hawaii, Basilone met with his brother, George, a member of the 4th Marines, recently returned from Saipan. After four months of training, the unit began loading up the transports in late December.

On their second day at sea, the Marines learned that their destination was Iwo Jima, a flat and featureless pork chop–shaped island of volcanic sand in the Bonin Islands. Dominated by Mount Suribachi, a dormant volcano that rose 555 feet, the island was needed as a landing and refueling site for American bombers en route to Tokyo, 650 nautical miles to the north. The existence of Japanese fighters and a radar installation on Iwo Jima were added incentives for the invasion. Because Iwo was native soil to the Japanese, American commanders understood that the defense would be fanatical. The Japanese were said to be entrenched in a series of interconnected fortified caves and blockhouses, consisting of 16 miles of lighted and ventilated tunnels connecting 150 fortified firing positions.[19]

Basilone's platoon was in the first wave to land on the beach on the morning of 19 February 1945. Basilone and another Marine walked upright under intense fire, kicking and dragging entrenched Marines to their feet, screaming at them to advance off the beach. The mission of C Company was to advance and capture Motoyama #1 airfield.

A fortified blockhouse blocked the advance, and Basilone gathered scattered troops and organized an assault, neutralizing the threat. After taking the airfield and positioning his men, then guiding tanks forward, Basilone returned to the beach to bring more troops forward. As he was returning, a mortar round exploded, mortally wounding Basilone and killing four others. It was 10:45 AM. He died of massive abdominal wounds, loss of blood, and shock twenty minutes later. Nominated for a second Medal of Honor, he was awarded the Navy Cross and Purple Heart, posthumously, the only enlisted Marine in World War II to earn all three.[20]

On 21 December 1945, Sgt. Lena Mae Basilone, as ship's sponsor, christened the USS *Basilone* (DD-824), a destroyer named in honor of her husband, at the Consolidated Steel Company Shipyard in Orange, Texas. It was commissioned on 26 June 1949. Other named honors for Basilone include a high school in New Jersey, a stretch of interstate highway in California, and a U.S. postage stamp issued on 10 November 2005. A plaque honoring Basilone was installed at the U.S. Navy Memorial in Washington, D.C., on 25 May 2006.[21]

Initially buried on Iwo Jima, Basilone's remains were returned to the United States and interred at Arlington National Cemetery, Section 12–Site 384, on 20 April 1948.

ENDNOTES

1. Navy Cross citation for GySgt. John Basilone, www.homeofheroes.com/valor/1_citations/03_wwii-nc/nc_06wwii_usmc.html.

2. Jim Proser and Jerry Cutter, *"I'm Staying with My Boys": The Heroic Life of Sgt. John Basilone, USMC* (Hilton Head: Lightbearer Communications Co., 2004).

3. James Bradley and Ron Powers, *Flags of Our Fathers* (New York: Bantam Books, 2000).

4. Samuel Eliot Morison, *History of United States Naval Operations in World War Two*, vol. 5, *Guadalcanal* (Boston: Little, Brown, 1969).

5. Ibid.

6. Telephone interview with Jerry Cutter, nephew of John Basilone and author, in August 2006.

7. Proser and Cutter, *I'm Staying with My Boys*.

8. Jon T. Hoffman, *Chesty: The Story of Lieutenant General Lewis B. Puller, USMC* (New York: Random House, 2001).

9. OPERATION ORDER No. 7-42—First Marine Division, Fleet Marine Force, Wellington, N.Z. [20 July 1942].

10. "World War Two in the Pacific: Timeline of Events 1941–1945," The History Place, http://www.historyplace.com/unitedstates/pacificwar/timeline.htm 1999.

11. John Whiteclay Chambers, ed., T*he Oxford Companion to American Military History* (New York: Oxford University Press, 1999).

12. Robert Hargis and Starr Sinton, *World War Two Medal of Honor Recipients,* vol. 1*, Navy & USMC* (Osceola, Wis.: Osprey Publishing, 2003), 20–22.

13. John T. Hoffman, "Battle for Henderson Field: Lt. Colonel Lewis B. Puller Commanded the 1st Battalion, 7th Marines," *World War Two Magazine*, November 2002.

14. Proser and Cutter, *I'm Staying with My Boys*.

15. Richard Tregaskis, *Guadalcanal Diary* (New York: Random House, 1943).

16. Telephone interview with Jerry Cutter.

17. Proser and Cutter, *I'm Staying with My Boys*.

18. Ibid.

19. Ibid.

20. Ibid.

21. Alec MacGillis, "Honoring One Marine to Remember Them All: WWII Hero Gets Plaque at Navy Memorial," *Washington Post*, May 29, 2006, p. B1.

NAVY CROSSES AT GUADALCANAL

Medals of Honor and Navy Crosses Awarded
for the Guadalcanal Campaign

THE GUADALCANAL CAMPAIGN (7 August 1942–8 February 1943) demonstrated courage and American resolve under extremely difficult and hazardous conditions on the ground, at sea, and in the air. The victory on Guadalcanal, the first defeat of the Japanese on the ground, raised morale at home and overseas and resulted in awards in recognition of extraordinary acts of valor.

Twelve Medals of Honor were awarded, six posthumously. The living recipients included Merritt "Red Mike" Edson, who also won two Navy Crosses; "Manila John" Basilone, the first enlisted Marine to win both the Medal of Honor and Navy Cross in World War II; Anthony Casamento, a 5th Marine corporal who was wounded fourteen times while manning a machine gun; Charles W. Davis, a captain with the Army's 25th Division; Joe Foss, a record-setting ace who shot down twenty-three Japanese aircraft at Guadalcanal; and Alexander Vandegrift, legendary general and commandant.

The following Medal of Honor awards were posthumous: Kenneth Bailey, a major with the First Raider Battalion; Harold William Bauer, commanding officer of VMF-212, who downed eleven planes; William Fournier, a sergeant with the 25th Division, who with Lewis Hall held off the Japanese; Norman Scott, a Navy rear admiral who destroyed eight enemy vessels; and Douglas Munro, the only Coast Guardsman so honored.

There were 214 awards of the Navy Cross, 72 being posthumous. One hundred fourteen of those went to Marines, 96 went to Sailors, 1 to a Coast Guardsman, 1 to a member of the Army, and 2 went to New Zealanders. Eleven went to Marine aviators, 10 to corpsmen, and 4 to medical officers. Two rear admirals were awarded the medal—Carlton Wright and Willis A. Lee (posthumously).

In total, 111 officers, 34 non-commissioned officers, and 69 enlisted men were awarded the Navy Cross for Guadalcanal.

Rear Adm. Roy M. Davenport, USN (Ret.)

Submariner awarded five Navy Crosses during the Following War Patrols

1. June to August 1943: off Palau and the Caroline Islands
2. September 1943: off the Truk Islands
3. October to November 1943: off the Truk Islands
4. September to October 1944: Tokyo Bay
5. November to December 1944: off Luzon, Philippines

IN ADDITION TO HIS five Navy Crosses, during his thirty-year career as a submariner, Rear Adm. Davenport was also awarded two Silver Stars, two Letters of Commendation with ribbon, two Presidential Unit Citations, a Navy Unit Commendation, the submarine combat insigne indicating ten successful war patrols, the area campaign medal, and the Philippine Liberation medal.

Who was this extraordinary seaman who reached the heights of a Navy career while fighting a dangerous and determined enemy in eastern Pacific waters? Was he just a superb leader of men, extremely knowledgeable in every facet of the boats he commanded, a man of patience, and a tactical genius? Yes, he was all that, and more. His reputation among his men was that he would always bring his crew safely home to port. And he did. He was a deeply religious man who attributed his good fortune and that of his men to the Almighty. He was often chided by his fellow skippers that God was on his side when he returned to port with a "clean sweep" (a broom attached to his submarine's mast, signifying a successful patrol) when they had realized minimal success.[1]

Roy Milton Davenport was born in Kansas City, Kansas, on 18 June 1909 to Virgil Oscar and Inez Florence Davenport. He attended Wyandotte High School and Kansas City Junior College before being appointed to the U.S. Naval Academy.[2] He graduated from the Academy, where he was nicknamed "the professor" by his midshipmen classmates, in 1933. In the 1933 *Lucky Bag*, the Academy's yearbook, he was described as "one of those practical minded men who knows what he wants and sets out to get it, an inveterate seeker after facts . . . and one who had an inherent liking for the ladies."[3]

During his career, Rear Adm. Roy M. Davenport, a submariner, would be awarded five Navy Crosses, two Silver Stars, two Letters of Commendation with ribbon, two Presidential Unit Citations, a Navy Unit Commendation, the submarine combat insigne indicating ten successful war patrols, the area campaign medal, and the Philippine Liberation medal. (Naval Historical Center)

After graduation Rear Adm. Davenport served aboard the battleship USS *Texas* (BB-35) for three years, then entered submarine training at the submarine base at New London, Connecticut. He was next ordered as a gunnery officer to the submarine USS *Cachalot* (SS-170), which was attached to Submarine Division 13, Submarine Force, based at Pearl Harbor. Although his assignment was as gunnery officer, he soon found himself manning the vessel's TDC (torpedo data computer), a device that determined the gyro settings of torpedoes. He was the only man aboard trained in the use of the system. He returned to the States in the fall of 1941 and reported for duty in connection with the fitting out of the USS *Silversides* (SS-236). Captain Davenport was about to begin his war on the enemy.[4]

The *Silversides* was commissioned on 15 December 1941, eight days after the surprise attack on Pearl Harbor. Captain Davenport was the *Silversides'* executive officer during her first fifty-two-day patrol (30 April–21 June 1942). Operating off Honshu, Japan, she sank one enemy submarine, one trawler, two supply ships, and one naval auxiliary, totaling 25,627 tons. The boat additionally damaged one tanker of 10,000 tons. Captain Davenport subsequently received a Letter of Commendation, with authorization to wear the Commendation ribbon.

Japanese merchant ship settling by the bow after she was torpedoed by a U.S. submarine. The photo was taken through the sub's periscope. (National Archives)

Captain Davenport was still serving as executive officer on the *Silversides* on her second patrol of fifty-five days (15 July–8 September 1942), in the area of Ichiye Saki, when she sank two passenger freighters and two trawlers, totaling 15,250 tons, and damaged one tanker and one trawler, totaling 5,750 tons; on her third war patrol of fifty-four days while operating in the waters off Truk, New Ireland, and Burka, she sank one freighter transport, the Japanese *Manila Maru*, one other vessel of 1,300 tons; and on her fourth war patrol of forty-five days, starting on 17 December 1942 in the area of New Ireland, she sank one tanker of 10,010 tons and damaged two supply ships (*Omedono Maru* and *Urabaya Maru*) and one submarine (SS I-1 Class), totaling 14,300 tons. It was during the boat's fourth patrol that an emergency appendectomy operation had to be performed, despite limited facilities, on a crew member while the submarine was far below the surface of the ocean not far from Tokyo. Captain Davenport kept the crew advised of the progress of the operation, which took five hours to perform.

For services on the first four war patrols of the *Silversides*, Captain Davenport was awarded the Silver Star Medal.

During his subsequent command of the USS Haddock, a crewman suffering from appendicitis (a common occurrance on submarines on extended war patrols) was transferred via rubber raft to a waiting PBY patrol bomber to be flown to Midway Island for hospitalization. (National Archives)

World War II USS *Haddock* (SS-231) Battle Flag on display at the Submarine Library, New London, Connecticut. (Naval Historical Center)

Following his detachment from the *Silversides* in March 1943, Captain Davenport assumed command of the USS *Haddock* (SS-231) at Midway Island on 5 March 1943. He commanded that submarine on her fourth war patrol of thirty-nine days in the Truk and Palau Island area, starting on 11 March 1943. He sank two passenger-cargo ships and one transport during the patrol. For his service on that patrol, he was awarded a Gold Star in lieu of a second Silver Star medal.

During the fourth patrol of the *Haddock*, the sub was damaged by an enemy depth charge and forced to return to port. Captain Davenport received a second Letter of Commendation for his conduct in evading the enemy and bringing his boat successfully to port.

The *Haddock*, still under Captain Davenport, commenced her fifth war patrol (forty-one days) on 30 June 1943. While patrolling in the areas of Palau and the Caroline Island group, she damaged all five ships in a convoy totaling 35,606 tons, and sank one transport of 10,936 tons. For his service in command of this patrol he was awarded the Navy Cross with the following citation:

> For extraordinary heroism as Commanding Officer of a United States Submarine during operations against enemy Japanese forces in the Pacific area. Throughout numerous war patrols in enemy infested waters, Lieutenant Commander Davenport pressed home his attacks with cool and courageous determination and despite intense and persistent hostile opposition, succeeded in sinking over 10,500 tons of enemy shipping and damaging over 35,500 tons. His aggressive fighting spirit, inspiring leadership and the splendid efficiency of his men in his command contributed immeasurably to the success of our operations in this vital area and were in keeping with the highest traditions of the United States Naval Service.

Captain Davenport continued to deal the enemy devastating blows during his sixth and seventh war patrols, for which he was awarded Gold Stars in lieu of his second and third Navy Cross medals.

On 22 May 1944 he took command of the USS *Trepang* from the time of her commissioning until the following December. At the launching of the new boat, which Mrs. Davenport sponsored, she said, "I christen thee *Trepang*, and may God bless thee!" On the *Trepang*'s first patrol while operating just south of Honshu, the Japanese home island, she sank a destroyer and two tankers, and damaged a 35,000-ton battleship, earning Davenport his fourth Navy Cross.

Since Captain Davenport's wartime exploits thus far have been treated in a rather expeditious manner, the authors deemed it appropriate to relate selected entries from his logbook during the *Trepang*'s second patrol. His heroism during that patrol earned him his fifth Navy Cross. The excerpts are taken from his 1986 book, *Clean Sweep*.

The second war patrol of the *Trepang* was to be conducted in the area north of Luzon in the Philippines. The *Trepang* along with the USS *Segundo* (SS-398) and the USS *Razorback* (SS-394) were to form a coordinated attack group with me as the group commander. The group was known as "Roy's Rangers."

USS *Trepang* (SS-412) under the command of Capt. Roy M. Davenport off Mare Island Naval Shipyard, California, on 12 July 1944. (Naval Historical Center)

1330, November 16 - Departed Majuro Atoll for second war patrol in company with USS *Segundo* (SS-398) as part of Coordinated Attack Group 17.15, known as Roy's Rangers. Set course via safety lane to lat. 20-00 N, long. 169-00 E, to rendezvous with *USS Razorback*. Made trim dive.

2005 - Radar contact at 23,000 yards, with range closing rapidly. *Segundo* and *Trepang* increased speed to avoid while escort closed with vessel to identify. Vessel identified as friendly by escort. Escort did not rejoin. We continued up safety lane.

0000, December 1 - Entered (patrol) area. The *Trepang* patrolling east of Babuyan Island with the *Segundo* to the north and the *Razorback* to the south. Distances between submarines was 20 miles.

0050, December 6 - SJ radar contact on two ships bearing 185 degrees T., range 6,500 yards. Stationed radar tracking party and commenced tracking ahead of ships. As we could not hear echo ranging from these targets and they were extremely small, we hoped they might be submarines.

0153 - submerged for approach; bright moonlight night. Made radar approach from side away from moon in to 4,000 yards and then to 2,000 yards at periscope depth. Echo ranging could now be heard and the targets were both identified as small patrol boats. They were in column zigzagging on base course of 030 degrees T., making 8 knots, lat. 20-18 N, long. 120-29 E. The sea was too rough to attempt a shallow torpedo depth setting; therefore we broke off approach and evaded at periscope depth.

0259 - Surfaced.

0525 - Submerged for periscope patrol off coast of Luzon. Our position was between Cape Bojeador and Mayraira Point, the *Razorback* was to the west of Cape Bojeador, and the *Segundo* was to the east of Mayraira Point. Submerged to test depth for check on density layers. Found none. Before we dove the weather changed abruptly and the sea became calm. Prior to surfacing in the evening it started to blow up again. Sea condition No. 3.

1058 - Sighted patrol plane identified as 'Emily,' lat. 18-53N, long. 120-40.5 E.

1829 - Surfaced; commenced surface patrol.

1844 - SJ radar contact on convoy bearing 328 degrees T., range 19,700 yards, lat. 19-01 N, long. 120-36 E. Seven ships were first sighted by radar and later three more, the latter being small escorts. These ships were later identified as three AKs (cargo) one large AP (transport), one large AO (oiler), one AE (ammunition), and one AO, AP or whaler, together with three small patrol vessels.

Stationed radar tracking party and commenced tracking. The night was dark; therefore a surface approach was possible. Convoy was tracked on course 200 degrees T., at 9 knots.

1950 - Obtained receipt from the *Segundo* and the *Razorback* for the *Trepang's* 061137, reporting convoy.

2006 - Went to battle stations torpedo.

2020 - The convoy had now taken a base course of 120 degrees T., at a speed of 5.5 knots, which headed them for Babuyan Channel. Neither boat had reported contact; however, with the convoy on its present course, I believed that the *Segundo* would make contact very soon. Considering the possibility that the convoy had already been alerted by our first transmission and had changed course, I decided against sending further information until after attacking to avoid a possible delay in delivering the initial attack. If this convoy was to be prevented from entering Babuyan Channel, an attack would have to be made soon.

The convoy was in two columns of three and four ships respectfully with escorts ahead and on each flank. Fortunately the ships were grouped extremely close together and the four ships were in column on our side.

The starboard escort was on the starboard quarter of the No. 1 ship. Just prior to attacking, our position was sharp on the escort's starboard bow at 3,000 yards. We placed him on our starboard bow, and when abeam of him turned toward the convoy picking Nos. 2 and 3 ships as our targets for the bow tubes. These were two large AKs, while the target for the stern tubes, the No. 4 ship, was a large AO. All torpedoes set for 6 feet.

2044 - Attack No. 1. Commenced firing the six bow tubes at Nos. 2 and 3 targets, which were overlapping.

2046 - First of five hits from the bow tubes, three on No. 2 target and two on No. 3 target. Two hits had been obtained before the stern tubes were fired.

2046 - Attack No. 2. Commenced firing the four stern tubes.

2048 - Observed two hits in the No. 4 target, which set him afire amidships. The Nos. 2 and 3 targets could no longer be seen and radar further reported that they sank right after firing the stern tubes. We now opened the range to trail astern of the convoy. The ships were grouped so close together that it was surprising that more of them weren't hit.

2135 - The burning ship damaged in Attack No. 2 had now dropped astern of the convoy, so while the *Segundo* made her approach (to the convoy) the *Trepang* closed this ship to finish her off. One escort was patrolling astern; his speed was two knots.

2145 - Observed four or more explosions in main part of convoy. This was *Segundo* attacking. A series of explosions took place on the No. 4 target that we were closing, range 4,000 yards. The No. 4 target sank without the expenditure of additional torpedoes.

2152 - Commenced approach on single ship that had broken off from convoy and was to the north of the *Segundo's* attack position. Another ship was seen to be heading south from this position. The seas had now increased to condition No. 5, and with our making nineteen knots to close this ship, we had a very wet bridge. The officer of the deck said that it was the fastest he'd ever gone submerged, and further stated that the diving officer had broached us a couple of times.

From the deposition of the remaining ships it was clear to the *Segundo* and the *Trepang* as to which ship each should go after. Therefore it was not necessary for me to designate the targets. We both got our respective ships at about the same time.

2241 - Attack No. 3. Commenced firing tubes Nos. 3, 4, 5, and 6 set at seven feet with torpedoes spread 50 yards between torpedoes. There were no hits. All torpedoes were heard to explode at end of run.

The target now steadied on course 050 degrees T., making 6.5 knots. We were ready for our second attack from a position on the target's starboard bow, using our four stern tubes.

2300 - Attack No. 4. Commenced firing the four stern tubes with torpedoes set at 10 feet.

2301 - First of three hits distributed over length of the target was observed from the bridge. The target took a slight list to starboard, but did not look to be in particular difficulty although smoke was rolling out of her forward and after holds. With the target now so close to a haven of safety and with the moon making it brighter every minute, decided that further torpedo fire was required to assure sinking this valuable target.

2326 - Attack No. 5. Presenting a very small angle on the bow, approached the target on the surface to within 1,000 yards and commenced firing tubes Nos. 1, 2, 3, and 4.

2327 - Observed the first of two good hits, one in the middle and one in the well deck aft. The latter hit set the after part of the vessel on fire. There were many internal explosions in this ship and finally at 2332 it began to sink stern first. Following an explosion in the bow, Target sank in almost vertical position.

2336 - Observed explosion bearing 185 degrees T., which was in the direction of the *Segundo*'s last target and now possibly the target the *Razorback* was making an approach on.

2337 - Started to close the position where our last target sank to attempt rescue of survivors. The state of the sea was not encouraging, but as there still were no escorts in the vicinity and no planes, decided it was worth the try.

2348 - Backed emergency to avoid ramming a large amount of wreckage and debris in the water. Heard many yells from ahead and to port and starboard from people in the water. It was a weird yell in a high voice and sounded like, 'Ooyee!' 'Ooyee!' We asked if they wanted to be picked up, and a great many came back with, 'Yes! Yes!' Although there was not much oil on the water, it was next to impossible to see anyone in the water. We saw a few human shapes on logs big enough to hold a person, but these were all twenty or thirty yards from the side of the ship. We called to them to swim to the ship, but we couldn't detect any movement in our direction. Although there were plenty of voices in the beginning, now there were none. It was so rough that these survivors couldn't live in the water for long, and it was my opinion that drowning kept most of them from calling or swimming to the ship. We had to keep our rescue squad on the cigarette deck, for it wasn't safe to go to the main deck.

0000, December 7 - Maneuvered into another position among a lot of wreckage. One of our men saw a man with a white jacket clinging to a board ten yards off the lee side. He threw him a life ring with an attached line. The ring dropped right alongside the man. He placed one arm inside the ring and with the other still held to the board. We pulled him over to the side of the ship and told him to hold on tight to the life ring. Although he probably didn't understand us, common sense should have told him to hold tightly to the life ring. He was still holding on to the board as we pulled him up on the side of the ship. With him practically aboard, he lost his grip on the ring and fell back into the water. He may have done this intentionally when he realized he was going aboard a submarine! He then drifted away from us to a point where we couldn't see him. We tried to get him to yell so as to locate him, but he never did utter a word, not even when he was hauled part way aboard. We couldn't risk using any kind of a light in our rescue operations.

0029 - Sighted ship burning to the south.

0040 - Having spent over an hour trying to pick up survivors, decided that any further attempt was futile.

0043 - Secured from battle stations and radar tracking party, and set course to close the burning ship. Observed first of a series of many explosions from the burning ship that lasted over the next few hours.

0135 - Exchanged recognition signals with the *Segundo* and asked if she had attacked ship that was burning to the south. The *Segundo* reported that she had stopped it, but that the *Razorback* had then set him on fire. The *Segundo* reported two sunk, one damaged. With our four, this accounted for the entire convoy.

It was truly a beautiful three hours of action with ships blowing up simultaneously all around the horizon. To have had the pleasure of seeing this entire convoy destroyed was something we'd always hoped to see. The three escorts couldn't be called friendly, but on the other hand, they weren't unfriendly. Although there were many explosions, none were identified as depth charges.

All five of the *Trepang's* attacks were made on the surface, and it is believed that the Segundo made all surface approaches. The *Razorback's* approach was made at radar depth; however she was on surface shortly after firing. We all seemed to escape repercussions from the enemy.

0454 - Submerged. Too rough for periscope patrol; made infrequent observations to check the weather. Rolled 10 - 15 degrees at 100 feet. After obtaining reports from the *Segundo* and *Razorback*, there was insufficient time to make our report of the attack to ComSubPac prior to daylight.

1755 - Surfaced.

1815 - Commenced sending the *Trepang's* first (report) to ComSubPac, reporting results of attack. With only two torpedoes remaining forward, I considered it advisable to clear the area and permit another boat to enter with a full load, therefore permission was requested to return to Pearl Harbor for refit.

1935 - Received ComSubPac's serial 62 ordering the *Trepang* to return to Pearl Harbor for refit via circuitous route. With the *Razorback* ordered to Saipan for a reload and the *Segundo* ordered to continue schedule operating independently. I was relieved of my duties as Commander Task Group 17.15. Departed area and set course for Pearl Harbor at two-engine speed. Seas extremely rough.

0700, December 22 - Rendezvoused with escort and set course for Pearl Harbor.

1100 - Moored at submarine base, Pearl Harbor, T.H., with a broom at the mast indicating a "clean sweep."

The following is a list of the five ships the *Trepang* sank, together with the record of the *Razorback* and the *Segundo*:

12/6/44 1-(IJN) Jinyo Maru (cargo)	6,862 tons sunk
12/6/44 1-(IJN) Fukuyo Maru (cargo)	5,462 tons sunk
12/6/44 1-(IJN) Banshu Maru No.31 (cargo)	748 tons sunk
12/6/44 1-Large AO (EU)	10,000 tons sunk
12/6/44 1-Large AP (EU)	10,000 tons sunk
Total 5 ships*	33,073 tons sunk

*Following the war the *Trepang* was credited with a fifth enemy ship sinking during operations on 12/6/44. This was due to a review and correlation of data contained in the two most reliable sources of Japanese ships sunk by U.S. submarines during World War II, namely: "The Master List of War Patrol Successes Prepared by ComSubPac during the World War II Era" and "Japanese Ship Losses in the Imperial Japanese Navy (IJN) in World War II."

RAZORBACK

12/5/44 1-DD (EU) Probable	1,500 tons sunk
12/6/44 1-Large AO (EU)	10,000 tons sunk
Total 2 ships	

SEGUNDO

12/6/44 1-Large AK (EU)	7,500 tons sunk
12/6/44 1-Large AE (EU)	7,500 tons sunk
Total 2 ships	

AFTER BEING DETACHED from command of the *Trepang* in December 1944, Captain Davenport returned to the United States, where on 8 February 1945 he reported for duty on the staff of the U.S. Naval Academy. Following his tour at the Academy, Captain Davenport attended programs at the Naval War College; was assigned as assistant operations officer for the submarine group at Pearl Harbor; assumed command of Submarine Division 52; was assistant operations officer for amphibious operations on the staff of the commander of Naval Forces Far East; and was involved in the planning of troop operations for the Inchon and Wonson invasions during the Korean War. He served on the staff of the Western Sea Frontier and was assistant inspector general for the Western Sea Frontier director. He commanded the USS *Uvalde* (AKA-88) from December 1953 to 1955, and served as planning officer of the staff of the 12th Naval District.

Captain Davenport retired from the U.S. Navy in November 1959 as a rear admiral. He passed away on 24 December 1986 at the age of 77.[5]

It is doubtful that any U.S. naval officer in the future will be awarded five Navy Crosses. He was the first to receive the awards in a fiercely fought global war. He will be remembered as the first and last to be so honored for his "extraordinary heroism."

ENDNOTES

1. Roy M. Davenport, *Clean Sweep* (New York: Vantage Press, 1986), 6–7.
2. Capt. Roy Milton Davenport, USN. U.S. Navy Official Biography, 1963. (Operational Archives, Naval Historical Center, Washington, D.C.)
3. *U.S. Naval Academy Lucky Bag* 1933 (Rochester, N.Y.: The DuBois Press), 251.
4. Davenport, *Clean Sweep*, 14–188.
5. "Last Call," *Shipmate Magazine*, March 1987, p. 105.

Lt. Joseph P. Kennedy Jr., USNR

One Mile East of Blydhburgh, Suffolk, England
12 August 1944

For extraordinary heroism and courage in aerial flight as pilot of a United States Navy *Liberator* bomber on 12 August 1944. Well knowing the extreme dangers involved and totally unconcerned for his own safety, Lieutenant Kennedy unhesitatingly volunteered to conduct an exceptionally hazardous and special operational mission. Intrepid and daring in his tactics and with unwavering confidence in the vital importance of his task, he willingly risked his life in the supreme measure of service and, by his great personal valor and fortitude in carrying out a perilous undertaking, sustained and enhanced the finest traditions of the United States Naval Service.[1]

Navy Cross citation for Lt. Joseph P. Kennedy Jr., USNR

OFTEN CALLED "THE FORGOTTEN KENNEDY," Joseph P. Kennedy Jr. aspired to be the first Catholic president of the United States. Born on 28 July 1915 in Nantasket, Massachusetts, Joe was the oldest of the nine children of the Hon. Joseph P. Kennedy Sr. The elder Kennedy served as ambassador to England prior to World War II, but his admiration for the National Socialists in Germany and his support of isolationism came into conflict with the Roosevelt administration, and he resigned his post. Joe visited Germany in the late 1930s with his younger brother Jack (the future American president), but they differed in their perception of Nazi Germany, with Joe taking his father's position. As the German war machine caught fire in Europe, Joe realized that America in its effort to support England would eventually join in the conflict. Congress passed the first peacetime conscription bill, and three weeks after entering Harvard Law School Joe registered for the draft, hoping that he could finish law school before being drafted. When his number came up, he signed up for the Naval Aviation Cadet Program in May 1940. He passed the preliminary physical and psychological tests, and was granted a delay until his semester was over. On 24 June he was sworn in as a seaman second class, U.S. Naval Reserve.

Joe reported to the Squantum Naval Air Facility near Boston, one of the Navy's "elimination bases" where candidates for aviation training are weeded out. The V-5 Pre-Flight Program had recently been turned over to professional and college athletes and coaches for the physical training. Ground school for potential naval aviators had

Lt. Joseph P. Kennedy Jr., USNR, often called "the forgotten Kennedy," was the oldest son of nine children of the Hon. Joseph P. Kennedy Sr., ambassador to England, and brother of President John F. Kennedy. (National Archives)

always been more difficult than the other services. Flight training for Navy pilots was longer, since all cadets had to qualify aboard aircraft carriers during their primary training, then learn airborne navigation. Also unlike the Army, the Navy's candidates had to have a college degree. With "jocks" running the program, they were also expected to be exceptional athletes. Cadets underwent commando training that included push ups, rope climbing, exhaustive daily swimming, boxing, and endless marches. They had to march double time when going to class and adhere to strict military discipline.[2]

This was all rather easy for Joe, because he had been participating in sports since he was a youngster, having spent many sunny afternoons at the Kennedy Hyannisport compound playing touch football and other games with his brothers and sisters. While at Harvard he played rugby, was a member of the varsity football squad, and won his Harvard "H" for sailing—not exactly the football "H" he had hoped for, but it was much to his father's delight because he too had lettered while at Harvard. Joe graduated cum laude in 1938.

Being the oldest child in the family, he felt that much more was expected of him in every endeavor he undertook. Early on, the competitiveness between him and his younger brother Jack emerged and remained with Joe for his entire life. They both admired each other and their accomplishments, but there was always that "edge."[3]

After completing pre-flight training, Joe was ordered to the Naval Air Station at Jacksonville, Florida, and entered primary flight training. While many of his friends wanted to become fighter pilots, Joe chose bombers; he liked the feel of large aircraft and the camaraderie of a crew. But it would take him many months to win his wings of gold and join the fleet. At the same time that Joe was sworn in as an aviation cadet, Jack, who had graduated from Harvard magna cum laude, passed his Navy physical and was commissioned an ensign. In his quest to remain first in family honors, Joe was not pleased when his brother suddenly outranked him.

After six more weeks of ground training Joe finally began his flight training in a biwing open cockpit Stearman aircraft, commonly known as the "Yellow Peril." After soloing in the Stearman, he graduated to a "real airplane," the SNJ Texan, a low-winged aircraft with retractable landing gear. Upon completion of his primary training, Joe entered advanced training, where he flew PBY Catalina twin-engine seaplanes off the St. Johns River. Although he had been considered an average student in primary flight, his instructors noted a definite improvement in his flying skills once he was at the controls of the Catalina. Eventually he mastered the aircraft, passing all his test rides with noticeable self-confidence and apparent enjoyment. He graduated from flight training after logging 192 hours in the air. His father was invited to address the graduates of his class and to pin on Joe's wings of gold.[4]

Joe received his operational training on the PBM Mariner (twin-engine seaplane) at Banana River, Florida. He was considered to be an exceptional PBM pilot, one who took the time to learn the complete mechanics of the aircraft. He was designated as an instructor pilot, and after six months was ordered to his first operational squadron, VP-203 (Mariner squadron) stationed in San Juan, Puerto Rico. About this same time brother Jack (now a lieutenant junior grade) had left his Washington desk job and joined a torpedo-boat squadron headed for Tulagi in the Pacific.

Joe made patrol plane commander (left-seat pilot) as an ensign, which was rare at the time. There were complaints about his impatience and a tendency to display arrogance. Because of his New England accent and known wealth, there were some who took an immediate dislike to him. Joe was a perfectionist, and he expected the same of his crew, which often caused strained relations. But Joe found many friends in the Navy and met many old acquaintances who visited Puerto Rico. After almost a year of hunting for German U-boats without success in the South Atlantic, Joe's squadron was ordered to Norfolk in 1943. Six more months of patrol flying out of Norfolk provided only one sub sighting, and Joe wanted to go where the action was. Jack had already seen action against the Japanese. Joe hoped that he would be ordered to England, where antisubmarine warfare raged in the Bay of Biscay.

German U-boats departing from their concrete pens along the French coast first had to navigate the Bay of Biscay to reach the Atlantic to stalk and sink allied shipping. The RAF Coastal Command was tasked with stopping the U-boats, but there were so few available aircraft, and the patrols were so infrequent, that a great many U-boats reached the Atlantic unscathed. The U.S. Army attempted to help, but its pilots were not trained in antisubmarine warfare operations. Furthermore, the Army needed its aircraft for bombing missions over Europe and wanted out of the antisubmarine business. The Navy attempted to improve the situation by assisting the Coastal Command using PBY Catalina flying boats to patrol the Bay, but the reliable but limited ninety-knot aircraft were unsuccessful in their effort. At the time, U-boats often stayed on the surface during their transits and fought it out with attacking Allied bombers, sometimes successfully. The Navy eventually added B-24 aircraft to its inventory to relieve the Army and get into the fray, which was rightfully a Navy mission. It was decided that the first contingent of pilots would come from Joe's squadron, VP-203. The new squadron that would assume antisubmarine duties in Europe would be VB-110 with PB4Y-1 Liberator bombers.[5]

Joe was selected to the new VB-110, and he quickly checked out in the four-engine bomber. Under a tight schedule, he began to ferry new aircraft from San Diego to the East Coast to fill out VB-110's complement of aircraft. About this time, brother Jack became a national hero when he rescued his PT boat crew after it was sunk by a Japanese destroyer in the Blackett Strait. He was subsequently awarded the Navy and Marine Corps medal. Although they were both lieutenants, Jack was now a combat veteran and a war hero. This inspired Joe to get into the action as soon as possible and perhaps match his brother's achievements. His eagerness was not lost on his squadron mates.

VB-110 deployed to England in September 1943 and was based at Dunkeswell in Devon. The pilots soon found out that flying antisubmarine patrols over the Bay of Biscay could be dangerous. German fighter aircraft flew from Luftwaffe airfields located on the Brittany Peninsula, which projected across the flight path of VB-110 aircraft on their antisubmarine patrols. Since the Liberators flew their patrols alone and unescorted, their best evasive tactic when jumped by enemy aircraft was to seek cloud cover. As the patrols continued through 1943 and into 1944, the squadron lost a number of planes and crews to enemy fighters. During the war VB-110 pilots and crews won two Navy Crosses, four Distinguished Flying Crosses, twenty-seven Air Medals, and two Purple Hearts. Two bombers were lost to enemy fighter aircraft, and ten lost to weather and mechanical failure. Sixty-eight men were killed in action.

Assigned to Bombing Squadron VB-110 based in England, Lt. Joe Kennedy flew numerous anti-submarine patrols over the Bay of Biscay. Pictured here is a VB-110 PB4Y-1 Liberator on patrol. (National Archives)

Joe's tour ended after his thirty-fifth patrol. He had not sunk a U-boat, shot down an enemy aircraft, or engaged in an encounter that would reward him with a personal decoration. He volunteered for a second tour and was involved in crucial D-day operations.[6]

To prevent German U-boats from entering the English Channel during the D-day invasion, U.S. and Royal Naval planners instituted Operation CORK. Under it, Allied antisubmarine bombers would fly tight patrols between Plymouth and Brest to prevent the U-boats from entering the channel from their French bases. The operation was a success; not a single U-boat made it into the Channel during the month of June, though many tried.

A week after D-day, England was hit by the first German V-1 "buzz bomb." Hundreds more followed, many falling on London. On the final patrol of his second tour (he would have a total of fifty missions for the two tours), Joe flew close to the island of Guernsey off Brest and was driven off by antiaircraft fire. Back at Dunkeswell, he packed his gear and prepared to depart. Though at times he threw caution to the wind in an attempt to strike the enemy a blow that would win him a decoration, it was not to be. Disappointed, he would go home without the medals he sought. But as fate would have it, Joe would fly one more wartime mission, highly secretive and extremely dangerous.

In 1939 British intelligence had received an anonymous letter stating that the Germans were developing gyro-stabilized rockets that would be used against England in great numbers. Subsequent interpretation of photographs collected by British reconnaissance aircraft flying over Peenemunde, on the German coast, depicted a small T-shaped object on what looked like a ramp. Greater magnification brought into focus a small airplane with no cockpit and short wings. Further reconnaissance flights over the Pas de Calais and Cherbourg areas displayed images of huge concrete bunkers with tracks leading to what appeared to be launch pads. The Pas de Calais site tracks were aimed directly at London, the Cherbourg pads at Bristol. A number of additional new camouflaged sites were identified along the French coast. The potential threat of these sites caused great concern among Allied commanders, and a massive bombardment of these areas began. Dubbed Operation CROSSBOW by Churchill, air operations aimed at eliminating these installations began in 1943. On 15 December over 1,000 Allied bombers dropped 1,700 bombs on 23 sites. Assessment of these sites revealed that little damage had been achieved. In the months preceding D-day, hundreds of flight hours were spent photographing the occupied coastal areas adjacent to England. In fact, large mosaics of areas of interest were created and updated almost daily. A year before the first V-1 rocket was launched against England, six hundred RAF bombers blasted Peenemunde and killed several hundred Germans, including both military and rocket-specialist personnel. The attacks slowed down the development of the new V-2 rocket program, but the V-1 "buzz bomb" became operational. The Germans had planned to launch their first V-1 flying bombs on the morning of the Allied invasion. They missed their launch date, however, by several days.[7]

Meanwhile, in the United States the German bunker sites had been replicated, and every army aircraft and bomb was tested against them. Out of the tests came the recommendation that damage could be inflicted only by low-flying attack aircraft. Following that recommendation, Army pilots flew P-47s at low altitudes and attacked the sites around Calais. Although all the aircraft returned safely to their base, German antiaircraft fire had been intense, and pilot survival became a factor.

To counter the V-1 blitz, Gen. Dwight D. Eisenhower, Supreme Allied Commander of the Allied Expeditionary Force, reasoned that Marine or Navy dive bombers such as the Douglas Dauntless might prove effective against the German bunkers. But these aircraft lacked the needed explosive power, so forty veteran B-17 bombers were gutted and equipped with basic remote-control radio equipment and flown to Winfarthing-Fersfield Airdrome near Anglia. The aircraft were to be loaded with explosives and flown by a crew of two, a pilot and technician. Once the plane was under control of a mother ship, the crew would bail out, and the bomber would be directed to strike a V-1 launch site. The drone operation was called APHRODITE.

Gen. James Doolittle, commander of the 8th Air Force, had learned of the Navy's use of drone torpedo bombers (TBMs) loaded with explosives against the Japanese during the invasion of Truk in the Pacific. The Navy could perhaps provide added expertise in the APHRODITE venture, and he contacted Adm. Ernest J. King, Chief of Naval Operations in Washington.

In early July 1944 a secretive group of radio-control experts were stationed at the Naval Air Station in Traverse City, Michigan. Two pilots, Cdr. James A. Smith and Lt. Wilford Willy, were briefed on APHRODITE and ordered to select pilots experienced in controlling drones, and accompanying crewmen, for two twin-engine Lockheed PV-1 Ventura mother ships (VK12 and VK13) that were equipped with radio-control electronic equipment, a radarscope, and a television screen. Smith and Wilford were also to transport pilot replacements, technicians, gunners, and radiomen to England for the secret operation. The drones to be used were Navy PB4Y-1 Liberators fresh off the assembly line in San Diego. The first of these aircraft, with the plane's designator T-11 painted on both sides of its forward fuselage, was flown to the Naval Materiel Center in Philadelphia and fitted out with a specially designed fail-safe arming panel, a remote control system, a radio receiver, and a television camera in its nose to permit the mother ships to guide it to its target. A television screen in the mother ship would allow the guiding crew to watch the approach to the target as if they were in the drone itself. The functions of controlling the drone and arming its explosives would be initiated by means of radio signals sent from the mother ship.

Joe Kennedy was selected to fly T-11 on its perilous mission.

Smith, Willy, and an armament engineer flew to Dunkeswell, arriving as a ferry pilot landed T-11 at the field. In the meantime Joe and a skeleton crew were transferred to Special Attack Unit One (SAU-1), destined to be stationed with the Army Air Corps APHRODITE team at Winfarthing-Fersfield Airdrome. The code name assigned to the Navy segment of operation of APHRODITE was Project ANVIL. Anvil initially consisted of three aircraft—two Venturas and one PB4Y-1 drone.

By the end of July 1944, T-11 was ready for a test flight. Instead of flying a short prescribed test hop, Joe, anxious to join the Navy unit at Fersfield, completed the test phase while flying T-11 to Fersfield. As he approached the airfield, he was impressed with the enormity of the base. While he taxied to his spot on the line, he noticed the intense activity of hundreds of personnel around him. Twenty naval officers, sixteen enlisted men, two Venturas, and his PB4Y-1 were dwarfed in a base housing forty APHRODITE B-17 bombers, their Liberator mother ships, and crewmen. On base there were a thousand Air Corps personnel and another thousand or so RAF, Czech, Pole, and Free French military men.

On 2 August Joe flew T-11 on its first test flight, carrying fifteen thousand pounds of sandbags to ensure the aircraft could handle the added weight. Though sluggish on take-off, the aircraft flew satisfactorily with the added weight. Subsequent flights were made under radio control of the Ventura mother ships to accustom Joe to the robot-like movements of the aircraft while being flown by the pilots in the other aircraft.

Two days later Joe noticed a quickened pace on the base. Air Corps brass and an array of personnel were massed around a parked B-17. Four of the APHRODITE aircraft had been loaded with explosives during the night. Joe's hope that the Navy would be the first to attempt the mission faded as the veteran Fortresses rumbled down the runway. They were followed by B-24 mother ships and P-38 fighters to provide cover for the mission.

The B-17s were nicknamed Snowbirds because their upper wings and fuselage were painted white so their controller aircraft could clearly spot the bombers. Manned by a pilot and technicians, the Snowbirds and their ten tons of RDX explosives headed for launch sites near Calais. All four aircraft failed to reach their targets. One exploded off the coast of France, one crashed shortly after the pilot bailed out, and two others were shot down by enemy aircraft. One pilot was killed, and another broke his back as he hit the ground after bailing out over England. The fifth and sixth Snowbirds were launched the following evening against a V-weapon site a mile and one-quarter from the village of Watten. One pilot lost an arm after it became mangled as he left his aircraft; the mother plane flew his bomber into the Channel, unable to control it. The other plane exploded after its pilot successfully bailed out.

Finally, Joe and Willy were given the nod to fly their mission with T-11. It was loaded with twelve tons of Torpex (twice as lethal as an equal amount of TNT). The aircraft was so crammed with boxes of explosives that Willy had to stand behind and to the right of Joe during the mission because his copilot's seat had been removed to allow more space for explosives. It was decided that the two would stay with T-11 for an extended flight pattern. They would fly southeast to Framlingham for twenty-three minutes, northeast to Beccles for twenty minutes, and then turn south towards Dover and the Channel. After they flew over Manston field, about ten miles north of Dover and the Channel, Joe and Willy were to bail out through the nose wheel well. Their target was the V-1 site closest to England, Mimoyecques. President Roosevelt's second son, Elliot, would fly wing on them in one of two British Mosquito photo reconnaissance planes, together with two B-17 bombers (one to scout the target area, the other to guide the group of aircraft through Anglian airspace to the bailout point and to recover Joe and Willy), two P-38 Lightnings (one carrying the base commander), and four P-51 Mustangs to provide fighter cover.

In one of the mother ships, control pilot John Demlein wondered if they would be able to find the target on their television screens because the bunker was nestled among farm houses and hilly terrain. To make spotting even more difficult, all of the villages in the area looked alike. After careful study of the target area, however, a huge concrete bunker was identified, complete with tracks directed toward London. The exact location of the target was later confirmed by a P-38 pilot who flew a reconnaissance flight over the area that same evening. All was ready to launch the first ANVIL mission. The T-11 engines roared to life, and most of the base personnel turned out to watch and cheer as the aircraft lumbered down a runway before lifting off.

Before taking off, Joe successfully tested the remote control system with the mother ships. Once in the air, he continued to test the system and everything functioned as expected. T-11 flew over Framlingham guided by control pilot Anderson, then was turned northward toward Beccles. Five minutes after turning north, T-11 edged off course, flying east of the planned flight track. Anderson put T-11 into a slow left turn. As the plane responded, it suddenly exploded. Two distinct blasts were heard by people on the ground below and were witnessed by the accompanying aircraft, some of which were damaged by flying debris. The explosion occurred in the area of Newdelight Covert, between Dunwich and Blythburgh, and the falling remains of the aircraft damaged 147 properties.

At the crash scene, wreckage was spread over an area of one square mile. American airmen of the 3rd Bombardment Division arrived in jeeps and began looking through the debris. Nothing was collected because all that remained of the bomber were small bits of metal. The largest piece of wreckage found was a piece of a torn bay door, which was picked up by a local inhabitant who took it to his home in Southwald. No one was able to find out what happened in the skies above them. Military personnel, sworn to secrecy, offered no information about the explosion. Later, the engines and a landing-gear actuating assembly were found scattered amid the countryside.

Subsequent informal and official investigations into the cause of the T-11 explosion revealed that a number of factors could have been responsible—radio static, a jamming signal, excessive vibration, overheating in the electrical circuitry of the arming panel, or an enemy radio signal that might have prematurely triggered the mishap. One plausible conjecture was that the most powerful jamming station in England went on the air just before the explosion, causing its pulses to affect the remote-control system or the arming mechanism in the aircraft. Eventually, nothing could be pinpointed as the cause of the incident, and the official finding recorded the cause as "unknown and undetermined." With hindsight, the whole mission took on an element of tragic irony, because the RAF's 617 Squadron of Lancaster had bombed Mimoyesques with 12,000-pound "Tall Boy" bombs a month earlier, scoring one direct hit and four very near misses. That information did not reach the U.S. 8th Air Force headquarters before the T-11 mission with Joe Kennedy.

An hour after the blast, the next of kin of both pilots were informed that Joe and Willy were missing and presumed dead. Both pilots were recommended for the Medal of Honor. Navy officials later downgraded the award to the Navy Cross. Both men were also awarded the Air Medal.

Before a second ANVIL mission could be planned and flown, all rocket sites along the French coast had been evacuated or occupied by Allied ground forces.

The Navy turned its ANVIL effort to attacking German U-boat pens without success. More Snowbird missions were flown against oil refineries and cities in northern Germany. All missed their targets. Seventeen army and two navy flying bombs had launched from Fersfield during the life of the secret operation. Nothing had been accomplished militarily. APHRODITE and ANVIL operations were subsequently terminated.[8]

Joseph P. Kennedy Sr. and Mrs. Kennedy receive their son's posthumous Navy Cross. (National Archives)

On 15 December 1945, the USS *Joseph P. Kennedy, Jr.* (DD-850), a 2,400-ton destroyer, was commissioned. Joe's brother Bobby served aboard the ship as a seaman in the ship's gunnery department. During the Korean War the ship joined Task Force 77, and from February through April 1951 it screened attack carriers as they pounded enemy positions and supply lines. The following month the *Kennedy* stood off Wonsan lending bombardment support during the Allied siege and occupation of the harbor islands. The ship received two battle stars for its Korean service. While on blockade duty during the Cuban missile crisis, the *Kennedy* stopped the Greek freighter SS *Marucla*, which was subsequently boarded and searched by a party from the destroyer. The *Kennedy* is now a museum in Battleship Cove, Fall River, Massachusetts.[9]

To honor their son, Ambassador and Mrs. Joseph P. Kennedy established the Joseph P. Kennedy Jr. Foundation in 1946. The mission of the Kennedy Foundation is to provide leadership in the field of mental retardation, for those born and unborn and their families. The foundation commemorates the deep love Joe had for his sister, Rosemary, who suffered from mental retardation.[10]

ENDNOTES

1. Official Biography of Lieutenant Joseph P. Kennedy Jr., United States Naval Reserve. Operational Archives, Naval Historical Center, Washington, D.C.
2. Hank Searls, *The Lost Prince: Young Joe, the Forgotten Kennedy* (New York: World Publishing, 1969), 114–79.
3. Ibid., 82–109.
4. Ibid., 179–89.
5. Official Biography of Lieutenant Joseph P. Kennedy Jr.
6. Searls, *The Lost Prince*, 190–201.
7. Ibid., 209–34.
8. Administrative Report of PB4Y-1 Airplane, Bureau No. 32271. Officer-in-Charge, Special Air Unit ONE, 14 August, 1944.
9. www.battleshipcove.com
10. www.jpkf.org

Lt. Cdr. Charles H. Hutchins Jr., USNR

Commanding Officer, USS *Borie* (DD-215)
31 October 1943

For extraordinary heroism as Commanding Officer of the USS *Borie* during action against two enemy submarines in the Atlantic on the night of 31 October 1943. While engaged in escort operations, Lieutenant Hutchins made sound contact with a hostile submarine and immediately maneuvered to attack with depth charges which forced the enemy vessel to surface and caused her subsequently to sink stern first. Contacting a second large submersible three hours later, the *Borie* again launched a fierce attack, her well placed depth charges bringing the enemy to the surface and her four-inch guns blazing as she forged full speed ahead, rammed her foe forward of the conning tower and held fast. In the ensuing battle, Lieutenant Hutchins' command waged a gallant fight at close quarters using every available weapon against a desperately determined enemy until the two vessels drifted apart. After more than one hour of continuous gunfire on both sides, the *Borie*, although unnavigable and badly holed the entire length of her port side, brought the submarine to a dead stop by exploding three depth charges almost directly under her and ending all resistance with the surrender and eventual sinking of the enemy vessel.[1]

Navy Cross citation for Lt. Cdr. Charles H. Hutchins Jr., USNR

IN LATE OCTOBER 1943, Task Group 21.14, consisting of the aircraft carrier *Card* (CVE-11) and the destroyers *Borie* (DD-215), *Barry* (DD-248), and *Gaff* (DD-247), received reports of a German U-boat fueling concentration in North Atlantic waters between the Azores Islands and Iceland. The task group was ordered to proceed immediately to the reported position. The *Borie* was an old "four stacker" launched in 1919 that had joined the U.S. Naval Detachment in Turkish waters for service in the Black Sea in the 1920s and subsequently operated for an extensive period in the Pacific. After patrol duty in the Caribbean, in June 1943 she became a member of an antisubmarine hunter-killer group centered around the *Card*. With the introduction of ASW task groups in the Atlantic, the tide of the Battle of the Atlantic turned, and the German hunter became the hunted. Since the beginning of 1943, forty U-boats had been sent to the bottom by Allied forces. To gain mastery of the Atlantic, the Allies were forced to use every escort combatant that was operational, which included the four stackers. The *Borie* was commanded by Lt. Charles

Lt. Charles H. Hutchins Jr. receiving the Navy Cross. (National Archives)

H. Hutchins Jr., U.S. Naval Reserve, was the youngest commanding officer of a destroyer in the U.S. Navy at the time.

The task group arrived at the reported area, and aircraft were launched from the carrier while the escorts searched for underwater contacts. On the afternoon of 30 October, one of the aviators spotted two U-boats, one being refueled by a "milch cow" (the term for large U-boat refuelers). One of the U-boats was sunk by an air-dropped acoustic homing torpedo (Fido) while the other submerged and successfully escaped the area. Thinking that the fleeing U-boat was the refueler, the task group commander ordered the *Borie* to search for it. (Not known at the time was that the milch cow, *U-584*, was the boat that had been sunk and the other, *U-91*, was an attack submarine.) During the early evening hours the *Borie* made sonar contact with a U-boat and dropped a depth-charge after losing contact at 150 yards. The destroyer was rattled by a heavy explosion, which caused the ship's sound gear to fail. After blown fuses were replaced, a second attack was made, but sound contact was lost. The crew detected the odor of oil, and though no evidence of destruction was found, it was assumed that the attack was successful. Hutchins sent the following message to the task group commander: "Scratch one pig boat."

Following the war, recovered U-boat logs revealed that the *Borie* had attacked the *U-256*, which was not sunk. Although badly damaged, *U-256* was able to return to its base in Brest, France. The *U-91* was long gone, and was subsequently sunk the following February by British escort destroyers.

USS *Borie* (DD-215) under way. (U.S. Naval Institute Photo Archives)

The *Borie* continued hunting, and it soon made another underwater contact, which led to a surface battle that is still regarded as one of the most astounding naval engagements of the war. That action, which occurred during the night hours of 1 November 1943, is best related by leading FC1 (and gun director) Robert A. Maher, USN, who was stationed immediately above the bridge, where he had a clear view of events throughout the battle. In numerous interviews with co-author Wise, Maher described the battle as follows.[2]

> We continued hunting and—bingo! "Radar contact, bearing 170, range 8,000 yards" was called out by our radarman. Captain Hutchins immediately ordered, "All ahead full, come left to course 170." Our helmsman responded. "Left to 170, sir." The sea was moderate, it was about 2:00 AM, and the ship's speed increased to twenty-seven knots. Everyone in the crew felt the excitement building. At about two thousand yards we lost radar contact, but again we heard the returning echoes.
>
> We got the order to release depth charges. Because of a malfunction, all the depth charges in the two racks rolled into the sea at once. The

resulting explosions lifted our stern and caused the ship to surge forward. But the job was done. Nothing could survive that, right? Wrong.

Looking back toward the marker flare, I was the first to see it: the conning tower of the *U-405*. I cried out, "There it is—about forty feet to the right of the flare."

We made radar contact and with that we turned on our 24-inch searchlight. Using radar bearings, we were able to keep the *U-405* illuminated for the one-hour battle to follow.

The conning tower appeared just off the port quarter, and we could see the image of a large, white polar bear. Only gun number four could bear on the target. As I remember it, we got the order to fire as we moved away to regain sound contact. When we turned and moved in at twenty-five knots, the range was more than a thousand yards. As leading fire-controlman, my battle station was director pointer. In director-controlled fire, the director (another crewman) aimed and fired all the main battery in unison with the pointer (me) pressing the firing key. As all guns came to bear, the order came: "Commence firing!"

I pressed the key, and three four-inch projectiles exploded as one in the vicinity of the *U-405*'s main deck gun, obliterating it before its crew could man it. Depending on the range, the main battery gun fire control switched from director control to local control throughout the battle. As the main battery continued, 20-mm guns opened up with devastating power, made even more spectacular by the one in five tracer bullets that made it possible to follow all the streams from the machine guns. Watching the results was both horrifying and fascinating. While the four-inch projectiles yielded terrific explosions, I really believe that the machine gun fire sweeping across the deck is what finally doomed the U-boat.

Apparently, the *U-405* could not submerge, as she tried to escape into the darkness, with men manning their machine guns. In the first few moments, our machine gun fire wiped them off the conning tower gun platform. For some reason men started to come out of the forward hatch, about five at a time, and make an impossible dash of about 30 feet to get to their guns. No one ever made it, as they were knocked over the side, arms and legs flailing. They kept trying however.

The speed and evasive tactics of the *U-405* were impressive, we tried to maintain a parallel course to keep all guns bearing on target. The sub's turning circle was smaller than ours, and I learned later that she could do seventeen-and-a-half knots on the surface. The *U-405* made good use of both features.

When I was not busy, I watched the sub as she tried to point her torpedo tubes in our direction or perhaps just to escape, as she twisted and turned first in one direction, then the other. Captain Hutchins managed to keep the guns bearing most of the time in spite of our larger turning circle.

At one time, I was sure that we were going to collide, not ram. I don't know if we attempted to ram this time, but I could see that we were on a collision, almost parallel course. I realized then the surface speed of the *U-405*. Just as we were about to collide, the U-boat appeared to turn on all her power, picking up enough speed to pass us. Looking down, I could see clearly the faces of the Germans still on the bridge.

We kept up a continuous fire with all guns that could bear, giving the *U-405* a monstrous hammering. Many of her men were dead, and damage was extensive, especially to the conning tower. I wondered how long they could endure this savage beating.

At one time, a number of pistol rounds appeared to come from the conning tower, which was a recognition signal unknown to any of us. It seemed also that the *U-405* either stopped or at least slowed, almost dead in the water. A man appeared on the bridge in the bright shining beam of our searchlight and started to wave his arms in a crossing movement. Fate again interceded. Shortly before this, a gun captain's telephone lines had become entangled in the empty shell casings that were rolling around the deck. Frustrated, he had torn off his phones and thrown them to the deck. Seeing the man on the deck of the *U-405* waving, Captain Hutchins commanded, "Cease fire!" But the galley deck house four-inch gun continued to fire. Hutchins than tried to shout directly across to the gun crew, and we on the firing bridge could plainly hear, "Cease fire! Cease fire!" Unfortunately, no gunners could hear above the noise on the galley deck house, and the big gun continued to boom out its deadly fire.

Watching this one man stand alone amidst all the destruction, with big guns firing, was awesome. It was not to last. Within moments his body stood there momentarily, arms extended over his head, then his head disappeared. It was a sight that gave me nightmares for months. Had the tangled phone lines caused this man's death? Had he been the bravest of the brave in volunteering to expose himself so that he could give a signal of surrender? We shall never know, for the *U-405* picked up speed again and started evasive maneuvers.

The battle continued much as before, with the U-boat attempting to get away, or train a torpedo tube at us, or both. Meanwhile, we were trying to close range either to ram or to drop depth charges.

"Stand by for a ram!" Our gunnery officer gave the order to me to relay to the rest of the gunnery division over the fire-control phone system. The last five minutes or so had been a frustrating but exciting period.

Because the range had closed to almost point blank, we were unable to use the gun director. For a short time we were only spectators.

I watched at first as if it were a game, the beautiful arching tracers of the 20-mm guns and the smashing four-inch projectiles hitting the sub or careening off the rounded hull into the darkness as a dull wobbly glow. I saw the German sailors being knocked over the side as they tried to man their machine guns. As one went over, another would take his place.

"Stand by for a ram!" suddenly brought me back to reality, as I passed the word on to the men at their battle stations. Instant chatter on the system from all stations stopped at once, as I anticipated more urgent orders.

Looking over the wind screen—only about three feet high—I could see our bow crashing up and down, rapidly closing on the U-boat still in our searchlight beam. I started to think that if we hit her at this speed I was going to sail right over the screen and on down to the forecastle. I got behind the range finder and placed my hands on it in front of me. Then I thought. "Hell no, this way I'll get my face smashed." I moved in front and put my arms over the range finder behind my back and prepared for the crash.

As we got closer and closer, with as many of our guns firing as we could bear on the target, I watched and waited for the inevitable sudden stop.

From my vantage point I could see everything. I could see the number one gun crew (bow gun) and wondered what they were thinking, as they would be closest to the sub when we collided, bow on, and most likely to be fired on just before ramming. I could see the Germans in the bright light still trying to muster some kind of defense, scurrying about in and near the conning tower. No one could deny their great courage.

Closer and closer we came, and I watched the sub get larger and larger. I held my breath, waiting for the crash. Almost at the moment of impact. The *U-405* made a sudden turn to the port side, trying to run parallel to our course and make us miss. The move was too late. We went at the U-boat at about a thirty-degree angle. I closed my eyes, held my breath, and prayed. Sneaking a peek with one eye, I saw our bow about to crash into the U-boat and the fear in the eyes of one German as he tried to get out of the way. Holding tighter, I waited . . . nothing. I looked up and saw that we were astride the sub with our bow just forward of her conning tower. Just before impact a large wave had caused us to rise above and over the U-boat's deck

For a moment there was a stunned lull in everyone's actions and thoughts. Then all hell broke loose on both sides. To our regret, the flying bridge had no small arms, so except for phone messages, we were only spectators. In fact from our vantage point directly below the large search-light and looking straight down on the conning tower encircled by the bright beam, it looked more like a Hollywood epic than an actual battle.

I could see the polar bear symbol clearly and also the machine guns they had been trying to keep manned. One quadruple mount and four single mounts all were firing sporadically.

One of our crewmen started in with his 20-mm mount, depressing it so that first he had to shoot away the wind screen before firing into the men on the deck of the U-boat. Although the action report of the battle says otherwise, my recollection was that no four-inch gun could be depressed far enough to bear, so all firing came from the 20-mm guns and small arms. Upon hearing the ram order, the small arms steel locker was broken open and weapons were passed out to the men on deck.

I saw one of our men open up and watched the first shots explode through the wind screen. One of our crew threw a four-inch shell casing into the group of men standing in the conning tower. From below the bridge, I saw a flash from a Very pistol and watched a bright ball of fire arc across into a man's chest. He went down and rolled over with his chest still burning.

An order was called from the bridge, "We will not board, we will not board!" I was then contacted by the fire controlman at the fire-control switchboard which was isolated by dogged down hatches, "What the hell is going on up there?" He didn't even know that we had rammed the U-boat.

I saw one German reach out with his hand as if he wanted help to board the *Borie*. No one offered to help. Small wonder, as they were still firing their machine guns.

Two gallant crews were engaged in fierce battle using every kind of weapon at their disposal. There was no sign of fear or disorder anywhere in the *Borie*. Everyone went about his duty with the utmost confidence. I felt great pride in being a member of the crew. I was to be even more proud by the time the action was over.

We on the flying bridge did not know it yet, but the *Borie* had sustained serious underwater damage to both engine rooms. In fact, the forward engine room was already flooded by the time we separated.

The U-boat made a mad dash into the night, with us firing whatever guns we could bring to bear. We saw a four-inch shell explode in the sub's starboard diesel exhaust, but it did not seem to slow the boat, as she took advantage of her smaller turning circle and opened her range to about five hundred yards. We fired one torpedo but missed because of one of her fast, tight turns.

The *U-405* continued circling in a turn that our ship could not match. The *Borie* movements were also hampered by the flooded engine room. We did, however, manage to maintain our murderous shelling, having killed between twenty and thirty of the sub's crew as they tried to man their deck guns.

Unable to close our range because of the U-boat's circling maneuvers, Captain Hutchins used a clever ruse. He ordered the searchlight turned off. Of course, the U-boat immediately tried to escape in the dark. We tracked her by radar until she reached a position to our advantage. With our entire starboard battery bearing on the fleeing boat, Captain Hutchins ordered, "On searchlight. Commence firing!" The *U-405* once again came under heavy damaging gunfire.

We started to close to ram again, but before we hit, the *U-405* turned into our starboard quarter. Seeing an advantage, Hutchins swung our ship hard to port, using both rudder and engines. The move brought us to a parallel course with the U-boat and within range of our depth charge projectors. Three charges were fired, one over and two short, a perfect straddle. All three exploded at thirty feet. We not only heard the explosions; since we were dead in the water, they almost knocked us over. What we felt was nothing compared to what it must have been like in the U-boat. The boat appeared to lift out of the water and almost stopped, thus ending what appeared to be an attempt to ram us. But to our surprise, the Germans came on again, heading directly into our heavy gunfire. They just would not give up.

Again they turned toward our stern and apparently tried to get away. But their speed just was not good enough. They were on our starboard side, heading aft of us. To close on them again, we started to circle around to our port side, so at first the range opened up. At about seven hundred yards Hutchins ordered, "Stand by to fire torpedoes!" At just about firing time, a full salvo of the main battery let go with the usual jolt throughout the ship, causing the engine room hatch to jump open. The open hatch stopped the tracking of the tube just before we heard the whoosh of the fish leaving its tube. All of us on the bridge could see the shallow torpedo charge through the water on its deadly mission, and we watched in fascination as another tableau emerged. This time fate was on the side of the *U-405*. The torpedo slithered by her bow, missing by about ten feet.

In the meantime, we were still firing all guns. Shortly after the torpedo miss, we again hit the sub's starboard diesel exhaust, which finally brought her to a standstill. Out of the conning tower came a shower of

Very stars, splashing the night with white, red, and green lights, indicating that the Germans were at last ready to surrender. This time we all heeded Captain Hutchins' order to cease fire, and the night was silent after more than an hour of mayhem.

One or two U-boat crewmen appeared and started to throw yellow two-man, rubber life rafts into the water. They were tied together and gave the appearance of a string of very large hot dogs. The *U-405* was settling fast by the stern. What was left of the crew, about twenty, managed to get off and over to the rafts just before she went down. An underwater explosion rumbled soon after.

The German survivors in their rafts continued to fire as we moved slowly toward them, still illuminating them with our searchlight. We thought they were signaling another sub, as a white star shone in the distance.

With the survivors just off our port bow—so close we could see their faces—our sound man reported suddenly, "Torpedoes, bearing 220." Captain Hutchins ordered, "Hard to port, heading 220, all available speed." Unfortunately, this heading caused us to cut through the group of survivors. I vividly remember seeing the face of one young boy straight below me. His eyes were wide and his mouth open in a silent scream, as he extended both arms, hoping we would pick him up. It was not to be, however, as someone reported seeing the torpedo traveling along our port side.

We had been without sleep for twenty-one hours, but our ordeal was not even close to being over. We left the battle area making ten knots at best and turned in evasive zigzags to get away from a possible sub attack while we assessed our damage, which was considerable.

Only then did we on deck learn about the courage and ingenuity of the men who had been struggling below during the battle. When we rammed the *U-405* we did not realize the havoc being wreaked below. A large hole in the forward engine room started to flood immediately. While the guns boomed above, the men below, in water up to their necks, had to maintain the ship's speed as they tried to repair the damage. The men in the after engine room also did an outstanding job in operating their plant while they repaired two holes in the ship's hull. At the same time other men in the damage control party, with their backs to the hot boilers, shored up the bulkhead between the forward and after engine rooms, which were in danger of collapse as the forward engine room flooded rapidly.

No sleep was in store for our tired crew; we tried to make our way back to the *Card* carrier group on a course of 000 degrees true and a speed of ten knots. We radioed this information to the *Card* at 4:52 AM, still not knowing the severity of the damage. With the forward engine room completely flooded, we had lost all but emergency radio power, which we used to send our message to the *Card*. This, too, did not last very long. The loss of all electrical power would make it extremely difficult to run the ship and make repairs. We could not recover feed water for the boilers, so we began to relate to each other that we might be in a lot of trouble.

At dawn, we found ourselves in a lot of trouble. Emergency radio power was gone, a heavy fog was hemming us in, and we were taking on water rapidly. We had to use all available gasoline to keep the pumps running so we could try to stay ahead of the incoming water; none was available for our radio generator.

To help keep the ship afloat, Hutchins gave the order to lighten ship. All hands turned to. Bucket brigades worked at a furious pace. Specific pieces of equipment were ordered jettisoned. We dumped our boats. Saving ten rounds per gun, the gunner's mates threw over all the rest of the four-inch shells. They also threw several machine guns overboard. The torpedo men dumped their torpedo mounts—quite a feat. The boatswain department let go all our anchor chain, which went to the bottom with a long, rattling roar.

Captain Hutchins called me to the bridge and gave me the order, "I want you to dump the gun director over the side, and I don't want it to come down on my bridge." I really had no idea what the gun director weighed, but considering its size and the fact that the base was made of bronze, a fair estimate would be between one and two thousand pounds. The navigational bridge, below, extended about five feet out on both sides of the flying bridge. I could see no way to swing it out from above. In spite of serious doubts, I replied, "Aye, aye sir."

I cannot remember who helped us, but the fire control director and I could not handle the task alone. I disconnected all the wires coming out of the base into the junction box on the bridge overhead. We then started to lift the director with pry bars, inserting wedges wherever possible. Gradually, the director started to lean to starboard until finally it was almost balanced on edge. For once the large waves were an advantage. As we rolled to starboard, we all pushed; it dropped neatly into the sea—without coming close to Hutchins' bridge.

By mid-morning, still in fog, our headway dropping slowly but steadily because we were using seawater in our boilers, abandoning ship became a distinct possibility. Hutchins ordered the chief torpedoman to drop depth charges off the stern racks. I remembered once meeting a sailor who had abandoned a destroyer going down, only to be injured seriously when the depth charges exploded.

Two charges were dropped. They exploded at a shallow depth, lifting our stern and shoving us forward. Our already stricken ship rattled and groaned. Hutchins roared, "Set them on safe." We felt the concussion and surged forward again. Hutchins screamed, "God damn it, I said set them on safe!" The chief yelled back, "God damn it, they *are* on safe!" As I remember, they had to remove the detonators to keep them from exploding.

At least once we thought we heard the sound of an aircraft above the fog. It well could have been, because at 8:50 AM the *Card* had catapulted four aircraft on antisubmarine patrol with orders to be on the lookout for the *Borie*. They could not see the *Borie* or anything else. So at 9:50 AM the aircraft still in the air were directed to look for DD-215. Because of the bad weather all airplanes were back on board the carrier by 10:00 AM with negative results.

By that time we were practically stopped and for the most part standing around, wondering when and if we would be found or whether another sub might get us first. Sometime before 11:00 AM one of our officers thought of collecting all the lighter fluid, kerosene, and alcohol on board the ship and using the whole mess to run the emergency radio generator. It worked!

At 11:10 AM the *Card* received our message, "Commenced sinking." The high-frequency radio direction finders picked up our signal, and two Avenger aircraft set out to search the area along our bearing. Despite the limited visibility, they found us fourteen miles away from the *Card* at 11:30 AM.

Upon receiving the report of our sighting, the *Card* group changed course to our bearing and sped toward us at eighteen knots. By the time they arrived, we were wallowing in the troughs of huge waves. We were happy to see our fellow warrior, the USS *Goff* (DD-247), coming close at about noon. At last we were no longer alone in sub-infested waters. We were dead in the water, and the *Card* was moving slowly with only one escort, the USS *Barry* (DD-248). At 4:30 PM, with the weather getting worse and darkness setting in, Hutchins had no choice but to abandon ship—even though we appeared not to be in danger of immediate sinking. With the bulkheads bulging and the waves getting larger (running about twenty feet or greater), the danger of capsizing was always there. We immediately began to abandon ship per the captain's orders and since we had thrown away our boats trying to save the ship, we climbed down lines on the port side, and swam to life rafts that had been cast over the side. Some made it into the rafts while others hung to the sides.

Bemedaled officers of Task Unit 21.14 examine the *Borie*'s newly won Presidential Unit Citation pennant. Left to right: Lt. Cdr. Herbert D. Hill, USNR, commanding officer (CO) of the USS *Barry;* Lt. Howard M. Avery, USN, CO of VC-9 (composite air squadron); Lt. Charles H. Hutchins Jr., USNR, CO of the *Borie;* and Lt. Cdr. Ira Smith, USNR, CO of the *Goff*. (U.S. Naval Institute Photo Archives)

Dusk had set in, and although none of the rescue ships were in sight, we began to take the situation in stride. Suddenly, someone saw the silhouette of a destroyer bearing down on our raft. We all started to cheer. But soon stopped when we realized that no one in the ship had seen us. One of the guys in the raft pulled out a cheap flashlight (that never worked) and flashed it toward the destroyer. It worked. The *Barry* veered to port, but not soon enough. The starboard side hit our raft on the side opposite me. It was a terrible sight. Some men scrambled up the side of the ship—many were killed between the ship and the raft. The destroyer showed up again. This time the crew saw us and as it came alongside, it became a mad scramble, as we all tried to climb aboard.

Taken below, we were looked after by the ship's doctor and a medic, cleaned up, and moved to a bunk. Best of all, they fed us a large shot of "legal" brandy.

The next morning we went on deck. The sea was quite heavy, and we were surprised to see that the *Borie* was still afloat. But the ship was down by the stern and wallowing heavily in the troughs. Orders were given to sink her. Torpedoes and shell fire hurtled toward the ship, but the heavy seas rendered both methods inaccurate. Bombs from *Card*'s planes finally sank her. It took three depth charges close aboard before she went down swiftly by the stern at 9:55 AM.

Regarding the *Borie* crew, 22 were on the *Barry* and 107 were on the *Goff.* We were subsequently transferred to the *Card* by pulley line.

TWO CREWMEN OF the *Borie* went down with the ship, and twenty-five were lost at sea during rescue operations. The task force arrived in Norfolk, Virginia, on 9 November 1943, and received the Presidential Unit Citation. Captain Hutchins, who in true Navy tradition made one last inspection and seized the ship's colors before abandoning ship, was awarded the Navy Cross. Two more Navy Crosses, two Silver Stars, and one Legion of Merit were also awarded.

ENDNOTES

1. From the personal collection of CPO Robert A. Maher, USN (Ret.).
2. Numerous interviews of CPO Robert A. Maher, USN (Ret.), by James Wise in 1997 and 2006.

Lt. Cdr. Quentin R. Walsh, USCG

Cherbourg, France
26–27 June 1944

The Navy Cross is presented to Quentin R. Walsh, Lieutenant Commander, U.S. Coast Guard, for extraordinary heroism as Commanding Officer of a U.S. Naval party reconnoitering the naval facilities and naval arsenal at Cherbourg June 26 and 27, 1944. While in command of a reconnaissance party, Commander Walsh entered the port of Cherbourg and penetrated the eastern half of the city, engaging in street fighting with the enemy. He accepted the surrender and disarmed 400 of the enemy force at the naval arsenal and later received unconditional surrender of 350 enemy troops and, at the same time, released 52 captured U.S. Army paratroopers.[1]

Navy Cross citation for Lt. Cdr. Quentin R. Walsh, USCG

THE NAVY CROSS WAS AWARDED to only six U.S. Coast Guardsmen during World War II. Lt. Cdr. Quentin Walsh is almost certainly the only Coast Guardsman in any war to be awarded the Navy Cross for actions involving close combat with the enemy on land. When he was tasked with assessing the condition of the port of Cherbourg on the coast of France, he played an unscheduled, but major, role in its capture.

Born near the sea in Providence, Rhode Island, on 2 February 1910, Walsh graduated the U.S. Coast Guard Academy at New London, Connecticut, on 15 May 1933. His first assignment was aboard the USS *Hernon* (DD-198). A *Clemson*-class destroyer, the *Hernon* was commissioned in 1920 for the Navy, but was transferred to the Treasury Department in 1930 for use by the Coast Guard as part of the "Rum Patrol" from Cuba to Nova Scotia to interdict "rum runners" attempting to smuggle liquor into the United States. In September 1940 it was "loaned" under the Lend-Lease Act to the British as the HMS *Churchill*. Earlier, the *Hernon* had taken part in U.S. naval operations off Cuban waters during the 1933 revolution, protecting American lives and property.[2]

In September 1934 Walsh reported aboard the USS *Yamacraw*, a Coast Guard cutter out of Savannah, Georgia, and was the boarding officer when it captured the rum runner *Pronto* off the coast of South Carolina, carrying a cargo of alcohol worth $20,000. He remained aboard the *Yamacraw* until April 1937. After a brief assignment at U.S. Coast Guard Headquarters, he was assigned as a Coast Guard inspector aboard the whaling factory ship *Ulysses* during a voyage from Gothenburg, Sweden, to the Antarctic, to Capetown, South Africa, and back to New York. At one point, he was at sea 132 days without making a landfall, believed to be a record for a Coast Guard officer at sea. His observations during the voyage of thirty thousand miles helped shape the U.S. Department of Commerce's policy opposing modern commercial whaling.[3]

Leaving the *Ulysses* in April 1938, Walsh was attached to the Coast Guard Academy until September, when he reported for line duty aboard the USS *Cayuga* at Boston, Massachusetts, and was officer of the deck when a hurricane struck the Boston Navy Yard. He temporarily served as commanding officer of the USS *Kickapoo* during ice-breaking operations along the Atlantic seaboard in the winter of 1938–1939. He was a delegate to the International Whaling Conference in London, England, and served as navigator and gunnery officer aboard the cutter USS *Campbell* during her neutrality patrols and for operations in Lisbon, Portugal.[4]

In June 1941 Walsh was assigned as navigator on the attack transport USS *Joseph T. Dickman* (APA-13) and participated in the original U.S. Navy amphibious training operations at Onslo Bay, North Carolina. From October to December 1941 the *Dickman* helped transport twenty-five thousand British troops from Halifax, Nova Scotia, to Bombay, India.

After America's entry into World War II, Walsh, as a lieutenant commander, was sent to England as a member of the Navy's Logistic and Planning Division in London, on the staff of the commander of U.S. Naval Forces in Europe. He arrived in England in May 1943. He was cleared by both U.S. and British intelligence and granted a "Bigot A" security clearance for Operation OVERLORD, Phase Neptune. It was not unusual for Coast Guardsmen to be attached to naval commands during the war. As plans were developed for the eventual invasion of Europe, it became clear to planners that establishing deep-water ports in northern France was critical. Without a steady flow of supplies, any forward momentum would be lost, and functioning ports were essential to assuring the expeditious shipment of supplies to the advancing Allied armies.

The Germans, also aware of the Allies' need, planned to defend ports as long as possible, then destroy any facilities before abandoning them. As part of the planning team for Operation OVERLORD, the Allied invasion of Europe, Walsh participated in the planning for "Gooseberries, Mulberry A, Phoenixes" (artificial harbors), and the plan to capture the French port of Cherbourg on the northern edge of Normandy's Cotentin peninsula. Walsh volunteered to lead a specially trained naval reconnaissance unit, Navy Task Unit 127.2.8, to scout Cherbourg shortly after the invasion began. On 10 June 1944, D-day plus three, Walsh and his unit of fifty-three specially selected men stepped ashore at Utah Beach, attached to the 7th Corps, U.S. Army.[5]

Walsh's mission was simple: scout the port, assess the damage, and determine the work necessary to get it functioning and operational. The team endured shelling and a torrential storm that turned the roads to mud puddles until they finally linked with elements of the U.S. 79th Division outside Cherbourg. They traveled in jeeps and slept in foxholes.[6]

When Walsh's team arrived in Cherbourg, they found that the Germans had tried to destroy the port's facilities. The gates to both canals had been destroyed, the tracks in the rail yard were uprooted and bent, the harbor was mined, and the water-ways were obstructed with sunken ships and wrecked derricks. To further delay and hinder reconstruction, many of the sunken ships were booby-trapped with explo-sives. In addition, Walsh's team was hindered by the fact that the western half of the city remained under the control of the Germans, including a naval arsenal and fort overlooking much of the port.[7]

There was still house-to-house fighting going on when Walsh and his team arrived at Cherbourg, and they joined in the street fighting to reach the waterfront on 24 June, where they set up temporary headquarters. Unable to proceed with clearing and repairing the harbor while under German guns, Walsh volunteered to lead a sixteen-man man raiding party on the naval arsenal.

On 26 June Walsh and his party, armed with bazookas, grenades, and subma-chine guns, worked their way through sniper-filled streets toward the arsenal. Making it to the heavy steel doors of the bunker, they used explosives to blow the doors open. Convinced that they were facing a superior force, the German garrison of about four hundred surrendered. Unwilling to leave the job half-finished, Walsh resolved to capture Fort du Homet, the fortress overlooking the port.[8]

History is silent on the question of how proficient a poker player Walsh was, but events indicate he had a superior understanding of the art of bluffing. Walsh forced a captured officer to lead his command through a minefield and the rubble of the waterfront to the gates of the fort. According to his information, the garrison of 350 Germans held some 50 American paratroopers prisoner within the fortress.[9]

When his second-in-command, Navy Reserve Lt. Frank Lauer, questioned the wisdom of storming a fortified stronghold with a force of eleven men, Walsh is said to have first asked the young officer if he ever played poker, then raised a white handkerchief above his head to signal his desire for a truce.

A German officer escorted Walsh and Lauer inside the fortress, and they met with the German commander. Keeping a poker face, Walsh informed the officer that Cherbourg had been surrendered and he was there to accept the surrender of the fortress. There was some confusion, for the German officer had assumed that Walsh was surrendering to him. Walsh insisted it was the German's duty to surrender now that Cherbourg had fallen. The Germans tried to negotiate safe passage to German lines in exchange for the release of the fifty-two American paratroopers, but in the end Walsh negotiated the release of the prisoners and the unconditional surrender of the garrison by convincing the Germans he commanded a force of eight hundred men. One can only imagine the German commander's consternation upon discovering he'd surrendered to a dozen Sailors. For his actions in capturing two installations and over 750 of the enemy, Walsh was awarded the Navy Cross.

With the threat removed, Walsh set up permanent headquarters, surveyed the location of the mines in Cherbourg, then repeated his work at the ports of Roscoff, Morlaix, and Brest, reporting to Gen. George Patton's 3rd Army and Gen. Troy Middleton's 8th Army in Brittany. He again came under fire when carrying out a reconnaissance of LeHavre while attached to the 1st Canadian Army. He remained as senior naval officer at LeHavre until 17 September, when he entered the hospital.[10]

In England's damp climate, Walsh had developed emphysema in December 1943. He was returned to the States aboard the USS *Wakefield* and assigned to public relations duties for the Merchant Marine, in the office of the commandant. Following the end of the war, Walsh was medically discharged on 1 June 1946, and he retired to Arizona. He was recalled to active duty on 2 February 1951 for service in the Korean War, and he served at Coast Guard Headquarters in Washington, D.C., and as an aide to the assistant secretary of the Treasury until his retirement as a captain on 1 August 1960.

After retirement, Walsh taught high school science and worked as a probation officer until retiring in 1975. He passed away on 18 May 2000 in Denton, Maryland. Walsh's funeral was held in the church in which he had married his wife, Mary Ann Knotts, fifty-seven years earlier. In his eulogy, his grandson, Bill Zolper, describing the "forceful personality" of his grandfather, recalled that he commanded his family as he would a Coast Guard cutter: "It was a swell ship for the captain, a hell of a ship for the crew."[11]

ENDNOTES

1. Navy Cross Citation for Lt. Cdr. Quentin R. Walsh, USCG, www.homeofheroes.com/valor/1_Citations/03_wwii-nc/nc_06wwii_uscg.html.
2. Official Biography of Captain Quentin R. Walsh, Office of the Historian, U.S. Coast Guard, Washington, D.C.
3. Robert F. Dorr and Fred L. Borch, "Damn the Torpedoes! Walsh's Heroic Gamble Led to German Defeat," *U.S. Army Times*, 8 May 2006.
4. Official Biography of Captain Quentin R. Walsh.
5. Ibid.
6. "Captain Quentin R. Walsh USCG 1910S2000," Biographies Section, U.S. Coast Guard Historian's Office, Washington, D.C., http://www.uscg.mil/hq/g-cp/history/ BIO_Quentin_Walsh.html.
7. *The Story of Quentin Walsh at Cherbourg.* U.S. Coast Guard Historian's Office, Washington, D.C., http://www.uscg.mil/history/Lov/DOT.html.
8. Ibid.
9. Bethanne Kelly Patrick, "Coast Guard Officer Played Poker with the Germans Who Held Cherbourg Fortress–and Won," www.Military.com/content/morecontent?file=ML_Walsh_bxp.
10. *The Story of Quentin Walsh at Cherbourg.*
11. Paul Stillwell, "A True Coast Guard Hero," *Naval History Magazine*, August 2000, p. 4.

Col. Gregory Boyington, USMC(R)

New Britain Islands Area/Rabaul
3 January 1944

The Navy Cross is presented to Gregory "Pappy" Boyington, Major, U.S. Marine Corps (Reserve), for extraordinary heroism as Commanding Officer of Marine Fighting Squadron TWO HUNDRED FOURTEEN (VMF-214), during action against enemy aerial forces in the New Britain Island Area, 3 January 1944. Climaxing a period of duty conspicuous for exceptional combat achievement, Major Boyington led a formation of Allied planes on a fighter sweep over Rabaul against a vastly superior number of hostile fighters. Diving in a steep run into the climbing Zeros, he made a daring attack, sending one Japanese fighter to destruction in flames. A tenacious and fearless airman under extremely hazardous conditions, Major Boyington succeeded in communicating to those who served with him, the brilliant and effective tactics developed through a careful study of enemy techniques, and led his men into combat with inspiring and courageous determination. His intrepid leadership and gallant fighting spirit reflect the highest credit upon the United States Naval Service.[1]

Excerpt from Navy Cross citation for Col. Gregory Boyington, USMC(R)

GREGORY "PAPPY" BOYINGTON was the leader of the legendary "Black Sheep" squadron, a "Flying Tiger" (mercenary civilian pilot) in China, and one of only sixteen men to win the Medal of Honor and *at least* one Navy Cross during World War II. Known as the "bad boy" of World War II, Boyington was one of the top Marine aces (or *the* top ace, depending on how you count), and the only man to be twice awarded the Medal of Honor for the same act, once posthumously.

Gregory Boyington was born in Coeur D'Alene, Idaho, on 4 December 1912, and was part Sioux Indian. His early years were spent in St. Maries, Idaho, a small logging town where he lived with his mother and alcoholic stepfather, whom he believed at the time to be his natural father. Only later did he learn his birth father was Charlie Boyington. In 1926 the family moved to Tacoma, Washington, and Boyington graduated from Lincoln High School, where he excelled in wrestling.

He entered the University of Washington in 1930, where he won the collegiate wrestling title for his weight. He was known then as Greg Hallenbeck, the name of his stepfather. He met his first wife, Helene, while a student at the University of Washington. During the summers he worked at mining and logging camps in Idaho. Boyington was a member of the Reserve Officers Training Corps, serving as a cadet captain, before graduating with a degree in aeronautical engineering in December 1934, shortly after which he married Helene. Their first son, Gregory Clark Boyington, was born ten months later. They were later divorced.[2]

Following his graduation, Boyington served on active duty as a second lieutenant in the U.S. Army Reserve, assigned to the 630th Coast Artillery at Fort Worden, Washington, before accepting an appointment as an aviation cadet in the U.S. Marine Corps Reserve. After passing elimination training in 1935, he received orders for flight training at the Pensacola Naval Air Station, Pensacola, Florida, where he reported on 27 January 1936. By then, Hallenbeck had changed his name. Although naval aviators were required by regulation to be single, his recent name change to Boyington meant there was no record of his marriage, although at that time he was still married.

As part of class 88-C, Boyington learned to fly in a floatplane version of the Consolidated NY-2, then progressed to the Vought O2U and SU-1 scouting biplanes. Although he had a hard time with flight training and had numerous rechecks, he graduated and was designated as a naval aviator (#5160) on 11 March 1937. He was sent to the Marine Barracks, Quantico, Virginia, to join Air Squadron One Fleet Marine Force, where he flew FB4-B biplanes. He was discharged from the Marine Corps Reserves on 1 July 1937 and commissioned a second lieutenant in the regular Marines the following day.

During the next year, Boyington was assigned first as an engineering officer at Quantico and then as a materiel officer at Parris Island. In July 1938 he entered the ten-month Marine Corps Basic School in Philadelphia, after which he was transferred to the 2nd Marine Aircraft Group at San Diego, California. He served aboard the USS *Yorktown*, going on field exercises to Puerto Rico, and aboard the USS *Saratoga* during exercises off California's coast. Following a promotion to first lieutenant on 4 November 1940, Boyington returned to Pensacola as a flight instructor.[3]

Despite being a competent flier, and few would dispute that he was, Boyington's personal life interfered with his Marine career. Almost a caricature of the hard-fighting, hard-drinking Marine, his involvement in drunken brawls (he once decked a superior officer in a fight over a girl who was not his wife) and mounting debts had all but extinguished his chances for advancement. It is said that the Chinese ideogram for crisis is made up of two characters meaning danger and opportunity. In the crisis in China, Boyington would find both danger and opportunity.

In 1941 the U.S. government, looking for ways to help the Chinese in their war with Japan, created a partnership with a private company, the Central Aircraft Manufacturing Company (CAMCO), to supply fighter planes and pilots to fly missions against the Japanese. CAMCO recruiters visited military aviation bases seeking volunteers for the American Volunteer Group (AVG). The AVG recruited

Maj. Gregory "Pappy" Boyington, USMC(R), is shown strapped in the cockpit of an F4F Wildcat fighter at a forward base in the South Pacific. (National Archives)

pilots from all of the military services as "volunteers" to form three pursuit squadrons under Gen. Claire Chennault. The group, known as the "The Flying Tigers," flew Curtiss P-40 Warhawk fighters out of Burma on missions against the Japanese in China.

Boyington later admitted that he was motivated to join the Flying Tigers not so much by a desire to fight the Japanese as for the money, including the bonuses paid for downed Japanese aircraft. Pilots earned $600 a month, and flight leaders $675, not counting bonuses. He was deep in debt, supporting his ex-wife and children, and was a first lieutenant with little chance of making captain due to his admittedly rowdy behavior. He resigned from the Marine Corps on 27 August 1941 to accept an offer of employment with the AVG in China, with a secret agreement with the Marine Corps that he would be reinstated upon his return or should America enter the war. Boyington left the Corps, traveled to San Francisco, and departed with twenty-five other pilots for China aboard a Dutch freighter, the *Boschfontein*, on 24 September 1941. Their passports described them as members of the clergy. They traveled from Singapore to Rangoon, Burma, then inland to the village of Toungoo, arriving on 13 November 1941.[4]

Boyington was assigned to the 1st Pursuit Squadron, nicknamed "Adam and Eve," at Toungoo, where he battled scorpions, mosquitoes, and snakes, as well as the Japanese. The unit moved to Kunming, China, after Pearl Harbor and watched as the Japanese invaded Hong Kong, the Philippines, and Wake Island, and moved closer to Singapore. With every Japanese advance, the Burmese people became more pro-Japanese, and the unit moved back to Mingaladon Field, Rangoon, on

2 February 1942, then in March evacuated inland, north to Magwe, all the while continuing to fly support and strafing missions.

Controversy surrounds the question of how many victories Boyington accrued while with the Flying Tigers. Admittedly, poor records were kept in the confusion of the war. Boyington claimed until his death that his record was six kills; Chennault and the AVG credit him with four-and-a-half kills, as documented below in a citation signed by General Chennault:

27 April 1942:

On 6 February 1942, in company with other members of his squadron, Vice Squadron Leader G. Boyington, AVG, engaged in combat with a number of Japanese pursuit planes near the city of Rangoon, Burma. In the combat which ensued, he personally shot down two enemy fighters in the air. On 24 March 1942, in company with five other pilots of the AVG he attacked the airdrome at Chiengmai, Thailand. As a result of this flight's attack, 15 enemy planes were burned, and the credit for the attacked [sic] shared equally, giving Vice Squadron Leader Boyington credit for destroying two and one half enemy aircraft. This pilot has destroyed a total of four and one half enemy planes; two of which were destroyed in aerial combat, and two and one half burned on the ground. He is commended on his performance and achievement in combat.[5]

But the above citation illustrates the unreliability of AVG records. If, as Boyington claims, the fifteen Japanese planes destroyed on the ground during the raid on Chiang Mai on 24 March were destroyed by four planes, among them Boyington's, then he should have been credited with three and three-quarter kills. If Chennault decided that the credit should be shared equally among all ten pilots who took part in that unfortunate raid (Chennault incorrectly cites six planes in his correspondence), the credit would have been one-and-a half, not the two-and-a-half credited.[6]

Boyington and Chennault had little respect for each other. Boyington's ability to antagonize and alienate superiors in the AVG echoed his performance in the Corps, with his reputation for insubordination, drinking, and rowdy behavior. According to Boyington's account, Chennault reneged on the agreement to return the pilots to their former service in the case of war, and instead offered them the choice of commissions in the Army Air Corps or paying their own way home. In late May 1942, upon hearing rumors that the remaining AVG pilots were to be inducted into the Army Air Corps in the coming July, Boyington took a DC-3 out of Kunming and flew over the Himalayas to Calcutta. From there he traveled to Karachi, where he sailed aboard the SS *Brazil* around Africa to New York City, arriving in July 1942.

He promptly traveled to Washington, D.C., to be reinstated into the Marine Corps. He was told to return home and await orders. He was appointed a first lieutenant in the Marine Corps Reserve on 16 September 1942, effective date of rank of 1 July 1940, but remained assigned to a general service unit in the 13th Reserve District.

When he had still received no word in November, Boyington sent a three-page telegram to the undersecretary of the Navy. The contents of that telegram are unknown, but three days later, on 16 November, Boyington received orders to report to San Diego with a commission as a major in the Marine Corps Reserve. By January he was en route to Nouméa, New Caledonia, aboard the SS *Lurline*, a liner converted into a troopship. From there he traveled aboard the *Henderson*, an army transport, to Espiritu Santo, New Hebrides, and on to the island of Tontuda, assigned to Marine Aircraft Wing One.

On Tontuda he was assigned as an assistant operations officer of a squadron of fighters (VMF-121) flying operations over Guadalcanal. By May 1943, Boyington was executive officer of the VMF-222, tasked with flying fighter support to escort bombers through "the slot," the area between Guadalcanal and Bougainville. The unit flew Grumman Wildcat fighters, and Boyington took over as commanding officer of the squadron for six weeks before taking rest and recreation in New Zealand.

Major Boyington (fourth from the left standing in front of the aircraft) with pilots of VMF-214 wearing baseball caps sent to them by the St. Louis Cardinals. Ball caps were traditionally worn by Marine pilots in the South Pacific during the war. (U.S. Marine Corps / TSgt. Douglas Q. White)

Boyington returned to his unit to find the Wildcats replaced by a new fighter, the F4U Corsair. Before he could resume flying combat missions, he snapped his ankle in a football game and was evacuated by hospital ship to New Zealand and admitted into the Mobile Six Hospital at Auckland in June. After treatment, he was given a series of administrative positions as commanding officer of squadrons rotating back to the United States, completing paperwork and other details.

Finally in August, when the need for fighter squadrons became critical, Boyington, along with Maj. Stan Bailey (later executive officer), was able to persuade higher headquarters to allow him to create a temporary fighter squadron from unassigned pilots. Contrary to legend, the majority of his pilots were not disciplinary cases but rather unassigned, replacement, and desk-bound pilots. At the age of thirty, Boyington was the oldest, hence the nickname "Pappy."

He took command of the new squadron, VMF-214, nicknamed the "Black Sheep" squadron, in September 1943, and took it to the Solomon Islands campaign, arriving on 12 September. On the first mission, his men downed eighteen enemy planes, with Boyington accounting for five kills. He continued to rack up kills, approaching Capt. Eddie Rickenbacker's World War I record of twenty-six downed enemy planes. On one occasion, 17 October 1943, he led a flight of twenty-four planes over the enemy airfield at Kahili, issuing a challenge in Japanese to the sixty planes stationed there. When the Japanese planes accepted the challenge, his flight downed twenty enemy planes without a single loss.[7] On 17 December 1943 he commanded the first Allied fighter attack on fortified Rabaul.

Boyington tied Rickenbacker's record of twenty-six shoot-downs on 3 January 1944 as he led a mission of forty-eight fighters over Rabaul Island. Unknown until after the war, Boyington downed two additional planes, breaking Rickenbacker's record.[8] But his luck ran out over Rabaul, and his plane was shot down. He parachuted into the ocean, where he was strafed and wounded by enemy planes. He was able to inflate a life raft and floated until being taken prisoner aboard a Japanese submarine.

Now a prisoner, Boyington was first taken to Rabaul, then to the island of Truk, then to Saipan, before eventually ending up at the Ofuna Prisoner of War Camp in the suburb of Yokohama on the Japanese mainland, where he remained until April 1945. The Red Cross was not informed by the Japanese of Boyington's capture, and the United States was not aware that he was still alive until fourteen days after the war ended. Believed dead, Boyington was awarded the Navy Cross on 25 May 1944 and the Medal of Honor posthumously by President Roosevelt. This award almost cost Boyington his life, for he had convinced his captors that he was an operations officer, not a combat pilot, and that he had no kills to his credit. The newspaper accounts of his medal revealed the truth, for which he was severely beaten.

When Major Boyington was shot down, it was not known that he had survived and was a POW. Believed dead, Boyington was posthumously awarded the Navy Cross on 25 May 1944 and the Medal of Honor by President Roosevelt. Upon his return to the United States, he was presented his "posthumous" Navy Cross by the Commandant of the Marine Corps on 4 October 1945, and President Truman "re-presented" his Medal of Honor the following day. (National Archives)

Boyington remained a prisoner of the Japanese for twenty months, enduring almost daily torture, mistreatment, starvation, and illness. He was transferred to Camp Omouri in April 1945, where he remained until the end of the war. He was liberated on 29 August. Upon his return to the United States, Boyington was presented his "posthumous" Navy Cross by the commandant of the Marine Corps on 4 October, and President Truman "re-presented" him his Medal of Honor in a White House ceremony the following day. Boyington then went on a Victory Bond tour, but his time in captivity had taken a toll on his health, and he retired from the Marines on 1 August 1947 with a promotion to full colonel. (He'd been promoted to lieutenant colonel on 29 August 1945, effective as of 10 April 1944.)

Boyington found transition to civilian life difficult. He was married and divorced several times, and struggled with finances and alcohol. After a series of jobs, he found moderate success when he wrote *Baa Baa Black Sheep*, an account of his war experiences, which became a best seller in 1958. He narrated the TV series *Danger Zone* in 1960. His book was made into a television series, *Baa Baa Black Sheep*, which ran from 1976 to 1978. In it, Boyington was portrayed by the actor

Robert Conrad. He worked on the show as a technical adviser and occasionally had a recurring role as a mechanic.

Boyington died of cancer in Fresno, California, on 12 January 1988 and was buried in Arlington National Cemetery three days later with full honors, including a flyover by F-4s from the Marine detachment at Andrews Air Force Base.

In February 2006 a resolution recommending a memorial for Boyington at the University of Washington, his alma mater, was put before the student senate. After much debate, the senate chair broke a 45–45 tie, defeating the motion. A national controversy erupted when it was revealed that one student senator argued that the university already had enough monuments to "rich white men" (ironically, Boyington was never rich and was one-quarter Sioux), and another senator stated she didn't think a Marine was an "example of the sort of person UW wanted to produce." One wonders which side Pappy would have favored. He never considered himself a hero, and in his book he had written, "Name a hero, and I'll prove he's a bum."[9]

ENDNOTES

1. www.homeofheroes.com
2. Bruce Gamble, *Black Sheep One: The Life of Gregory "Pappy" Boyington* (Novato, Calif.: Presidio Press, 2001).
3. M. L. Shettle, *USMC Air Stations of WW II* (Roswell, N.M.: Schaertel Publishing, 2001).
4. Gregory Boyington, *Baa Baa Black Sheep* (New York: Putnam, 1958).
5. Daniel Ford, *Flying Tigers: Claire Chennault and His American Volunteers 1941–1942* (Washington, D.C.: Smithsonian Books, 2007), and Chennault Papers, Stanford University.
6. Ibid.
7. Frank Walton, *Once They Were Eagles: The Men of the Black Sheep Squadron* (Frankfort: University Press of Kentucky, 1996).
8. Again, these numbers depend on how you count and whom you believe.
9. Boyington, *Baa Baa Black Sheep*.

INTERIM YEARS

In the years between the end of World War I and the United States' entry into the World War II, the Navy Cross was awarded 308 times, to 170 sailors, 133 Marines, 1 Coast Guardsman, 1 Soldier, and 3 foreign nationals.

The first postwar awards of the Navy Cross went to fourteen Navy men (ten officers, four enlisted) and a Coast Guard officer for their participation in NC trans-Atlantic flights. The Navy Curtiss (NC) Flying Boat was a four-engine seaplane (three in front, one in the rear) that was built during World War I to protect shipping and to conduct antisubmarine patrols. Four were built, but the war ended while they were still being tested. Three of them were given the mission of attempting the first trans-Atlantic crossing. (The fourth, NC-2, was found to be unsatisfactory for the task.) On 8 May 1919, NC-1, NC-3, and NC-4 took off from Rockaway, New York, for Halifax, Nova Scotia, on the first leg of the trans-Atlantic journey to Lisbon, Portugal, by way of Newfoundland and the Azores Islands. The flight was under the command of John Towers, who was also commanding officer and navigator of NC-3. The 4,526-mile journey was completed in 53 hours, 58 minutes.[1]

Eight Navy Crosses were awarded to four Sailors and four Marines of the Byrd Antarctic Expeditions (1929 and 1933), which included the first historic flight to the South Pole in which Adm. Richard E. Byrd, along with pilot Bernt Balchen, copilot/radioman Harold June, and photographer Ashley McKinley, flew to the South Pole and back in 18 hours, 41 minutes.

Nine Marines were awarded the Navy Cross for their actions in Haiti in 1919 and 1920. In the Second Nicaraguan Campaign (1927–1933), 113 Navy Crosses were awarded. Thirteen of the awards went to naval personnel, including two doctors and three corpsmen. The one hundred awards to Marines included three to GySgt. William "Iron Man" Lee, two to Lt. Lewis "Chesty" Puller, and one each to Marine legends Merritt Edson and Evans Carlson. Six of the medals were awarded posthumously.

American ships had patrolled the Yangtze River and Chinese coast since 1854 to demonstrate an American presence in the region. The uprising by Chinese nationalists in and around Nanking in 1927 required the rescue of American and British civilians by American destroyers USS *William B. Preston* (DD-344) and USS *Noa* (DD-343), supported by the British cruiser HMS *Emerald* and destroyer HMS *Wolseyand*.[2] Three navy signalmen and a chief quartermaster were awarded the Navy Cross for the four-day rescue mission from 21 to 25 March 1927.

With relations between Japan and the United States deteriorating in the late 1930s, and with Japanese aggression in China, the USS *Panay* and other ships of the Yangtze River Patrol attempted to protect American interests in an increasingly complex and hostile political environment. In November 1937 American gunboats evacuated most of the U.S. Embassy staff from Nanking. The *Panay* was assigned as station ship to guard the remaining Americans and to evacuate them at the last possible moment. They came on board 11 December, and the *Panay* moved upriver to avoid becoming involved in the fighting. The next day, Japanese naval aircraft were ordered by their Army to attack "any and all ships" in the Yangtze above Nanking. Knowing of the presence of *Panay* and the merchantmen, the Navy requested verification of the order, which was received before the attack began about 1:27 PM that day. The *Panay* sank at 3:34 PM. The Japanese government later apologized for their "mistake" and paid a large indemnity. Three men were killed, and forty-three Sailors and five civilian passengers were wounded. Twenty-three Sailors, one Soldier, and two foreign nationals were awarded Navy Crosses. And it became clear that the extremists in Japan desired war with the United States.[3]

ENDNOTES

1. Douglas Sterner, Home Of Heroes Web site, Navy Cross database, http://www.homeofheroes.com.
2. *Dictionary of American Naval Fighting Ships* (DANFS). (Washington, D.C.: U.S. Government Printing Office, 1977), Vol. V, p.208; Vol. VIII, p.377.
3. Ibid.

WORLD WAR I (1914–1918)

When the United States entered World War I on 6 April 1917, the United States Marine Corps was composed of 462 commissioned officers, 49 warrant officers, and 13,214 enlisted men on active duty, for a total strength of 13,725. (It would expand to a wartime high of 75,101 actual strength, including reserves.) One hundred eighty-seven officers and 4,546 enlisted men were on duty beyond the continental limits of the United States, and 49 officers and 2,187 enlisted men were serving on board ships of the U.S. Navy. Despite tremendous logistical complications, on 14 June 1917, just five weeks after war was declared, 70 officers and 2,689 enlisted men of the 5th Marine Regiment, approximately one-sixth of the enlisted strength of the Marine Corps, sailed aboard the USS *Henderson*, *DeKalb*, and *Hancock* toward France, comprising one-fifth of the first American Expeditionary Force (AEF).[1]

Those forces were soon joined by the 6th Marine Regiment and the 6th Machine Gun Battalion, which was formed into the 4th Marine Brigade. As one of the two infantry brigades of the Army's 2nd Division, they engaged in no less than eight distinct operations in France, four of which were major operations: the Aisne defensive (31 May–5 June 1918), the Aisne-Marne offensive (18–19 July 1918), the St. Mihiel offensive (12–16 September 1918), and the Meuse-Argonne offensive (1–10 October 1918 and 1–10 November 1918).

At the time, the United States' sole decoration for valor was the Medal of Honor, and there were no awards for any sort of meritorious acts outside of combat. In 1918 Congress, with the support of President Woodrow Wilson, passed legislation that authorized the U.S. Army to award the newly-created Distinguished Service Cross (DSC) for valor in combat and the Distinguished Service Medal (DSM) for distinguished noncombat duty. Congress authorized the Navy Cross and the Navy Distinguished Service Medal for the U.S. Navy in February 1919, three months after the armistice.

A total of 1,838 Navy Crosses were awarded during World War I. One thousand two hundred ninety-eight were awarded to Sailors, 392 to Marines, 36 to Coast Guardsmen, 12 to the U.S. Army, and 100 to foreign naval personnel, almost exclusively officers.[2]

ENDNOTES

1. Maj. Edwin McClellan, *The United States Marine Corps in the World War*, Historical Branch, G-3 Division Headquarters, U. S. Marine Corps, Washington, D.C. (1920).
2. Fifty-nine were awarded to France, twenty-nine to England, nine to Italy, and one each to Japan, Brazil, and Portugal.

Lt. Cdr. Walter O. Henry, USN

USS *Fanning* (DD-37)

17 November 1917

For Distinguished Service in the line of his profession as officer-of-the-deck on the USS *Fanning* in initiating prompt and efficient offensive action on the occasion of the engagement with, and the capture of the German U-58 on 17 November 1917.[1]

Navy Cross citation for Lt. Cdr. Walter O. Henry, USN

WORLD WAR I (the "Great War") broke out in Europe in 1914. The following year, Great Britain established a blockade zone in Atlantic waters and around the home islands to protect its shipping as well as that of the United States and other nations that carried war cargoes to Britain. German U-boats, previously thought to be of little value in naval warfare, roamed the seas and sank thousands of tons of Allied shipping. On 7 May 1915 the German U-boat *U-20*, under the command of Kapitanleutnant Walter Schwieger, sank the British liner *Lusitania* off the coast of Ireland; among the dead were 129 Americans. Three months later, three more Americans lost their lives when *U-24* sent the British passenger steamer *Arabic* to the bottom. As additional Americans lost their lives on other foreign ships, tension began to mount between the United States and Germany, and by the spring of 1916 the situation had become so dire that President Wilson threatened to break diplomatic relations with Germany.[2]

The U.S. Navy, although boasting a formidable fleet of major combatants (first-line battleships), lacked small ships that would be effective in antisubmarine warfare should America join the Allied forces against the Central Powers. But events would push the United States into the war nonetheless. On 12 March 1917, the American steamer *Algonquin* was sunk without warning near the British Isles. Within a week, U-boats sank three more American ships. On 12 April 1917 President Wilson told Congress, "The world must be made safe for democracy . . . The right is more precious than peace, and we shall fight for the things which we have always carried nearest our hearts." Four days later the United States declared war.

The USS *Fanning* (DD-37) was one of numerous U.S. naval escort destroyers that accompanied transport ships carrying American troops and supplies to France during World War I. Based at Queenstown, Ireland, the *Fanning* was the first American warship to sink a German submarine. It did so while escorting a small convoy off Milford Haven, England, in November 1917. (Naval Historical Center)

American naval participation in the war was minimal. Aside from sending five battleships to Scapa Flow to reinforce the British Grand Fleet, operations were confined to providing escort ships that accompanied transport ships carrying American troops and supplies to France.[3] Among the American escort ships was the destroyer USS *Fanning* (DD-37). Eventually based at Queenstown, Ireland, *Fanning* and her sister destroyers patrolled the eastern Atlantic, escorting convoys and rescuing survivors of sunken merchant ships.[4] On 17 November 1917 a division of American destroyers (including the *Fanning*) sailed from Queenstown, escorting eight merchant ships. As the small convoy proceeded off Milford Haven, Lt. Cdr. Walter O. Henry, USN, who had duty as officer-of-the-deck on the *Fanning*, sighted a periscope close to one of the merchant ships, the 5,730-ton Dominion liner *Welshman*. Acting quickly on Henry's orders, the crew of the *Fanning* brought the ship around in a tight circle and dropped a depth charge on the spot where the periscope had been spotted. The destroyer *Nicholson* (leader of the division) dropped another depth charge just forward of the first charge. For fifteen minutes the crews searched the waters for floating debris or oil spills that would indicate they had destroyed the U-boat.[5]

Then, to everyone's amazement, the *U-58* broke the surface of the water, stern first, followed by the rest of the hull, and settled on an even keel. Both destroyers took the U-boat under heavy fire, and within minutes the U-boat crew came stumbling onto the main deck, all shouting "Kamerade!" Two of the German sailors disappeared below decks, and upon their reappearance the boat began to settle in the water. They obviously had opened the boat's strainers to flood the craft. The crewmen dived into the water and swam to the destroyers, where they were hauled aboard as POWs.[6]

A *Fanning* depth charge wrecked the *U-58*'s electric motors and jammed her rudders. The U-boat skipper had no choice but to blow the ballast tanks and surface. Under heavy fire by the *Fanning* and other American destroyers, the U-boat crew stumbled out of the boat onto the main deck, all shouting "Kamerade!" to indicate that they were friends, shipmates. (Naval Historical Center)

The captured German crew later recounted that as they were about to torpedo the *Welshman* they were suddenly attacked by the *Fanning*. The *Fanning*'s depth charge had wrecked the electric motors and jammed the rudders. The U-boat skipper, Kapitanleutnant Armberger, had two choices: sink to the bottom of the sea and perish or blow the ballast tanks, surface, and surrender.[7] This was the first of two U-boat sinkings by American naval vessels. The second occurred on 19 May 1918 when the destroyers USS *Patterson* and USS *Allen* sank the *U-119* west of Cardigan Bay. American naval escorts were also credited with the indirect destruction of other U-boats during the war.[8]

Ship's officers of the *Fanning* at the time of the capture of the *U-58*. Left to right: Lt. Robert B. Carney, USN; Lt. Cdr. George H. Fort, USN; Lt. Cdr. Arthur S. Carpender, USN; Lt. John A. Vincent, USN; and Lt. Cdr. Walter O. Henry, USN. (Naval Historical Center)

ENDNOTES

1. Harry Stringer, *The Navy Book of Distinguished Service: An official Compendium of the Names and Citations of the Men of the United States Navy, Marine Corps, Army and Foreign Governments Who Were Decorated by the Navy Department for Extraordinary Gallantry and Conspicuous Service above and beyond the Call of Duty in the World War* (Washington, D.C.: Fassett Publishing Company, 1932), 80.

2. E. B. Potter, *Sea Power* (Annapolis, Md.: Naval Institute Press, 1981), 223.

3. Ibid., 225–28.

4. *Dictionary of American Naval Fighting Ships (DANFS)*, vol. II (Washington, D.C.: U.S. Government Printing Office, 1977), 388.

5. R. H. Gibson and M. Prendergast, *The German Submarine War (1914–1918)* (Annapolis, Md.: Naval Institute Press, 2002), 226.

6. Ibid.

7. Ibid., 227.

8. V. E. Tarrant, *The U-Boat Offensive 1914–1945* (Annapolis, Md.: Naval Institute Press, 1989), 75.

Sgt. Maj. Daniel Joseph Daly Jr., USMC

First Sergeant, 73rd Company, 6th Regiment

Belleau Wood, France
5 June 1918

Sergeant [Daniel] Daly repeatedly performed deeds of heroism and great service on 5 June 1918. At the risk of his life he extinguished a fire in an ammunition dump at Lucylebocage. On 7 June 1918, while his position was under violent bombardment, he visited all the gun crews of his company, then posted over a wide portion of the front to cheer his men. On 10 June 1918, he attacked an enemy machine gun emplacement unassisted and captured it by use of hand grenades and his automatic pistol. On the same day, during the German attack on Bouresches, he brought in wounded under fire.[1]

Excerpt from Navy Cross citation for Sgt. Maj. Daniel Joseph Daly Jr., USMC

THE MEDALS OF SGT. MAJ. DANIEL DALY, USMC, were donated to the Marine Corps along with a large number of his citations, warrants, papers, several photographs, and other assorted memorabilia. Daly's nephew, Burton J. Loeb, of Massapequa, New York, presented the material to the assistant commandant, Gen. Samuel Jaskilka, at a ceremony arranged by the Marine Corps Public Affairs Office, New York. The office's public affairs chief, GySgt. Robert L. Hoffman, was instrumental in persuading Mr. Loeb to make his generous donation.

The medal collection contained Daly's two Medals of Honor, his Distinguished Service Cross, his Navy Cross, French decorations, and all of his campaign medals. The only medal missing was his Good Conduct Medal, which disappeared some years ago. The Daly collection is understandably of inestimable value to the Marine Corps. Sergeant Major Daly and Maj. Gen. Smedley D. Butler are the only two Marines to have been awarded the Medal of Honor for two different actions.[2] Daly once remarked that he disliked all the fuss made over him. He termed medals "a foolishness." Personally, he enjoyed a pipe crammed with cut plug tobacco, but did not drink.

Very little is known about Daly's early life other than the fact that he was born in Glen Cove, Long Island, on 11 November 1873. He was a newsboy on Park Row and something of a fighter for his weight and size (five feet, six inches tall, 132

Described by Marine Corps general officers as "the outstanding Marine of all time," Sgt. Maj. Daniel Daly was awarded two Medals of Honor for separate acts of heroism (during the Boxer Rebellion 1900 and in the 1915 Haitian campaign). He was awarded an Army Distinguished Service Cross and Navy Cross for heroic acts performed during World War I. (U.S. Marine Corps)

pounds). Nevertheless he cut a fine military figure, erect and well-proportioned. His keen gray eyes looked upon danger without fear. He was a strict disciplinarian, yet fair-minded and popular among his officers and enlisted men. He was known not only for his reckless daring but also for his constant attention to the needs of his men. Offered a commission on several occasions, he is said to have declined on the grounds that he would rather be an outstanding sergeant than just another officer.[3]

Dan Daly enlisted in the Marine Corps on 10 January 1899, at the age of twenty-five. His twenty-one years of active service were filled with wars large and small, expeditions, landings, and seven tours at sea.

In May 1900 he was serving as a member of Capt. Newt H. Hall's Marine detachment in the cruiser USS *Newark* (C-1) when a segment of disgruntled Chinese people facing starvation formed a secret society called the Fists of Righteous Harmony—or "Boxers," because they practiced the martial arts. The Boxers attracted thousands of followers and vowed to overthrow the government and get rid of all foreigners who were vying for trading rights and control of China. The Boxers roamed the countryside, killing foreign missionaries and Chinese converts, and began threatening the safety of the Peking legations. Daly disembarked the *Newark* at Taku Bar on 15 May along with Captain Hall and twenty-five other detachment Marines and, with Capt. John T. Myers' USS *Oregon* (BB-3) detachment, headed north. On 31 May the Marines entered Peking, accompanied by a mixed force of French, Russian, Austrian, Japanese, Italian, and German sailors and marines. On 6 June the Boxers cut the rail to the south. A week later the siege of the legations began in earnest; it was to last fifty-five days.

On the night of 15 July, Hall and Daly, who was a private at the time, set out to reconnoiter a barricade position on the Tartar Wall. According to the plan, if the two were not attacked during their reconnaissance, a working party was to come out with sandbags and construct an emplacement. The reconnaissance was made, there was no attack, but the working party did not appear. Despite stray shots coming from front and rear and the isolation of the site, Daly volunteered to stay and hold off the Boxers while Hall returned for the working party. For his coolness and bravery under fire, Daly was awarded his first Medal of Honor on 11 December 1901.

He earned his second Medal of Honor in 1915 as a gunnery sergeant in Haiti. During a patrol by three squads of 15th Company, 2nd Regiment, the Marines were ambushed by a large Caco force (Haitian bandits) while fording a swift stream at the bottom of a deep ravine. Fighting their way to a good defensive position a mile away, the Marines were subjected throughout the night to continuous, albeit inaccurate, fire from the surrounding Cacos. The horse carrying the patrol's machine gun had been killed in the ambush, and Gunnery Sergeant Daly volunteered to retrieve the weapon. Crawling through Caco lines, he returned to the site of the ambush and, under fire, repeatedly dove to the bottom of the stream until he located the dead animal. Stripping the gun from its back, Daly then executed a harrowing return to the Marine lines. At dawn, with Capt. William P. Upshur, 1st Lt. Edward A. Ostermann, and Gunnery Sergeant Daly each in command of a squad, the Marines attacked outward in three different directions, scattering the Cacos.

Three years later Daly was in France serving as first sergeant, 73rd Company, 6th Regiment. On 1 June 1918 the regiment, as part of the 4th Marine Brigade, 2nd U.S. Division, was inserted in the line athwart the Paris-Metz road. The move was designed to plug the gap left by the shattered French 43rd Division and halt the headlong German advance on Paris. The Marines did not have to wait long. The next day, the crack German 28th Division hit the Marines' center but recoiled from deadly Springfield fire. After repeated attacks the Germans fell back, and on 5 June consolidated their position in the Belleau Wood. That same day, German artillery fire hit a Marine ammunition dump on the outskirts of Lucy-le-Bocage, a town adjacent to the wood. As ammunition boxes began burning, Sergeant Daly unhesitatingly ran into the dump and extinguished the blaze. The next day, operating under orders from General Jean Degoute, who commanded the French Sixth Army, the Marines went after the Germans in the wood. As the Marines advanced across open wheat fields, German Maxims cut them down by machine-gun fire, but they continued and reached the woods in the afternoon. It was on this hellish day that Daly, seeing a leaderless platoon pinned down by machine-gun fire, is reputed to have roared, "Come on, you sons of bitches! Do you want to live forever?"

In the fighting on 10 June around Bouresches, across Belleau Wood from Lucy-le-Bocage, Daly singlehandedly engaged a German machine-gun post. With a few grenades and a .45-caliber handgun, Daly attacked the position and blew it apart. For this act and for his heroism in the blazing ammunition dump, he was awarded not only a Distinguished Service Cross by the Army but also a Navy Cross. Daly was wounded soon afterward and evacuated under protest to a hospital. As soon as possible, he returned to his unit but was wounded once again.

Dan Daly was truly a legend in his own time. Maj. Gen. John A. Lejeune called him "the outstanding Marine of all time," while Maj. Gen. Smedley D. Butler said he was "the fightingest Marine I ever knew. . . . It was an object lesson to have served with him."[4]

Sergeant Major Daly remained unmarried all his life. In 1919 he was reported to have said, "I can't see how a single man could spend his time to better advantage than in the Marines." Following his retirement from the Corps in 1929, he took a job as a bank guard on Wall Street in New York City. He died at Glendale, Queens, Long Island, New York, on 28 April 1937. His remains were buried in Cypress Hills National Cemetery, Brooklyn, New York.[5]

In 1942 a destroyer was named after him, the USS *Daly* (DD-519). The *Fletcher*-class destroyer saw extensive combat action in the Pacific during World War II and served during the Korean War.[6]

ENDNOTES

1. U.S. Marine Corps, Historical Division Archives, U.S. Marine Corps Base, Quantico, Virginia.
2. *Fortitudine: Newsletter of the Marine Corps*, summer 1978, pp. 6-8, Historical Program, USMC Historical Division, 1978.
3. U.S. Marine Corps website, http://hqinet001.mil/HD/Historical/Whos_Who/Daly_DJ.htm
4. *Fortitudine: Newsletter of the Marine Corps*.
5 . U.S. Marine Corps Historical Division Web site.
6. "History of the USS *Daly* (DD-519)," in *Dictionary of American Fighting Ships*, (DANFS) vol. II (Washington, D.C.: U.S. Government Printing Office, 1966), 236.

BIBLIOGRAPHY

Abdelsamad, Ramy, and Gavin Hawe. "U.S. Occupation of Haiti, 1915–1934." Unpublished paper. Washington, D.C.: Naval Historical Center, 2005.

Administrative Report of PB4Y-1 Airplane, Bureau No. 32271. Officer-in-Charge, Special Air Unit ONE, 14 August 1944.

Allen, Lawrence. Interview by Scott Baron, 29 November 2006.

"Awards for Extraordinary Heroism in the War on Terror." www.freerepublic.com/focus/f-news/1434873/posts.

Bailey, Laura. "Honored with a Bronze Star, Cpl. James Wright Sets His Sights on Healing." *Marine Corps Times*, June 2004.

Bath Iron Works Corporation. "Launching of the Guided Frigate *Taylor* (FFG 50)." Bath, Maine, 5 November 1983.

Boyington, Gregory. *Baa Baa Black Sheep*. New York: Putnam, 1958.

Boyles, Denny. "A Marine's Bravery Earns Him Navy's Second-highest Medal." *The Fresno Bee*, 4 May 2006.

Bradley, James, and Ron Powers. *Flags of Our Fathers*. New York: Bantam Books, 2000.

Bray, N. N. E. *A Paladin of Arabia: The Biography of Brevet Lieut.-Colonel G. E. Leachman*. Unicorn Press, 1936.

Brinkley, C. Mark. "Finest of the Finest: Corpsman Awarded Navy Cross for An Nasiriyah Valor." *Marine Corps Times*, 23 August 2004.

———. "March 23rd Is a Day Remembered All Too Well." *Army Times*, 17 March 2004.

Burgess, Lisa. "This Is How Custer Must Have Felt." *Stars and Stripes*, 14 June 2005.

"Captain Quentin R. Walsh USCG 1910–2000." Biographies Section, U.S. Coast Guard Historian's Office, Washington, D.C. www.uscg.mil/hq/g-cp/history/BIO_Quentin_Walsh.html.

"Chontosh, Brian." www.snopes.com/politics/military/chontosh.asp.

Clare, D. "Honoring the Brave: Marine Sgt. Maj. Bradley A. Kasal." *DAV Magazine*, November/December 2006.

Cressman, Robert J. *A Magnificent Fight: Marines in the Battle for Wake Island* Marines in World War II Commemorative Series. History and Museum Division, U.S. Marine Corps, 2006.

Cutter, Jerry. Telephone Interview by Scott Baron, August 2006.

Davenport, Roy M. *Clean Sweep*. New York: Vantage Press, 1986.

Davis, Burke. *Marine! The Life of Chesty Puller*. New York: Bantam Books, 1991.

"Devereux, James Patrick." *Biographical Directory of the United States Congress.* Washington, D.C.: Government Printing Office. http://bioguide.congress.gov.

Dictionary of American Naval Fighting Ships (DANFS), Vol. II and V. Washington, D.C.: U.S. Government Printing Office, 1977.

Dodd, Matthew. "Running into Bullets: A Marine NCO's Valor." www.ptsdsupport.net/willie_copeland.html (15 August 2005).

Dorell, Oren, and Greg Zoroya. "Battle for Fallujah Forged Many Heroes." *USA Today*, 9 November 2006.

Dorr, Robert F. *Marine Air: The History of the Flying Leathernecks in Words and Pictures.* New York: Berkeley Publishing Group, 2005.

Dorr, Robert F., and Fred L. Borch. "Damn the Torpedoes! Walsh's Heroic Gamble Led to German Defeat." *Army Times*, 8 May 2006.

Evans, Stewart. "Aphrodite 2: Robot Missions." *FlyPast Aviation Monthly*, November 1996.

Executive Officer USS *Borie* to Commanding Officer USS *Borie*, Subject: Second Enemy Attack, Night of 31 October, 1 November 1943. Personnel report of 8 November 1943.

Fairburn, Tony, and Stewart Evans. "Kennedy's Fatal Mission." *Aircraft Illustrated* 10, no. 3 (March 1977).

Fairfield, Rupert T. Interview by Scott Baron, 29 November 2006.

"Fallen Heroes: Navy Petty Officer 2nd Class Danny P. Dietz." http://livinglegendteam.blogspot.com/2006/01/navy-petty-officer 2nd-class-danny-p.html.

Fischer, Ronald E. "The Navy Cross." *Journal of the Orders and Medals Society of America*, 45, no. 2 (March 1994).

Fisk, Robert. "Atrocity in Fallujah." *The Independent UK*, 1 April 2004.

Floto, Patrick J. "Wounded Marine Photographed in Fallujah Awarded Navy Cross." *Leatherneck*, July 2006.

Ford, Daniel. *Flying Tigers: Claire Chennault and His American Volunteers 1941–1942.* Washington, D.C.: Smithsonian Books, 2007; Chennault Papers, Stanford University.

Fortitudine: Newsletter of the Marine Corps. Summer 1978 Washington, D.C.: U.S. Marine Corps Historical Division.

Fuentes, Gidget, and John Hoellwarth. "Intense Firefight: Two Marines Earn Navy Cross during Fallujah Battle." *Marine Corps Times*, 23 May 2006.

Gamble, Bruce. *The Black Sheep.* New York: Presidio Press, 1998.

———. *Black Sheep One: The Life of Gregory "Pappy" Boyington.* New York: Presidio Press, 2001.

Gibson, R. H., and M. Prendergast. *The German Submarine War* (1914–1918). Annapolis, Md.: Naval Institute Press, 2002.

Hall, Wynton C., and Peter Schweizer. "Campus Rads vs. Our Vets." www.nationalreview.com/script/printpage.p?ref=/comment/hall_schweizer2005082.

Hammel, Eric M. *Aces at War: The American Aces Speak*, vol. 4. New York: Presidio Press, 1997.

———. *Chosin: Heroic Ordeal of the Korean War.* New York: Vanguard Press.

Hargis, Robert, and Starr Sinton. *World War Two Medal of Honor Recipients (1)–Navy & USMC.* Osceola, Wis.: Osprey Publishing, 2003.

Heinl R. D. Jr., *Marines in World War II: The Defense of Wake*. Historical Section, Division of Public Information, Headquarters, U.S. Marine Corps, 1947.

"History of the USS *Daly* (DD-519)." *Dictionary of American Fighting Ships*, vol. II. Washington, D.C.: U.S. Government Printing Office, 1966.

Hoffman, John T. "Battle for Henderson Field: Lt. Colonel Lewis B. Puller Commanded the 1st Battalion, 7th Marines." *World War Two Magazine*, November 2002.

————. *Chesty: The Story of Lieutenant General Lewis B. Puller, USMC*. New York: Random House, 2001.

Home of Heroes. www.homeofheroes.com/brotherhood/seals.html. (Full text citations for award of the Navy Cross in the war on terror, Vietnam, Korea, World War II, and World War I.)

Hubbs, Mark E. "Massacre on Wake Island." *Naval History Magazine*, February 2001.

"In His Own Words: Marine Sergeant James 'Eddie' Wright." www.Blackfive.Net (19 November 2005).

"Inside the Battle at Qala-I-Jangi." http://time.com/time/ nation/article/0,8599,186592,00. html.

"Iraqis in Deadly Clash with U.S. Troops." *Leatherneck Magazine*, August 2006. www.cnn.com/World, (29 April 2003).

"John 'Jack' Bolt, 83; Double Ace Fought in WWII, Korean War." Obituary, *New York Times*, 14 September 2004.

Kasal, Sgt. Maj. Bradley. Interview on KETV, Omaha, Nebraska.

The Joseph P. Kennedy Jr. Foundation. http://www.jpkf.org

Kerrigan, Evans. *American Medals and Decorations*. New York: Mallard Press, 1990.

Knox, Frank, Secretary of the Navy (William Franklin Knox). Navy Cross Citation to Lieutenant Commander Charles H. Hutchins, United States Naval Reserve, 2 February 1944.

————. Presidential Unit Citation to Task Unit Twenty-One Point Fourteen, 9 November 1943.

Langille, SSgt. Jeffrey. "Trailbrazing Reserve Unit Demobilizes." U.S. Department of Defense, News about the War on Terrorism, 19 June 2003. http://www.defendamerica.mil/ articles/june2003/a062003a.html.

"Last Call." *Shipmate Magazine*, March 1987. (Obituary of Rear Adm. Roy Milton Davenport, USN [Ret.].)

Lenens, Jess. "Marine Thrives on Army Roots: Military Experience Leads Former Soldier to Top Honors in Recruit Training." Marine Corps Recruit Depot, San Diego, 7 November 2003.

Lowry, Richard S. "The Battle of An Nasiriyah." Military History Online, 2004. http://www.militaryhistoryonline.com/desertstorm/annasiriyah/default.aspx.

————. *Marines in the Garden of Eden*. New York: Berkeley, 2006.

MacGillis, Alec. "Honoring One Marine to Remember Them All: WWII Hero Gets Plaque at Navy Memorial." *Washington Post*, 29 May 2006.

Maher, CPO Robert A. Numerous interviews by James Wise in 1997 and 2006.

Maher, Robert A., and James E. Wise Jr. *Sailors' Journey into War*. Kent, Ohio: Kent State University Press, 1998.

Maib, Cara. "Navy Cross Recipient Talks about Experiences with Rota Sailors." *Navy Newsstand*, 22 November 2004.

McClellan, Maj. Edwin. *The United States Marine Corps in the World War*. Washington, D.C.: Historical Branch, G-3 Division Headquarters, U.S. Marine Corps, 1920.

"Medal of Honor Statistics." Home of Heroes Web site. http://www.homeofheroes.com/ moh/history/history_statistics.html.

Memorial to LCpl. Lance T. Graham. http://www.corpsstories.com/graham-whatwhen where1.htm.

Milks, Keith A. "Marines Take Care of One Another in Fierce Afghan Firefight." *Stars and Stripes*, 8 June 2004.

———. "Second House of Hell Survivor Awarded Navy Cross for Iraqi Action." *Leatherneck*, October 2006.

———. "War among the Rocks: Battlefield Standout Wins Navy Cross." *Leatherneck*, June 2006.

Montoya, Scott. Interview by Scott Baron, 28 January 2007.

Morison, Samuel Eliot. *History of United States Naval Operations in World War Two*. Volume V: *Guadalcanal*. Boston: Little, Brown, 1969.

Navy Cross citation for Capt. Brian R. Chontosh, USMC. www.homeofheroes. com/valor/ 1_Citations/nc_21wot.html.

Navy Cross citation for Cpl. Joseph B. Perez, USMC. www.homeofheroes.com/valor/1_ Citations/ nc_21wot.html.

Navy Cross citation for Senior Chief Petty Officer Britt Slabinski, USN (SEAL). www.freerepublic.com/focus/f-news/14373/posts.

"Navy Honors Four Marines' Valor in Combat." www.signonsandiego. com/news/ military/20040504-9999-Im4awards.html.

"Navy SEAL from Colorado dies in Afghanistan." www.militarycity.com/valor/958396. html.

"Navy SEAL Heroes." www.floppingaces.net/2005/07/10/navy-seal-heroes.

Naylor, Sean. *Not a Good Day to Die*. New York: Penguin, 2005.

"Never Quit: Marine Corps Community for USMC Veterans." www.leatherneck.com/ forums/archive/index.php/t-39300.html.

Official Biography of Maj. John Bolt, USMC. USAF Air University, Maxwell-Gunter AFB, Montgomery, Alabama. www.au.af.mil/au/goe/eaglebios/97bios/bolt97.htm.

Official Biography of Capt. Roy Milton Davenport. U.S. Navy. Operational Archives, Naval Historical Center, Washington, D.C.

Official Biography of Lt. Joseph P. Kennedy Jr., United States Naval Reserve. Washington, D.C.: Operational Archives, Naval Historical Center.

Official Biography of Maj. Stephen W. Pless, USMC. History and Museums Division of the United States Marine Corps.

Official Biography of Lt. Cdr. Jesse Taylor Jr., USN, 8 November 1971. U.S. Naval Institute Archives, Annapolis, Md.

Official Biography of Capt. Quentin R. Walsh. Washington, D.C.: Office of the Historian, U.S. Coast Guard. www.uscg.mil/history/BIO_Quentin_Walsh.html.

Official Navy Cross citation for John F. Bolt. www.homeofheroes.com.

Official Navy Cross citation for James C. Breckenridge. www.homeofheroes.com.

Official Navy Cross citation for Hospital Corpsman Apprentice Luis Fonseca Jr., USN. http://patriotfiles.org/hallofheroes.html.

Official Navy Cross citation for Lt. Gen. Lewis Burwell Puller, USMC, 19 November 1951 (second award). www.homeofheroes.com.

Official Statement of SSgt. Lawrence H. Allen, USA. www.popasmoke.com/stories/pless_Crew.html.

Official Statement of Capt. Rupert E. Fairfield (#085242), USMC, (Copilot). www.popasmoke.com/stories/pless_Crew.html.

Official Statement of LCpl. John G. Phelps (#1209285), USMC (Crew Chief). www.popasmoke.com/stories/pless_Crew.html.

Official Statement of Capt. Stephen W. Pless (#079156), USMC (Pilot). www.popasmoke.com/stories/pless_Crew.html.

Official Statement of GySgt. Leroy N. Poulson (#2076835), USMC (Gunner). www.popasmoke.com/stories/pless_Crew.html.

"Operation Anaconda." www.time.com/time/covers/110102318/popup.

"Operation Enduring Freedom." www.globalsecurity.org/military/ops/enduringfreedom.htm.

Operation Order No. 7-42–First Marine Division, Fleet Marine Force, Wellington, NZ, 20 July 1942.

Oxford Companion to American Military History. Edited by John Whiteclay Chambers. New York: Oxford University Press, 1999.

Page, Eric. "William A. Lee, 98, Marines' Acclaimed Ironman." Obituary, *New York Times*, 2 January 1999.

Page, Lt. Col. John U. D. www.military.com/Content/MoreContent?file=MLjpagebkp.

Patrick, Bethanne Kelly. "Coast Guard Officer Played Poker with the Germans Who Held Cherbourg Fortress–and Won." www.military.com.

PBS American Experience. "Vietnam: A Television History–Timeline." http://www.pbs.org/wgbh/amex/Vietnam.

Perez, Joseph B. Interview by Casey Wian. CNN, "Lou Dobbs Tonight," 25 November 2004.

Perry, Tony. "Marine Hero to Be Decorated for His Bravery." *Marine Corps Times*, 1 May 2006.

Phelps, John G. Interview by Scott Baron, 25 November 2006.

Potter, E. B. *Sea Power*. Annapolis, Md.: Naval Institute Press, 1981.

Poulson, Leroy. Interview by Scott Baron, 26 November 2006.

Princeton University Army ROTC. "Medal of Honor Citation: Lieutenant Colonel John U.D. Page, U.S. Army." www.princeton.edu/-armyrotc/alumni5.htm.

Proser, Jim, and Jerry Cutter. "*I'm Staying with My Boys*": *The Heroic Life of Sgt. John Basilone, USMC*. Hilton Head, S.C.: Lightbearer Communications, 2004.

Paul A. Putnam Papers. Special Collection #313, Joyner Library, East Carolina University, Greenville, North Carolina.

Recommendation letter for the Medal of Honor dated 26 August 1967, by Lt. Colonel Joe Nelson, Commanding Officer Marine Observation Squadron 6, Marine Group 36, 1st Marine Air Wing. www.popasmoke.com.

Renda, Mary A. *Taking Haiti: Military Occupation and the Culture of U.S. Imperialism, 1915–1940*. Chapel Hill: University of North Carolina Press, 2001.

Searls, Hank. *The Lost Prince: Young Joe, The Forgotten Kennedy*. New York: World Publishing, 1969.

"Sergeant Marco Martinez to Be Recognized by City Council." www.las-cruces.org/news/news_item.asp?NewsID=94.

"Sergeant 'Scuff' McGough, Royal Navy Special Boat Service (SBS)." Obituary, Telegraph UK. http://www.telegraph.co.uk/news/main.jhtml?xml=/news/2006/06/24/db2403.xml.

Sherrod, Robert. *History of Marine Corps Aviation in World War II*. Washington, D.C.: Combat Forces Press, 1952.

Shettle, M. L. *United States Marine Corps Air Stations of World War II*. Roswell, N.M.: Schaertel Publishing, 2001.

"The Siege of Fallujah." *Guardian Unlimited*. http://www.guardian.co.uk/flash/0,5860,1193510,00.html.

Sims, Lydel, and W. Scott Cunningham. *Wake Island Command*. Boston: Little, Brown, 1961.

"The Soldiers You Never Hear About." www.nationalreview.com/script/printpage.p?ref=/kob/kob200405280824.asp.

Steinkopf, Eric. "Marines Saved during Battle at An Nasiriyah." *Jacksonville* [North Carolina] *Daily News*, 12 August 2004.

Stevens, Paul Drew. *The Navy Cross: Vietnam, Citations of Awards to Men of the United States Navy and the United States Marine Corps 1964–1973*. Forest Ranch, Calif.: Sharp & Dunnigan Publications.

Stillwell, Paul. "A True Coast Guard Hero." *Naval History Magazine*, 1999.

"The Story of Quentin Walsh at Cherbourg." Washington, D.C.: U.S. Coast Guard Historian's Office. www.uscg.mil/history/Lov/DOT.html.

Stringer, Harry R. *The Navy Book of Distinguished Service: An official compendium of the Names and Citations of the Men of the United States Navy, Marine Corps, Army and Foreign Governments Who Were Decorated by the Navy Department for Extraordinary Gallantry and Conspicuous Service above and beyond the Call of Duty in the World War*. Washington, D.C.: Fassett Publishing Company, 1932.

Summers, Harry G. *The Vietnam War Almanac*. Novato, Calif.: Presidio Press, 1985.

Sutton, SSgt. Kurt. "Chesty Puller: Everyone Needs a Hero." *Marine Magazine*, August 1998.

Tarrant, V.E. *The U-Boat Offensive 1914–1945*. Annapolis, Md.: Naval Institute Press, 1989.

Telfer, Gary, Keith Fleming, and Lane Rogers. *U.S. Marines in Vietnam–Fighting the North Vietnamese 1967*. U.S. Marine Corps History Division. Washington, D.C.: Government Printing Office, 1984.

Third Battalion/25th Marines Unit History. www.usmc.mil/13thMEU/thunderingthird.htm.

"Three Marines, One Sailor Killed in Hadithah." www.centcom.mil (9 May 2005).

Toomey, Vurlee A. "Wake Island, Island of Valor." www.geocities.com/vurleeb/wakeisland.htm.

Tregaskis, Richard. *Guadalcanal Diary*. New York: Random House, 1943.

"Trio Face Enemy Fire in Battle for Baghdad." www.usatoday.com/news/nation/2006-11-09-medal-battle-baghdad_x.htm.

"Two SEALs Receive Posthumous Navy Cross Awards." *Navy Newsstand:* The Source of Navy News. www.navy.mil/search/display.asp?story_id=25573.

Tyson, Ann Scott. "Two SEALs Receive Navy Cross." *Washington Post*, 14 September 2006.

"Uprising at Qala-I-Jangi: The Staff of the 3/5th SF Group." *Special Warfare Quarterly*, September 2002.

Urwin, Gregory J. W. *Facing Fearful Odds*. Lincoln: University of Nebraska Press, 1997.

United Nations Office for the Coordination of Humanitarian Affairs, Integrated Regional Information Network (IRIN). "Iraq: Fallujah Situation Improving Slowly," 21 March 2006.

U.S. Department of Defense. "Army Awards Medal of Honor to Officer for Action in Korean Fighting." News release, 19 December 1956.

———. "Executive Summary of the Battle of Takur Ghar." News release, 24 May 2002.

U.S. Department of the Navy. "Lieutenant Joseph P. Kennedy, Jr., USNR, and Lieutenant Wilford J. Willy, USN, Lost Their Lives in Heroic Mission of 'Drone' Plane." Press release, 24 October 1945.

U.S. Naval Academy, *Lucky Bag 1933*. Rochester, N.Y.: DuBois Press.

USS *Taylor* (FFG 50). http://navysite.de/ffg/FFG50.HTM.

"Vice President's Remarks at a Rally for the Troops." www.whitehouse.gov/news/releases/2004/07/20040727-3.html.

Viggiani, Anthony. Interview by Scott Baron, 5 November 2006.

Vought, Cpl. Jeremy M. "3/5 Marines Awarded for Heroism." *Marine Corps News*, 13 May 2004.

Walton, Frank. *Once They Were Eagles: The Men of the Black Sheep Squadron*. Frankfort: University Press of Kentucky, 1996.

Weinberger, Caspar, and Wynton C. Hall. *Home of the Brave: Honoring the Unsung Heroes in the War on Terror*. New York: Tom Doherty Associates, 2006.

West, Owen. "A Ghost is Born: Dispatches from Fallujah." *Slate*, 28 July 2004.

———. "Leadership from the Rear: Proof that Combat Leadership Knows No Traditional Boundaries." *Marine Corps Gazette*, 1 September 2005.

Whitcomb, Darrel D. *The Rescue of BAT 21*. New York: Dell, 1998.

Wood, Trish. *What Was Asked of Us: An Oral History of the Iraq War by the Soldiers Who Fought It*. New York: Little Brown, 2006.

Wooldridge, Capt. E. T. Interview, 5 December 2006.

Workman, Jeremiah. Interview by Scott Baron, 20 January 2007.

"World War Two in the Pacific: Timeline of Events, 1941–1945." The History Place. www.historyplace.com/unitedstates/pacificwar/timeline.htm 1999.

Ziezulewicz, Geoff. 'There Was Just No Way I Was Leaving My Boys'–Shot to the Leg Couldn't Get Marine Out of the Fight." *Stars and Stripes*, 14 June 2006.

Zimmerman, Beth. "Navy Cross, Silver Star Awarded for Actions in Deadly Firefight." *Marine Corps Times*, September 2006.

INDEX

ABOUT THE AUTHORS

JAMES E. WISE JR., a former naval aviator and intelligence officer and Vietnam veteran, retired from the U.S. Navy as a captain. His other books include *Stars in Blue* and *U-505: The Final Journey*. He lives in the Washington, D.C., metropolitan area.

SCOTT BARON, a U.S. Army veteran of the Vietnam War and former law enforcement officer in California, is the author of *They Also Served: Military Biographies of Uncommon Americans* and coauthor with Wise of *Women at War: Iraq, Afghanistan, and Other Conflicts.*